Further praise for *From Character to Color*

"*From Character to Color* is an impressive literary project that critically examines the theoretical underpinnings of a race-obsessed ideology and seamlessly surveys its disgraceful ramifications for America and Americans of all descents. Writing with insight, persuasion, and hope, Dr. Ernest J. Zarra connects various divisive crystallizations of critical race theory (CRT), as both a scholarly field of inquiry and a pedagogy for far-left political activism, with broader socioeconomic, cultural, and political changes of our nation. In making the case for the timeless truth of "character over color," Dr. Zarra craftily demonstrates that the best tribute to any immutable characteristic is the triumph of our individuality and humanity over that characteristic. This book is a must-read for students, practitioners, and general readers who wish to gain a better understanding of race and America."

—Wenyuan Wu, PhD, Executive Director at Californians for Equal Rights, Director of Administration of the Asian-American Coalition for Education, and author of *Chinese Oil Investments in Peru and Ecuador: Social Responsibility, Host Government Regulations and Host Civil Society*

"Dr. Zarra takes us on a deep dive of the concepts, beliefs and background associated with CRT. With a commitment to serious research and background study, he introduces us to a logical and historical approach to analysis of a very political topic in education while accepting a wide range of beliefs and views. Full of notations, facts, and background, this book should trigger intellectual discussion on a very timely topic among professionals. Any program/school district that debates the introduction of CRT into their curriculum/program of study should require this text as expected reading for its professional staff prior to any decision-making and implementation. There is a lot to absorb, contemplate and debate. This book is timely, pertinent, and fact-filled. Anyone who takes CRT seriously should read this book."

—Ernest E. Brattstrom, MA, served forty-seven years in the field of education; was a New Jersey Teacher of the Year, teacher of the deaf, school administrator, superintendent of schools, and university instructor; and established the highly successful Learning Tree Educational Consultants

From Character to Color

From Character to Color

The Impact of Critical Race Theory on American Education

Ernest J. Zarra III

ROWMAN & LITTLEFIELD
Lanham • Boulder • New York • London

Published by Rowman & Littlefield
An imprint of The Rowman & Littlefield Publishing Group, Inc.
4501 Forbes Boulevard, Suite 200, Lanham, Maryland 20706
www.rowman.com

86-90 Paul Street, London EC2A 4NE, United Kingdom

British Library Cataloguing in Publication Information Available

Library of Congress Cataloging-in-Publication Data Available

ISBN 9781475864120 (cloth : alk. paper) |
ISBN 9781475864137 (pbk. : alk. paper) |
ISBN 9781475864144 (epub)

This book is dedicated to the children of previous generations who were labeled and traumatized because of the color of their skin, and remain scarred as adults. It is also dedicated to those children whose trauma is being inflicted today, because of someone else's past. May your saving grace be found in the One whose character includes the healing of human hearts.

Contents

List of Figure and Tables

FIGURE

TABLES

Preface

A seven-year-old child asks her mom if she was born a racist because she is white. The mom asks her child where she heard such a thing. The child replies that her teacher taught her that in social studies, and that all whites are born as racists. The perplexed child then asks her mom another question: "Mom, what's a racist?" Uncommon? Not in the least.

Critical Race Theory (CRT) was unheard of in common conversation until just a few years ago. Professors began to be hired for both newly created and long-standing departments at colleges and universities. Women's studies, queer studies, gender studies, black studies, and even critical race studies professors were hired in the humanities, particularly under the auspices of sociology. In Human Resources, professional developers and directors were hired to lead departments of Diversity, Equity, and Inclusion and offer regular training for faculty and staff.

New ideas brought about by groups of people sharing similar group grievances saw the opportunity to open the floodgates of academe and eventually spill their theory into the aqueducts of the rest of American society. Professors in other disciplines woke to the old ideas of Marxism and began to adopt a neo-Marxist approach to their own disciplines, all under the banner of Crit studies.

There was a perfect storm gathering and it struck with full force during the Trump administration. In cult-like fashion, proponents of race-based academics used an old approach to marginalize people. It seemed that everyone and everything that had any connections to Caucasians was deemed racist. But that was not enough. Black scholars began to delve into critical theory more deeply and carved out their own cult-like niches of critical race ideology. The mood was right for groups like Black Lives Matter (BLM) and individuals like Colin Kaepernick to take center stage.

The death of George Floyd served as a catalyst for anti-American groups to release their onslaught against the status quo. As a result, race, gender, sex, economics, and ableism-concerned groups began to realize the political benefits of the theory attached to their particular grievances. So, the nation went from kneeling during the national anthem, to tearing down statues, burning down parts of cities and looting, and assassinating policemen, all within the guise of a narrative that America is systemically and irreparably racist.

America's schools and school boards were gradually assumed by radicals who decided to deconstruct whiteness within what is taught in their districts, of course without parent input. Before they knew it, parents were answering questions about racism from their children and wondering what was taking place in schools. Online learning revealed much.

The COVID-19 pandemic revealed to some parents the answers they were seeking. The phrase *we do not teach critical race theory in our schools* was quickly put to rest when parents and teachers began to speak up. What was found was that *CRT is taught most everywhere*. This led to some states banning it outright for their public schools.

The growth of CRT is reminiscent of the type of growth of other fads that America has endured. These are written about at length in several of my other books. There is no mistaking the fact that the nation is more marginalized by race, weaker in character, fearful of speaking its mind in public, and slowly choking on a vengeance-oriented reverse oppression. With the conversion of people believing that one's skin color makes them inferior, America is slowly erasing the memory of a time when the civil rights icons fought to cut loose the bonds of melanin-driven bigotry.

The growth of the assumption that whites are racists is more than a fad. It is cancer to the soul of America, which has been purposely unleashed from the labs of higher education and has now metastasized in schools, businesses, entertainment, military, athletics, and the medical community.

From Character to Color: The Impact of Critical Race Theory on American Education draws a distinction between Martin Luther King Jr.'s call for the nation to examine the character of individuals and the current push to view people by the group to which they belong.

The old guard of the Black Civil Rights Movement of the mid-to-late twentieth century is dying off. A new movement has arisen that cares little about the values of the past, including those preached by MLK—and those for which he gave his life.

Rather than corrective measures, this new group wants to overthrow and dismantle constitutional principles that are the foundation of America. Many of these principles are those which the group relies upon to express dissent. However, the voices of the past are speaking with one last burst of energy to set the record straight: equality of individuals and their character trumps identification by skin color grouping.

THE REASONS FOR WRITING THIS BOOK

From Character to Color was written to explore CRT from logical, moral, and educational standpoints, as these relate to history, people, and racial groups. This book is also written to explain reasons why it is a bad choice to allow the CRT to grow unabated and continue to infect the nation. In attempting to accomplish these reasons, the following questions were considered important and are answered throughout the chapters:

- What are the definitions of critical theories, and CRT?
- Where did the critical theory and CRT originate?
- Why are critical theories so popular today?
- Why have race and racism become such important issues at this time in America's history?
- Who are the major black and white proponents and critics of CRT and antiracism?
- What have states done to promote and counter CRT?
- To what extent is CRT found in states' academic content standards and curriculum frameworks?
- What is antiracism and why is it being included in teacher training and as a consideration in teacher hiring in schools and in the corporate world?
- In what ways are critical race and common grace similar and different?
- How do parents and teachers really feel about CRT and BLM curriculum in their children's classrooms? What are the responses by parents at school board meetings once they are informed that CRT is being taught to their children?
- Is the United States really an institutionally and systemically racist nation? If so, what are the evidences?
- In what way is the focus on CRT inadequate and diminishes the quality of education in K-16 public learning institutions, as well as in private schools and colleges?
- What are some suggestions in recalibrating American education so that graduates are less activists and more merit-based competitors in the marketplace?

Schools are challenged in the book to return to using merit-based assessments in core subjects. They are also requested to shun the hours spent on diversity training and implicit bias to focus on teaching training in content, the development of soft and hard human skills, and the building of friendships. These are not bound to skin color and much more important for a healthy society.

All across America, parents are asking when schools will return to teaching the things that matter for children's futures. The idea that the adoption of any race theory claiming that traditional subjects like mathematics, science,

English-language arts, social studies, and advanced courses are in place to reinforce white supremacy is based on false premises. Hopefully, this book will serve as a catalyst for a new wave of activism—one that dispels errors and provides a return to that which values each person equally and righteously.

College is an important undertaking for most students. It is also a place where some faculty subscribe to neo-Marxist ideology, while a growing number claim postmodernism as their preferred ideology.[1] Postmodernism is essentially neo-Marxist, or as I refer to it, as cultural-Marxism-lite.

When it comes to college, Thomas Sowell proclaims that "teaching and learning are at the heart of what most people think of as the function of a college or a university."[2] The question for today is exactly what are faculty teaching at these institutions of higher education and what are students learning. Based on the rhetoric shared by professors in the humanities and, by the hires by colleges for the focus on Diversity, Equity, Inclusion, and also belonging and Collegiality, students are hearing more and more about what separates them and power imbalances based on skin color. This book is meant to give voice to those wishing to speak up and push back against what seems open season on America's students.

THE IMPORTANCE OF THIS BOOK

In terms of education, advocates of CRT contend that school programs, including advanced placement and higher-level mathematics classes, are racist in and of themselves. This book is extremely important as it attempts to set the record straight. M. K. Sprinkle writes,

> Critical Race Theory rests on the belief that mathematics is a tool of White oppression, inherently biased against Blacks. Therefore, to level the playing, Black children should be held to a different competency level. Mathematical approximations, as opposed to correct answers is the goal.[3]

Is this the type of thinking parents desire for their children?

George Floyd's death sparked a national outcry, and race groups took advantage of the moment. It is no accident that *The New York Times 1619 Project* was launched by the paper and Nikole Hannah-Jones around this time. Books such as *White Fragility*, *Nice Fragility*, *How to be an Antiracist*, and *Stamped from the Beginning* began to flood the shelves. Something very different began sweeping the nation. It swept across all sectors of government. The military and the corporate world were changed. Professional sports had gone *woke*. People began to find that, in order to keep their jobs, they had to undergo diversity, equity, and inclusion (DEI) training. Many people also had to take classes and seminars on deconstructing whiteness, white fragility, implicit bias, and some even apologized for being white.

The ideas from the books mentioned previously now flood the minds of students and teachers in most of America's public schools. Teachers' unions adopted the eventual materials that emerged in print for students and teacher trainings. During the COVID-19 pandemic, students online and in person began hearing about checking their privilege, and coming to terms with white supremacy.

The moment was there for the taking. In just fifty years, blacks have gone from being second-class citizens to fully equal under the law. Thanks in large part to the work of Martin Luther King Jr., the nation was slowly moving into the arena of tolerance and equality.

Then comes along Ibram X. Kendi, who wrote an important version of American history, titled *Stamped from the Beginning*. Kendi missed the point that all humans share in a common nature. We are fallen creatures, given to shortcomings, as well as blessings, and failures, and successes. None of these is dependent upon skin color or any other sociological or anthropological designation. Theology calls human nature as one given to sin, and it is original in us all by nature. The term is not popular, but it is true and will stand the test of time over the idea that all of a given race is inferior by its shade of melanin. Given time, it will out itself, no matter how hard we try. No race or amount of melanin has a corner on sinfulness.

In terms of CRT, the impact of American education has resulted in division. Those divided cross all races and backgrounds and share similar concerns about CRT. American education involves schools and administrators. Schools involve teachers, students, and parents. Education also involves a wider community, including churches and civic groups. Therefore, anything that impacts these stakeholders sends ripples into homes and local groups very quickly. CRT has caused many ripple effects.

Parents have formed groups to fight off what they view is the teaching of a form of racism, bigotry, and false ideas about humanity. CRT proponents view things differently, in that they claim that racism is an issue caused by whites and that it is impossible for blacks to be racists because they lack the requisite power to demonstrate it. Church pastors and civic groups hear about an unpardonable sin that has been committed by those with white skin. Some pulpits are filled with leaders that have begun to address the issue of racial divisions in society.

Critics of CRT are sometimes knee jerk, attaching whatever new idea they discover online or on a student's assignment to what they know about the theory. But, the reality is, CRT is illiberal and constraining, emotionally tattooing labels upon children even in the womb. CRT has done more to marginalize racial demographics since the Jim Crow era when the Democrats of the south fought hard to keep society separate.

The impact of CRT is real and has already been the cause of moral concerns among government workers, the corporate world, the military, college, and professional athletics, and now it is reaching its apex by injecting itself into schools. Few would dare come out and say they are teaching CRT to children. However, the concepts that grow from the heart of the theory are directly related to the tenets of CRT.

Parents who remember their public school days fondly are coming to terms with the shift in focus from academics to social justice and equity. Thomas Sowell captures this almost prophetically, when he writes,

> American education is undermined by numerous dogmas and numerous hidden agendas. The dogmas fall into two general categories—dogmas about education and dogmas about the larger society. Self-esteem, role models, diversity, and other buzzwords dominate educational policy—without evidence being either asked or given to substantiate the beliefs they represent.[4]

Sowell accurately identifies the issues surrounding CRT in American education today.

The fundamental importance of writing this book is captured in five important assertions.

1. CRT has grown significantly and has negatively affected American society. Children are being indoctrinated by a problematic set of assumptions about whiteness.
2. Parent groups and students in schools and colleges are expressing concern they are unable to offer dissent without being labeled as racists, targeted for violence, and shamed by teachers and faculty, both in person and on social media.
3. Schools that care about true education to move back to merit-based education and see students individually, rather than by color groupings.
4. CRT has assisted in further dividing America into tribes based on skin color and intersectionality. Segregation is not a positive direction and can have no beneficial outcome for the nation. Assimilating all into a more civic-minded America is unifying.
5. Dispelling the notion that the United States has to be deconstructed and that the nuclear family has to be destroyed must occur. Deconstruction and destruction are given to revolution and not national unity.

THE STRUCTURE OF THE BOOK

This book contains six chapters. Chapter 1 is titled "Critical Race Theory." This chapter examines the genesis and progression of critical theories (Crits), emerging from the Frankfurt School in Germany. The chapter also describes the impact Marxism had on theories and the point at which race became a mainstay under the banner of critical theories. This progression is highlighted by tables and an illustrated figure.

Chapter 1 defines terms like *postmodernism*, *intersectionality*, *white rage*, *spirit murder*, *white fragility*, and *white privilege*, and also addresses what is meant by the term *systemically racist*. Also in this chapter is a discussion of the principal figures behind the American proliferation of CRT. Principals such as Kimberlê Crenshaw, Robert Delgado, Derrick Bell, and Jean Stefancic are credited with efforts to launch CRT into the psyche of American academe.

The reader will be pleased to note that the five basic tenets of CRT are addressed. This will help to identify CRT by other names and by concepts, rather than by its title. A helpful table is included to assist in this identification. Finally, there is a hefty section on the impact of CRT upon K-12 schooling and higher education and the harm CRT has done in separating students by race.

Chapter 2 is given the title "What's the Matter with Melanin?" The purpose of this chapter is to examine whether melanin really matters in America, or whether focusing on skin color is the wrong approach. The chapter examines what happens when race becomes the most important factor of group and individual identity. As seen with America's past, such a focus fragmented the nation. The chapter presents the role of Paulo Freire in the development of CRT and the importance of his ideas in the construction of neo-Marxist ideology using race.

The third chapter of the book is an examination of CRT from an unconventional angle. The chapter is titled "Critical Race and Common Grace." The chapter begins with the sensible approach that all humans have the same nature and what one human is capable of is certainly within the capabilities of other humans. No race is free from this nature.

Common grace is presented as the reason why people of faith can work together in common with those not of the same faith, learn from each other, and share similar values. The chapter defines character and presents the case that human corruption has affected all aspects of American life. But the chapter is clear that all is not lost if grace is allowed to flourish and a return to the basic understanding and relationship with the One in whom grace resides by attribute.

There is a large portion of this chapter dedicated to tracing the life and biblical views of MLK on grace and its moorings in theology. King's approach to change in culture is then compared with what motivates twenty-first-century racial groups and some of the actions taken, as a result.

Chapter 4 consists of a lengthy and deep analysis of CRT and calls attention to its impact on American education. It does so by analyzing some of the strategies employed by proponents of CRT and their plans to indoctrinate the next generation toward race consciousness and activism. This chapter includes sections on the subjectivity of CRT, why *The 1619 Project* is debunked by scholars as it loses sight of history, a critique of Ibram X. Kendi's works on antiracism, and how CRT is playing out in the lives of Americans.

Chapter 5 provides a specific identification and examination of several of the *Critical Flaws of Critical Race Theory*. To name a few, CRT is illogical and based on fallacies; CRT is inconsistent in what it proposes, due to double standards; CRT promotes racial segregation; and CRT advances discrimination. Several others are also included in the chapter.

The last chapter of the book, "Communities Fighting Back," is a compilation and examination of community efforts to push back against the onslaught of CRT in America's schools. Grassroots efforts by parents are chronicled and strategies to battle with school boards are discussed. Real-life examples are shared and attention is given to those in the battle for our nation's children.

A tabular listing of many of these events is included in the chapter. The chapter is meant to (1) lobby for a return to character over color, (2) encourage a return to educating children in what really matters academically, and (3) draw a clear line about who actually has the responsibility to rear and educate America's children for a successful future absent discrimination.

In closing, there are three appendices, each of which adds additional information for one or more chapters of the book. These include "States' Legislative Decisions Regarding CRT," "Christian Colleges and CRT," and "Teachers' Associations and the Progressive Agenda of Washington State."

NOTES

1. Matthew Sharpe. "Is cultural Marxism really taking over universities? I crunched some numbers to find out." *The Conversation*. September 7, 2020. Retrieved November 11, 2021, from https://theconversation.com/is-cultural-marxism-really-taking-over-universities-i-crunched-some-numbers-to-find-out-139654.
2. Thomas Sowell. *Inside American Education*. New York: The Free Press, 1993, p. 202.
3. M. K. Sprinkle. "Sprinkle: Racist mathematics of racism propounded as antiracism? Commentary." *Baltimore Sun*. March 13, 2021. Retrieved August 8, 2021, from https://www.baltimoresun.com/maryland/carroll/opinion/cc-op-sprinkle-031321-20210313-m2lg4tomcndolfj5kebf6asike-story.html0.
4. Sowell. *Inside American Education*, p. 15.

Acknowledgments

This book would never have been written without the support of my publisher Rowman & Littlefield. I am grateful they are providing the opportunity to share my work and the platform upon which to offer my voice in print. The long-standing relationship with Tom Koerner and Carlie Wall at R&L has never been taken for granted. Their professionalism as individuals, and those with whom they work, is simply awesome! I have been blessed.

Authors know the weeks and months it takes from idea, to proposal, to research, and then on to manuscript. In my case, throughout this process, I was fortunate to have had my ideas shaped by experiences past and present. Many times an experience was questioned by friends, family members, and even complete strangers. Sometimes people without any knowledge of the person with whom they are speaking are more honest people an author can query.

The first group of significant people I would like to acknowledge is my group of online buddies and former colleagues. These folks are former teachers, professors, social media leaders, and professionals from various walks of life. They come from all backgrounds, races, religions, and genders. The discussions, Zoom calls, message chats, online forums, YouTube comments, and texts helped to provide an organized framework for this book.

The second group of significant people that I need to be acknowledged are those in the trenches, dealing with education issues that only an online school board meeting addict can appreciate. The opportunity to bounce ideas around with board members, local teachers, administrators, and parents assisted greatly in filling in the pieces that fit inside the framing of this book. I am indebted for your suggestions, desire, and willingness to help, and I deeply appreciate the time we spent together in discussions.

The last group of people is my immediate and church families. The various worldviews gathered from those with whom there are interpersonal relationships are often the most valuable. Each of us knows that ideas outside the box are welcome, and that being granted patience to be when needed most has broadened my understanding of common grace. Thanks so much for understanding the cave which authors enter and for providing the space for the research and writing required to make this happen. I love you all dearly, especially my 1970s New Jersey bride.

Thanks again to all and I pray each of you will be mightily blessed for your interest and assistance in dealing with CRT in our schools and culture.

On behalf of our children and grandchildren . . .

Chapter 1

Critical Race Theory

> CRT has been helpful, for instance, to point out the particular ways that white supremacy has mutated from legalized de jure institutional racism (explicit laws like separate by equal) to de facto institutional racism (implicit ways discrimination continues illegally), but attempts to use CRT to discredit anti-racism work is ahistorical and inaccurate.[1]

> Critical race theorists attack the very foundations of the liberal legal order, including equality theory, legal reasoning, Enlightenment rationalism, and neutral principles of constitutional law.[2]

There is an interesting, yet peculiar, theory, which has a clear foundation rooted in classical Marxism. Its origin dates back to early twentieth-century Germany.[3] This theory has evolved over time in the United States, impacting academe over the past few decades. The theory changed its look as it added issues to the original theoretical tenets.

Since the 1960s and 1970s, the United States has seen a steady rise in cultural and racial neo-Marxism. The latest appearance in the United States was largely at the higher education levels to begin and was referred to simply as critical theory. As the theory adopted race into its fold, this triggered the American Bar Association to claim "CRT is not a diversity and inclusion 'training' but a practice of interrogating the role of race and racism in society that emerged in the legal academy and spread to other fields of scholarship."[4]

The man credited by some for the rise of cultural Marxism and responsible for some of its clash with capitalism is the "Italian communist, Antonio Gramsci . . . Gramsci proposed that capitalism could be overthrown gradually, by infiltrating and transforming society's major institutions—e.g., education establishments, media, law, religion, and the family."[5] Cultural

Marxism, and the public's exposure to CRT, has grown exponentially in the United States within the last decade.

DEVELOPMENT AND PROGRESSION OF CRITICAL RACE THEORY (CRT)

Several dozen legal scholars

> met at a convent outside of Madison, Wisconsin, on July 8, 1989, as Public Enemy's *Fight the Power* topped the Billboard charts. They came together to forge an antiracist intellectual approach known as *critical race theory*. Thirty-year-old UCLA legal scholar Kimberlê Williams Crenshaw organized the summer retreat the same year she penned *Demarginalizing the Intersection of Race and Sex*. The essay called for *intersectional theory*, the critical awareness of gender racism (and thereby other intersections, such as queer racism, ethnic racism, and class racism). . . . One of the greatest offshoots of the theory was critical Whiteness studies, investigating the anatomy of Whiteness, racist ideas, White privileges, and the transition of European immigrants into Whiteness. Critical race theorists, as they came to be called, joined antiracist Black Studies scholars in the forefront of revealing the progression of racism in the 1990s.[6]

Helen Pluckrose and James Lindsay refer to Crenshaw's work and its growth as an American phenomenon, which formally rose to academic prominence in legal studies during the 1970s.[7] CRT "grew in the 1980s and 1990s. It persists as a field of inquiry in the legal field and in other areas of scholarship."[8] Gloria Ladson-Billings refers to CRT as deployment of "race and racial theory as a challenge to traditional notions of diversity and social hierarchy."[9]

A Theory Takes Shape

Matt McManus describes the environment in Germany in the early days of the University of Frankfurt Institute for Social Research, which later "became known as just the Frankfurt School of Critical Theory."[10] (See table 1.1). The interesting history

> of the Frankfurt School begins in 1930, when Max Horkheimer took over and recruited an eclectic array of Marxist inspired scholars into the institution's ranks; including luminaries such as Erich Fromm, Theodor Adorno, and Herbert Marcuse. These authors were largely inspired by two events. The first was the

Table 1.1 Principal Figures at the Frankfurt School

Name	*Important Publications*	*Historical Context*
Theodor Adorno	*Dialectic of the Enlightenment* (with Horkheimer)	The rise of nationalism in Europe and Asia, including the rise of Nazism in Germany, Fascism in Italy, and socialism/communism in Soviet Union/Russia, and Red China.
Walter Benjamin	*The Works of Art in the Age of Mechanical Reproduction*	
Erich Fromm	*Hope, Humanism, and the Future*	
Antonio Gramsci	*Prison Notebooks*	
Jurgen Habermas	*Knowledge and Human Interests* *The Structural Transformation of the Public Square*	
Max Horkheimer	*Critical and Traditional Theory* *Dialectic of the Enlightenment* (with Adorno)	
Gyorgy Lukacs	*History and Class Consciousness*	
Herbert Marcuse	*One Dimensional Man*	

Source: Ashley Crossman. "Understanding critical theory." *ThoughtCo*. October 15, 2019. Retrieved October 30, 2021, from https://www.thoughtco.com/critical-theory-3026623.

> failure of Marx's scientific prediction that a utopian revolution would emerge in developed Western states to overthrow the exploitative capitalist order. The most spectacular Marxist uprising—the infamous Bolshevik Revolution—began in underdeveloped feudal Russia. . . . The second event which inspired the Frankfurt School was the rise of fascism and Nazism in Western liberal democracies; most spectacularly in Germany, the homeland of the major authors . . . Adorno and Horkheimer published their seminal Dialectic of Enlightenment to try and explain how an enlightened liberal country could give rise to Nazism an the horrors of the Holocaust.[11]

Critics questioned the adequacy of critical theory. As a result, what was developed were three criteria to determine the theoretical applications. Therefore, critical theory is adequate only if it meets three criteria.

According to Horkheimer,

> It must be explanatory, practical, and normative, all at the same time. That is, it must explain what is wrong with current social reality, identify the actors to change it, and provide both clear norms for criticism and achievable practical goals for social transformation.[12]

Herbert Marcuse "is credited with hatching the Critical Theory ideology from which the racial, gender, and other Critical Theory-based movements were launched in America."[13] Marcuse believed that people had the right to use any means possible if the system did not allow the changes they demanded. Levin asserts,

KARL MARX: The Father of the ideas behind the school in Frankfurt, Germany. The purposes of the school included questioning and understanding the interworkings of power and cultural domination.

PURPOSE OF CRITICAL THEORY: to unearth the assumptions within society that prevent people from living their best lives and understand the functioning of the known world.

MAX HORKHEIMER laid out differences between critical theories and traditional theories.

A true critical theory must be certain to:

- give account to historical context, and
- seek comprensive critiques from all social science fields.

CRITICAL THEORY is different from a traditional theory in three areas. Critical theories must be

- *explanatory* (provide adequate explanations of social problems that exist),
- *practical* (offer practical solutions in response to identified problems), and
- *normative* (hold to the norms of criticism).

CRITICAL THEORY adopted in many other areas of study, including:

Ableism, Ageism, Black, Culture, Ethnic, Feminism, Gender, Media, Queer, Race, White

Developers of Critical Race Theory: Kimberle Crenshaw and Derrick Bell

Figure 1.1 The Genesis and Progression of Critical Theory. Author Designed.

> The inescapable conclusion is that in the end, Marcuse was urging the violent overthrow of American society in which the established hierarchy was using tolerance to perpetuate oppression against the minority. This nonsensical argument has served as the foundational catalyst for various critical theories that have grown into Marxist-related ideological movements—which in turn have been embraced and promoted by the Biden administration, the Democratic Party, the media, and institutions throughout our society and culture. One of the most destructive among these movements is Critical Race Theory . . . CRT is an insidious and racist Marxist ideology spreading throughout our culture and society.[14]

Basic Meanings of Critical Theory

There are two basic meanings that have arisen within philosophy for the term *Critical Theory*. The first is a narrow meaning of the term, which pertains to the "generations of German philosophers and social theorists in the Western Marxist tradition known as the Frankfurt School."[15] According to this group of theorists, "A theory is critical to the extent it seeks human 'emancipation from slavery,' acts as a 'liberating influence,' and works to 'create a world which satisfies the needs and powers of human beings.'"[16] The second basic meaning of critical theory is the broad view. The theorists which hold to the broad view of critical theory connect their ideas to social movements "that identify varied dimensions of the domination of human beings in modern societies."[17] In addition to these two basic meanings, "CRT incorporates scholarship from feminism, continental social philosophy, postmodernism, cultural nationalism, and a variety of social movements."[18]

CRT, Postmodernism, and Perspective

Over time, the American version of critical theory developed an acute awareness of social concerns pertaining to race, gender, sex, and others.[19] In contemporary fashion, "a fundamental change in human thought took place in the 1960s. This change is associated with several French Theorists . . . among them Michel Foucault, Jacques Derrida, and Jen-Francois Lyotard."[20] Eventually, a new conception on how to view the world becomes "known as *postmodernism.*"[21] This new idea remained difficult to define, as Pluckrose and Lindsay emphasize, "Postmodernism is difficult to define, perhaps by design. . . . The difficulties of defining postmodernism are not just philosophical; they are spatial and temporal because it has not been one unitary movement."[22]

Along with a postmodern perspective came a fundamentalist subjectivity and philosophical relativity to reality. As a result, there arose blatant rejections of objective truth as reality. Rejections included "the possibility of obtaining true knowledge [because] postmodernism insulates itself from criticism and obscures its logical inconsistencies."[23]

Postmodernism's continued influence on CRTs manifests itself "in claims that speech is violence (including microaggressions and cancel culture) and in claims that science, reason, and objectivity are white ways of knowing."[24] Richard Delgado and Jean Stefancic define microaggressions as "sudden, stunning, or dispiriting transactions that mar the days of women and folks of color."[25] Notice there is no room for whites when it comes to being microaggressed.

Lindsay Perez Huber and Daniel G. Solorzano provide a more detailed definition, referring specifically to racial microaggressions. They state,

> Racial microaggressions are a form of systemic, everyday racism used to keep those at the racial margins in their place. They are: (1) verbal and nonverbal assaults directed toward People of Color, often carried out in subtle, automatic or unconscious forms; (2) layered assaults, based on race and its intersections with gender, class, sexuality, language, immigration status, phenotype, accent, or surname; and (3) cumulative assaults that take a psychological, physiological, and academic toll on People of Color.[26]

As postmodern and critical theory groups emerged, they adopted the claim to "have something in common"[27] with each other. Each group brought with it an individual perspective or lens through which to examine life. Delgado and Stefancic describe this perception as "examining how things look from the perspective of individual actors . . . [to] understand the predicament of intersectional individuals."[28]

CRT and Intersectionality

The perspective described by Delgado and Stefancic refers to the idea of *intersectionality.* "Intersectionality accurately recognizes that it is possible to uniquely discriminate against someone who falls with an *intersection* of oppressed identities—say black and female—and that contemporary discrimination law was insufficiently sensitive to address this."[29] Herein lies one of the original uses of critical theory, in terms of legal studies in the United States.

Ange-Marie Hancock wrote at length about intersectionality, its historical points of origin, and the various popular definitions, impacts, and applications stemming from the conceptual to the actual. Hancock argues that intersectionality "is in the process of reaching maximal salience across academe,"[30] but one of its very real concerns is its connection to cancel culture, because such an association tends to equate it with what "whitens and memifies"[31] the very concept at its core. Ijeoma Oluo takes it a step further as she adds,

> But if you don't embrace intersectionality, even if you make progress for some, you will look around one day and find that you've become the oppressor of others. . . . It's not enough for you to personally believe in intersectionality. We need to start demanding intersectionality of all those who seek to join our social justice movements.[32]

CRT and Cultural Assimilation

There are two distinct characteristics of CRT and these are associated with perspective and cultural assimilation. Each is germane to critical theory. The first characteristic is "the notion of multiple consciousness, [whereby] the increasing number of multiracial individuals suggests that this concern will only increase."[33] As perspectives grow, characteristics change. Therefore, the question of cultural assimilation is equally as important.

A second area revolves around the concept of assimilation, especially in the area of race; it raises questions like (1) should blacks assimilate into what they perceive as nationalism and white culture? and (2) does a black perspective allow for any room for this "assimilation?"[34] Critical theory incorporated race almost from the beginning, and its additions of various domains are much more recent. Theorists have admitted that the theory has become somewhat bloated with an abundance of social subcategories.

Nationalism and Assimilation

In America,

> Debates about nationalism versus assimilation figure prominently in current discourse about race. One strand of critical race theory energetically backs the nationalist view, which is particularly prominent with the materialists. Derrick Bell . . . urges his fellow African Americans to foreswear the struggle for school integration and aim for building the best possible black schools.[35]

Interestingly, "Their struggle led directly to a conscious, racial form of nationalism. Nationalists of all types question the majoritarian assumption that northern European culture is superior."[36]

CRT was a tidy fit for an emerging racial nationalism. Several key ideas were advanced as outgrowths of the theory. Two of these outgrowths include nationalists who were

> apt to describe themselves as a nation within a nation and to hold that the loyalty and identification of black people . . . and a . . . position, embraced by a few sophisticated thinkers . . . [that] holds that minorities of color should not try to fit into a flawed economic and political system but transform it.[37]

Today, in terms of critical theory, whether the social issue is race or any other issue, there is an essential element of struggle that is common: "A search for the proper unit, or atom of social analysis and change."[38] As a result, we have the onset of beginnings of viewing people in groups. So, what exactly is the current version of CRT, and what is all the commotion about?

DRILLING DOWN ON CRT

Specifically,

> Critical Race Theory holds that race is a social construct that was created to maintain white privilege and white supremacy. This idea originated long before postmodernism with W.E.B. Du Bois, who argued that the idea of race was being used to assert biological explanations of differences that are social and cultural, in order to perpetuate the unjust treatment of racial minorities, especially African Americans. While other factors may have contributed, race and racism as we understand them today probably arose as social constructions, made by Europeans to morally justify European colonialism and the Atlantic Slave Trade.[39]

Allowing sociologists to define terms and speak authoritatively and objectively empowers the discipline to reject competitive ideologies. For example, theology recognizes differences as God-given and distinct, and theology was at one time the *queen of the sciences*. The idea that some theologians and scientists argue that "theology can still be regarded as queen of the sciences"[40] is rejected by most sociologists.

Kimberlê Crenshaw and CRT

One of the American originators of CRT—and who is also one of the innovators of the application of modern CRT to culture—is Kimberlê Crenshaw. Crenshaw

> wanted to keep the theoretical understanding of race and gender as social constructs and use deconstructive methods to critique them, *and* assert a stable truth claim: that some people were discriminated against on the grounds of their racial and sexual identities, a discrimination she planned to address legally, using identity politics. Crenshaw argues that (identity) categories have meaning and consequences . . . she distinguishes between a black person and a person who happens to be black.[41]

Crenshaw is the "critical race scholar who . . . most clearly advocates for a more politicized and actionable use"[42] of CRT. She is also "the progenitor of the concept of *intersectionality*. Intersectionality began as a heuristic—a tool that lets someone discover something for themselves—but has long been treated as a theory and is now described by Crenshaw as a *practice*."[43]

When intersectionality converges with social justice, there is a conceptual clash that results. The reason for this clash is that critical race theorists "try to combine pragmatist and utopian visions."[44] Social justice issues are important to utopian visionists. Pluckrose and Lindsay clarify, "The only way to be a virtuous person under Social Justice is to assume that these power imbalances and prejudices exist everywhere at all times, masked by the egalitarian false-premises of liberalism."[45]

Carol Swain and Christopher Schorr add,

> A corollary to Critical Race Theory is Intersectionality. This is a theory asserting that overlapping sources of oppression compound one another, rendering racial and ethnic minorities, gays and lesbians, and economically disadvantaged groups even more marginalized and victimized by society in proportion to their accumulating victim identities.[46]

Table 1.2 Terms and Concepts Associated with Critical Theory and Critical Race Theory

Critical Social Justice; Conscious, Explicit Bias; Unconscious Bias; Diversity Training; Microaggressions; White Privilege; White Fragility; Diversity, Equity, and Inclusion (DEI); Praxis	Critical Pedagogy; Institutional Bias; Systemic Oppression; Educational Justice; Internalized Racism; Institutional Racism; Systemic Racism; Multiculturalism	Anti-Blackness; Cultural Appropriation; Implicit Bias; Internalized White Supremacy; Social-Emotional Learning (SEL): Social Justice	Antiracism; Spirit Murder; Racial Centering; Explicit Bias; Oppressors; Oppressed; Intersectionality; Antiracist; Racial Justice	Centering; Cultural; Relevance; Oppression; Marginalized; Identities; Patriarchy; Systemic Bias; Woke

Source: Staff. "Glossary of CRT-related terms." *Center for Renewing America*. September 23, 2021. Retrieved October 30, 2021, from https://americarenewing.com/issues/glossary-of-crt-related-terms/.

Crenshaw, Swain, Schoor, and other critical theory researchers share an interesting commonality. That is, they agree that the theory has expanded beyond law school and into general culture. Some of the concepts that are included in an ever-expanding critical theory are found in table 1.2.

CONTROVERSIAL NATURE OF CRT

Swain and Schorr consider CRT

> a fundamentally racist worldview predicated on the claim that racism is in the DNA of American institutions and society, as well as, in effect, in the DNA of white Americans. It sees minorities, especially black Americans, as victims of systemic racism: racism permeating a vast network of impenetrable institutional structures and cultural stereotypes—all created by whites to give themselves unearned advantages.[47]

Stephen Sawchuk makes the point that not all critics of CRT are of the conservative ilk, politically. He does assess critics and claims that they "charge that the theory leads to negative dynamics, such as a focus on group identity over universal, shared traits, divides people into 'oppressed' and 'oppressor' groups; and urges intolerance."[48] Sawchuk believes that there is much confusion and controversy about CRT and what it means. In fact, he states, "To an extent, the terms 'critical race theory' is now cited as the basis of all diversity and inclusion efforts regardless of how much it's actually informed these programs."[49] A part of the controversy of CRT rests in the actions of its advocates in sheltering the theory from the public and the conscious effort to hide it within the guise of activism.

Some scholars are taking a different approach, rather than just trying to fight against CRT, as it relates to the triad of diversity, equity, and inclusion (DEI) of emphasis on college campuses. Two scholars are offering an interesting alternative program. Dorian Abbot and Ivan Marinovic of the University of Chicago and Stanford, respectively, have developed the MFE program: Merit, Fairness, and Equality. The professors say they want students to experience the university for the sake of learning, rather than a politicized version of it. MFE would ensure that student applicants "are treated as individuals and evaluated through a rigorous and unbiased process based on their merit and qualifications alone."[50] They hope to have it established within a decade. As one can expect, calls for terminations of the professors are well underway.

Examples of Control

Documents uncovered from the Office of DEI of the Wellesley Public School District revealed that leaders of the Massachusetts public school system "are encouraging students and staff to file complaints against one another for telling rude jokes, referring to the *China virus*, and committing microaggressions or other incidents of bias."[51] According to the documents, "Students are encouraged to report incidents of discrimination or any concerning pattern of biased behavior to any district staff member or a trusted adult."[52]

The Wellesley policy explains what incidents should be reported to adults, or teachers, by the students. In fact,

> An incident of bias is defined as any biased conduct, speech, or expression that has an impact but may not involve criminal action, but demonstrates conscious or unconscious bias that targets individuals or groups that are part of a federally protected class.[53]

The Wellesley policy is just one of many policies around the nation that encourages people to watch their neighbors very closely.

An example of one of the more destructively woke Departments of Education in America is the Oregon Department of Education (DOE).[54] The Oregon DOE published its *Pathway to Math Instruction Toolkit*, which delineates how math equity may be achieved within its public school districts.

According to the toolkit, mathematics equity can be achieved by "visibilizing the toxic characteristics of white supremacy culture with respect to math."[55] Two specific toxic characteristics include "(1) Focusing on the right answer, and (2) Independent practice valued over teamwork and collaboration."[56] Sawchuk demonstrates an interesting assumption when he writes, "Much of the current debate appears to spring not from the academic texts, but from fear among critics that students—especially White students will be exposed to supposedly damaging or self-demoralizing ideas."[57] Fear is not at issue and neither is demoralization. But assume for a moment that the latter is in play.

What if one of the self-demoralizing ideas, then, the result of absurd professorial claims? Laurel Rubel, Brooklyn College professor of math education, shared on a social media page the ridiculous statement that "2+2=4 reeks of white supremacist patriarchy."[58] Is logic demoralizing because it is white or because there are other acceptable answers to the equation? It would be highly interesting to see the response of this professor, should the bank in which she chose to place her money used its own demoralizing mathematics. One can be certain the numbers on her paycheck, and in her retirement fund, add up correctly.

Spirit Murder

The Abolitionist Teaching Network "incorporates language associated with critical race theory."[59] Abolitionist teachers are instructed to construct school cultures that "engage in healing and advocacy. This requires a commitment to learning from students, families, and educators who disrupt Whiteness and other forms of oppression. . . . It also discussed the *spirit murder* of people of color."[60]

Spirit murder is described by Patricia Williams. She claims,

> The truth is, black and brown children are spirit murdered daily, a term . . . coined to refer to the *disregard for others whose lives quantitatively depend on our regard.* Spirit murdering occurs every single day in many of our schools, virtually unnoticed, unchecked, and all in the name of some arbitrary norm created by a white person.[61]

Williams continues,

> We have to address these forms of oppression the same way we react to blatant murder. With time, I have learned that the guises for the slow cultural genocide (spirit murdering) often fall into one of four categories: communication and language, uniformity and safety, character, and systems.[62]

White teachers holding students to high standards in a classroom in terms of language, assimilation, calmness, unity, development of character and virtue, and self-control are assumed in the commission of spirit murder. Sadly,

Martin Luther King Jr. would have been accused of spirit murder upon his own children, since he lobbied for a colorblind society and one where character mattered as an American over the color of skin in a group.

This kind of rhetoric today would be met by King's detractors with accusations claiming the civil rights icon to be just another black face of white supremacy.[63] The reality is that today's activists are not like MLK's protesters. Both CRT and King may have existed in the 1960s, but each found its niche in different places and for varied social and racial purposes. Sadly, today's activists reject MLK's strategy that actually worked, as they instead favor the deconstructing and dismantling America.

FIVE CRT TENETS THAT HAVE IMPLICATIONS FOR AMERICAN EDUCATION

Delgado and Stefancic reveal the nucleus of CRT and lay out several tenets that currently affect our children and the American educational system. The authors begin with the premise of the first tenet with "racism is ordinary, not aberrational—*normal science*, the usual way society does business, the common, everyday experience of most people of color in this country."[64] R. R. Reno suggests that

> systemic racism is the hidden power that can explain our frustrations. The concept of intersectionality allows us to apply antiracist analysis widely. . . . The fact that one finds no discrete instances of discrimination or even conscious sentiment is of no moment. A system is at work.[65]

- The first tenet of CRT is that systemic racism is the normal, everyday way of doing business in America.

The second tenet which the authors submit is that "most would agree that our system of white-over-color ascendancy serves important purposes, both psychic and material, for the dominant group."[66] The reason this has not changed is "because racism advances the interests of both white elites (materially) and working class Caucasians (psychically), large segments of society have little incentive to eradicate it."[67] This is described as *interest convergence*.

In contrast, Janel George questions the use of the structural racism paradigm because it "dismisses the idea that racist incidents are aberrations but instead are manifestations of structural and systemic racism."[68] In terms of this first tenet, Gloria Ladson-Billings provides a bit of realism, when she writes, "few outside of CRT would declare that racism is normal."[69]

- The second tenet of CRT is that the dominant culture, which is ruled by whites, is set up as a comprehensive system for that very dominant culture and for the benefits that come along with status quo.

Next, in the third tenet, the authors express that "only aggressive, color-conscious efforts to change the way things are will do much to ameliorate the misery"[70] of blatant racism in the nation. As antiracist and CRT advocate Ibram X. Kendi puts it, "The only remedy to racist discrimination is antiracist discrimination. The only remedy to past discrimination is present discrimination. The only remedy to present discrimination is future discrimination."[71]

- The third tenet of CRT is that only conscious efforts to focus on color and actions of discrimination toward others can make significant differences toward dismantling the misery of racism.

Fourth, the authors share the idea that "society frequently chooses to ignore . . . scientific truths, creates races, and endows them with pseudo-permanent characteristics . . . no person has a single, easily stated, unitary identity."[72] Moreover, Joel Kotkin and Edward Heyman take Kendi to task for his assertions about meeting discrimination with discrimination. In Kendi's

> retelling of American history in *Stamped from the Beginning* . . . he uses it to rationalize and support his claim that African Americans have failed to attain the fruits of American life in the same way as whites—higher education, corporate leadership, home ownership and intergenerational wealth—but suggests that is due almost entirely to racist policies embedded in American institutions and law.[73]

This is a characteristic of the *social-construction* thesis, which "holds that race and races are products of social thought and relations. Not objective, inherent or fixed . . . rather, races are categories that society invents, manipulates, or retires, when convenient."[74]

- The fourth tenet of CRT is that society has constructed false characteristics about people and groups, their potential achievements, and, that race itself, is a pseudo-characteristic and social construct keeping people from success.

Critical race theorists make the claim in the fifth tenet:

> "that racism is codified in law, embedded in structures, and woven into public policy. CRT rejects claims of meritocracy or *colorblindness.* CRT recognizes

> that it is the systemic nature of racism that bears primary responsibility for producing racial inequality."[75]

This leads to the fifth tenet of CRT, which Janel George points out as one of the aspects of CRT found earlier in legal studies at American law schools.

- The fifth tenet of CRT is that racism is codified in American law and is responsible for producing racial inequality that now affects all aspects of life for people of color.

CRT HARMS SOCIETY

Swain and Schorr begin by expressing the dismissive nature of proponents of CRT. The authors share, "Concepts such as colorblindness, assimilation, and merit are dismissed as cynical means by which whites maintain their power and privilege in American society."[76] Likewise, in the text that included key writings that formed the initial critical race movement, it is stated that the *liberal approach of racial colorblindness* is to be rejected, in order to dream "beyond the colors of black and white."[77]

America has undergone large-scale reform, and this reform happened in the midst of a pandemic. The impetus of this reform was the tragic death of George Floyd. The new standard of current reform is now re-tethering to the more radical civil rights movement of the twentieth century. Instead of a person's character and the sum of his or her merits, people are being evaluated based on their grievances, skin color, numbers of oppressed categories into which they fit, and the fuzziness of the subjective application of a term *equity* or guaranteed outcomes.

A THEORY GONE WILD: WHITES AS RAGING RACISTS?

Attaching value added to skin color is harmful. Each person is unique and, although placed in various demographics, there is no replacement for any person in existence. Children need to hear the message that despite their external characteristics, they can achieve wonderful things in school, graduate, and go on to accomplish wonderful things as adults. They also need to hear that they are individuals with dreams and aspirations that do not have to fit those of any sociological grouping. However, they can achieve these things only if adults stop drilling into their heads how bad they are within a group of oppressors or how victimized they are in an oppressed group. This is where parents need to step in to counter the group-oriented indoctrination of their children.

The era of separate but equal is long gone in a legal sense. However, with CRT there is a similar new doctrine making headway across the land and it is infecting young minds. That is the doctrine that blends sociology, theology, and law. That blend combines a *new form of separatism*, *skin-color sinfulness*, and *inequality of outcomes*. This is the result of shifting from a focus on character to focusing on melanin. Not only does it affect younger children, but it leaves older students in a quandary about who and what they are.

Carol Anderson, in her book *White Rage*, writes,

> This is the moment now, when all of us—black, white, Latino, Native American, Asian American—must step out of the shadow of white rage, deny its power, understand its unseemly goals, and refuse to be seduced by its buzzwords, dog whistles, and sophistry. This is when we choose a different future.[78]

Anderson's rhetoric could easily be applicable to critical race theorists, antiracists, and groups like BLM. Instead, she focuses her research on whites only, and she does so in the following ways.

First, whites are considered racists because of the sins of America's past. White families whose relatives emigrated from Europe in the 1900s, or even more recently, are deemed just as racist as those whose families descended from the original British citizens who occupied the Original 13 colonies on the eastern seaboard of the United States.[79] Whites are also considered racists by default of their skin color at birth, and this includes those of mixed race, according to more fundamentally fervent CRTs. Thus, to the ardent among them, the assertion about whites is true whether a white was born in America or anywhere else. To paraphrase CNN commentator Van Jones, whites are born with racism as part of their biology and can be switched on and off at any time. In Jones's words, "So even the most liberal, well-intentioned white person, has a virus in his or her brain that can be activated at an instant."[80]

Jones's statement seems to imply racism has a DNA component to it. Taken to its absurd conclusions, babies are racists growing into their racism, by default. According to Jones, maybe the COVID-19 pandemic is secondary to the virus in the brains of developing children. Labeling has always been wrong, but this occurs more and more in our schools, involving both teachers and students. Labeling is also found in district-approved curriculum.

Allowing this labeling to continue diminishes human character and the uniqueness of people. These tactics devalue the educational experiences of children when they show up in classrooms across America. Students are not graded as a group, and there is no group dynamic that earns a diploma.

The second area Anderson focuses on reduces whites as racists for denying they are racists. Any effort that demonstrates defensiveness or to shun even the notion of the label is met with accusations of fragility and dismissal.

These accusations are based on the assumptions that whites are comfortable in their roles as *supremacists* and *oppressors*. Thus, it is the ease at which whites shun the accusations that leads to their denial. With irrational views such as those, there could easily be questions posed as to why groups of people assumed as oppressors are not angrier than they show. If whites were to demonstrate any such anger, the race-baiters would have them exactly where they expected. The fact that they do not should also imply how much stock is placed in Anderson's claim.

Nevertheless, Anderson argues the denial that they are racists means white powers are being challenged and they are psychologically defending themselves, in order to maintain their *fragile* whiteness over those whom they oppress. This cannot help but affect student learning, classroom decorum, and local civic unity.[81] The reason it affects students is because they will be left in a state of confusion, questioning themselves. The psychological impact would be quite significant.[82] Not surprisingly, even with such a risk, Adrienne D. Dixson, Celia Rousseau Anderson, and Jamel Donnor favor CRT because its "approaches allow us to rethink and reconstruct traditional school policy and practices around the insights of the greatest stakeholders—those who experience the brunt of educational injustice."[83]

Third, when whites agree they are racists, they are then shamed and called out for their implicit (unconscious) and explicit (conscious) bias. They can be doxed, lose their jobs and their families, and some even take their own lives. There can be a sacrifice of personal and real estate property—which might even be destroyed by violent mobs.[84] Such actions did occur between 2019 and 2021. Admissions by whites and confessions on behalf of past generations of racism are met with statements of "See, we told you so" and "You must check your privilege and deconstruct your Whiteness." Either way, whites are slotted to lose.

There seems no way out of being labeled a racist if a person is white. Ironically, the critical race theorist is not focused on acts of racism, per se. Yet, the reality is these actions are viewed as evidence of the existence of something systemic, which critical race theorists maintain affects all institutions in American society. This is another piece of evidence of the inconsistency of applying a theory to one group of humans.[85] But is this sensible? George affirms, "CRT does not define racism in the traditional manner as solely the consequence of discrete irrational bad acts perpetuated by individuals."[86]

Anderson concludes by summarizing what she thinks is the trigger point for the demonstration of white rage. She exclaims,

> The trigger for white rage, inevitably, is black advancement. It is not the mere presence of black people that is the problem; rather, it is blackness with ambition, with drive, with purpose, with aspirations, and with demands for full and

equal citizenship. . . . The truth is, white rage has undermined democracy, warped the Constitution, weakened the nation's ability to compete economically, squandered billions of dollars on baseless incarceration, rendered an entire region sick, poor, and woefully undereducated, and left cities nothing less than decimated.[87]

CRT AND ACADEME

Caitlin Bird writes,

> Critical race theory . . . is an academic framework that has been around since the 1970s. It is rooted in the idea that racism is systemic in institutions and public policies, like zoning, policing, banking, education, health care and more. Inequities, the theory contends, is not just demonstrated by individual people with prejudices.[88]

Christopher Rufo, a fellow at the Manhattan Institute, describes CRT as

> an academic discipline . . . built on the intellectual framework of identity-based Marxism. . . . Over the past decade it has increasingly become the default ideology in our public institutions. It has been injected into government agencies, public school systems, teacher training programs, and corporate human resources departments in the form of diversity training programs, human resource modules, public policy frameworks, and school curricula.[89]

CRT incorporates "a series of euphemisms deployed by its supporters . . . including *equity*, *social justice*, *diversity and inclusion*, and *culturally responsive teaching*."[90] Pluckrose and Lindsay expand this point: "A critical theory is chiefly concerned with revealing hidden biases and underexamined assumptions, usually by pointing out what have been termed *problematics*, which are ways in which society and the systems that it operates upon are going wrong."[91]

CRT Growth and Expansion

CRT means some things to some groups and other things to other groups. Supporters claim it is a factual way to view the world. Detractors argue that it is a teaching hatred and racism to children. George writes, "CRT is not itself a substantive course or workshop; it is a practice. It is an approach or lens through which an educator can help students examine the role of race and racism in American society"[92] There is one point of agreement regardless of the position one takes on CRT. Since its inception into the academy, CRT "has since been adopted in other fields in higher education."[93]

Academe served as the launching point of origin for the eventual spread of the theory into schools, the corporate world, medicine,[94] and even the US military. Institutions are now being instructed about the differences between race-based and race-conscious equity and practice. One of the latest examples of CRT in the medical field comes from the document *Advancing Health Equity*, from the American Medical Association. The document reads:

> It is critical to address all areas of marginalization and inequity due to sexism, class oppression, homophobia, xenophobia and ableism. Yet conversations about race and racism tend to be some of the most difficult for people in this country to participate in for numerous reasons, including a lack of knowledge or shared analysis of its historical and current underpinnings, as well as outright resistance and denial that racism exists.[95]

CRT is part of an ever-expanding group of studies categorized now as grievance studies, which amounts to "a loose collection of academic disciplines characterized by their emphasis on oppressive social and political institutions and the marginalized identities they victimize."[96] Philosopher Stephen Hicks perceives this as a formidable issue. He exclaims, "We are experiencing a period of *skeptical epistemologies*."[97] As a result, this skepticism leads Hicks to conclude that over time "a growing number of intellectuals came to align with Marxist and socialist political perspectives."[98] Hicks then argues that "there is a clear line through where the scientific pretensions of classical Marxism gradually gave way to the irrationalist critiques of the cultural Marxists, and finally converged with the overtly skeptical epistemologies of the postmodernists." Hence, the obvious pretenses of Marxism plus irrationalism do converge in postmodernism.

Pluckrose and Lindsay take a less rhetorical approach. They profess,

> It is becoming increasingly difficult to miss the influence of . . . *identity politics* or *political correctness*. Almost every day, a story comes out about somebody who has been fired, *canceled*, or subjected to public shaming on social media. . . . Sometimes the accusations are warranted. . . . However . . . often the accusation is highly interpretive and its reasoning tortuous.[99]

When those who act as bullies or authoritarians over what is said and done by the average person, they tend to "use everyday words differently from the rest of us."[100]

For example,

> When they speak of racism . . . they are not referring to prejudice on the grounds of race, but rather to, as they define it, a racialized system that permeates all interactions in society yet is largely invisible except to those who experience it or who have been trained in the proper *critical* methods that train them to see it.[101]

One must question whether the racist system actually exists, or whether those that speak of systemic concerns are working backward from a definition to make certain there is a fit.

How can CRT academicians argue against objectivity and preach the same to students, and then not admit their position against objectivity is actually an objective in-and-of-itself? In fact, how can they even infer such knowledge when their "theory holds that objective knowledge—that which is true for everyone, regardless of their identity—is unobtainable, because knowledge is always bound up with cultural values"?[102]

Contrasting Terms

CRT has spread neatly into nearly every facet of American society, and not the least of which is schooling. George asserts that some of the "most compelling demonstrations of how racism has been replicated through systems is within the education system."[103] Furthermore, some of the older concepts pertaining to discrimination and race, and dealt with in decades past under the law, are no longer in vogue to critical race theorists. "Equality . . . is explicitly rejected by critical race theorists. To them, equality represents *mere nondiscrimination* and provides *camouflage* for white supremacy, patriarchy and oppression."[104]

Standing in contrast to equality,

> equity as defined and promoted by critical race theorists is little more than reformulated Marxism. In the name of *equity*, UCLA Law Professor and critical race theorist Cheryl Harris has proposed suspending private property rights, seizing land and wealth and redistributing them along racial lines.[105]

Segregation is still around, and it is gaining renewed traction through the conscious efforts of CRT proponents. Pluckrose and Lindsay claim, "Segregated schooling is a particularly profound and timely demonstration of the persistence of systemic racism in education."[106] The late Derrick Bell was known for his cynical pessimism and viewed race issues through this perspective. "For instance, he . . . considered that white people had introduced desegregation, not as a solution to black people's problems, but to further their own interests."[107]

According to Bell, the 1955 Supreme Court case of *Brown v. Board of Education of Topeka*, Kansas, was decided the way it was because of what he terms *interest convergence*,[108] which is the recognition that the interests of Black people in achieving racial equality will be accommodated only when it converges with the interests of white people.[109]

As a clarion call to action for modern civil rights lawyers,

> an important consideration is that many of our nation's systems and structures—including the legal system—were created when people of color were denied full participation in American society. Therefore, as may critical race theorists have noted, CRT calls for a radical reordering of society and a reckoning with the strictures and systems that intersect to perpetuate racial inequality.[110]

Thus, CRT has expanded exponentially and factional advocates have set their sights on actively reordering American society.

CRT: A FACTION IN ACTION

According to CRT supporters, racism is inescapable and ingrained in society, as well as part of the DNA of all whites.[111] The claim is that there is a certain blindness that whites could not—and still cannot—fathom that racism exists. "Ambition was forbidden"[112] for blacks. In many cases, blacks were generally knowledgeable about the south's "Dixie limit, which made certain not to allow Blacks to advance in society."[113] But why are schools functionally repeating the failures of the past?

Poorly performing public schools and inadequate classroom teachers, combined with low-achieving students, lower the bar of teacher performance and academic expectations. As if to make matter worse, the bar of achievement is continuing to be lowered, in order to meet the new definitions of educational fairness and equity.

In addition to newly defined educational outcomes, there exists a bevy of social safety net programs that compete economically and financially as good alternatives to full-time employment. If ambition was forbidden in the past, then advancement is discouraged in the present, and sometimes this is the fault of governmental policy and decisions by local leaders.

For example, the state of Washington has been a progressive leader in forging ahead with the expansion of CRT. In order to demonstrate that there is a positive impact upon students, the teaching of CRT is coupled with the lowering of academic standards. In order to demonstrate positive outcomes with CRT, Washington's new learning standards have been released that focus on five core areas of study: English language-arts, history, social studies, math, and science.

These standards are "disguised by the label Ethnic Studies"[114] standards and "will replace Washington's academic learning standards with controversial Critical Race Theory content."[115] The new state standards will include "academic material according to four CRT domains: Identity, Power and Oppression, History of Resistance and Liberation, and Reflection and Action."[116] Furthermore, "In English, instead of teaching grammar, the new standards will teach the concepts of White supremacy, Institutional racism, Structural racism, and White privilege."[117]

The demonstration of the learning of these new standards includes a classroom environment that is both academic and activism oriented, with each encouraging "students to take action"[118] This is found in the literature of CRT that requires student action and special attention is paid to elements of social justice. In order for teachers to be ready to apply CRT in their curriculum, Washington State governor Jay Inslee signed "SB 5044 . . . to require the implantation of mandatory Critical Race Theory training for all teachers and staff at K-12 schools."[119] As a progressive state, Washington acted, while "politicians, educators, and pundits all [were] . . . arguing that the hundreds of thousands of students who did not go on to college were being *lost* to the nation."[120]

This type of progressivism caught the attention of now deceased, former Alabama congressman, Carl Elliott. He warned the nation that what is taught in America's public schools will be what America will face as a nation.[121] Education "can be transformative. It reshapes the health outcomes of a people; it breaks the cycle of poverty; it improves housing conditions; it raises the standard of living. . . . In short, education strengthens a democracy."[122]

Americans must stand up and proclaim the vision of the nation they wish to imagine. The problem is there are competing visions. According to Anderson, people must take ownership of the vision and work to

> defuse the power of white rage. It is time to move into that future. It is a future where the right to vote is unfettered by discriminatory restrictions that prevent millions of American citizens from having any say in their own government.[123]

Anderson believes "the future is one that invests in our children by making access to good schools the norm, not the exception, and certainly not dependent on zip code. . . . It's time to rethink America."[124] Anderson will have a difficult time convincing political leaders to fix the inner-city schools. They seem more concerned about one's color than they are about textbooks.

CRT WIDENS ITS UMBRELLA

Delgado and Stefancic posit that

> CRT is founded on two key principles: that racism is ordinary, not aberrational—normal science, the usual way society does business, the common, everyday experience of most people of color in this country; second, that our system of white-over-color ascendancy serves important purposes, both psychic and material. . . . CRT therefore holds that racism is embedded deeply in American life, unconsciously into White American psyches, and that it is impossible for White Americans to understand their own racism or that of the system, let alone remove it.[125]

CRT evolved beyond its original purpose in academe, as is the case with many theories that emerge from the ivory towers of universities. In fact, CRT proponents declare the theory "is not a diversity and inclusion training but a practice of interrogating race and racism in society that emerged in the legal academy."[126] However, they also admit that CRT had "spread to other fields of scholarship."[127]

Kimberlê Crenshaw, "who coined the term CRT, notes that CRT is not a noun, but a verb."[128] This implies that there is action involved at the root of CRT.[129] This should come as no surprise. CRT must become activated in practice in order for it to have any legitimacy as a change agent.[130] Progressives on college campuses now have their sights set on radicalizing K-6 students and also hope to turn out a teaching cohort of classroom teachers to accomplish their vision.[131]

The umbrella of CRT was opened wide by insightful whistleblowers and their reports. In an effort to tarnish one of the earlier reporters on CRT, the claim is made that Christopher Rufo had been working in tandem with the Trump administration to make "critical race theory toxic in the public imagination."[132]

According to critics, it was Rufo who wanted to expand the umbrella of CRT to larger audiences. He was reported to have written,

> The goal is to have the public read something crazy in the newspaper and immediately think critical race theory . . . We have decodified the term and will recodify it to annex the entire range of cultural constructions that are unpopular with Americans.[133]

However, this criticism is only a distraction. CRT needs no help in finding new avenues to infect. Examples of CRT used in public schools are found in table 1.3.

Table 1.3 Sample of Public School CRT and Race-Based Activities and Goals

Location	*Activities*	*Goal(s)*
Arizona State Department of Education	Created an equity toolkit for use district-wide.	(1) To point out that babies exhibit first signs of racism at three months of age and (2) that white children become are strongly biased toward whiteness and become full racists by age five.
Buffalo, NY Public Schools	Kindergarteners watch a video of deceased black children and are told that police are racists and could kill the black students at any time.	To teach all students all white people perpetuate systemic racism.
Charlotte-Mecklenburg, NC School District	Teachers take mandatory antiracist and implicit bias training courses.	Fulfillment of courses on Race, Bias, and Equity.
City Schools of Decatur, Georgia	Teachers required to read Ibram X. Kendi's book How to be an Antiracist. A two-day assignment was given and teachers were separated into racial groups.	Teachers required to complete a two-day workshop with a personal inventory taken of their white privilege.
Cupertino, CA Elementary School	Forced first graders to deconstruct their racial and sexual identities.	Students rank selves according to their understanding of power and privilege.
Montgomery, Maryland County Public Schools	In 2020, the district launched a no-opt-out psychoeducational lesson to teach children about a dual pandemic involving COVID-19 and systemic racism. Materials recommended that teachers buy Ibram X. Kendi's book *Antiracist Baby*.	To use Social-Emotional Learning and CRT to link up the severity COVID-19 and racism as equal in concern. To expose children to racial activism and politics by means of Ibram X. Kendi's controversial book on antiracism.
Norman, OK Public Schools	Spent taxpayer dollars on left-wing advocacy groups to instruct DEI training for teachers.	To strive for social justice, being culturally aware and achievement of equity for all.
Oregon State Department of Education	The ODOE is promoting and encouraging its educators to take a revised course that addresses how to dismantle racism in mathematics.	To rid mathematics instruction and content of the toxic characteristics of white supremacy culture.

(Continued)

Table 1.3 Sample of Public School CRT and Race-Based Activities and Goals (*Continued*)

Location	*Activities*	*Goal(s)*
United Nations International School New York	Students launched an anonymous social media campaign denouncing teachers and school consciousness for white Liberal racist thinking, and direct and repeated racial trauma upon students.	(1) Threaten to cancel the school adult oppressors through social media shaming, (2) decolonize the school curriculum, (3) create safe spaces for marginalized students, and (4) unseat Eurocentric academics.

Sources:

- Christopher F. Rufo. "Critical race theory: What is it and how to fight it?" *Imprimis*. March 2021. 50(3): p. 3. Cf. Rufo:
  - o *Critical race theory briefing book*. July, 2021. pp. 9–11. Retrieved August 1, 2021, from https://christopherrufo.com/crt-briefing-book/. "Failure Factory." *City Journal*. February 23, 2021. https://www.city-journal.org/buffalo-public-schools-critical-race-theory-curriculum.
  - o "Woke elementary." *City Journal*. January 13, 2021. Retrieved November 1, 2021, from https://www.city-journal.org/identity-politics-in-cupertino-california-elementary-school.
  - o "Manhattan's most privileged kids play victim—and their teachers cave." *New York Post*. January 27, 2021. Retrieved June 4, 2021, from https://nypost.com/2021/01/27/manhattans-most-privileged-kids-play-victim-and-teachers-cave/.
- Elizabeth J. Schultz. "The left is lying: CRT is peddling hate in our schools." *Bacon's Rebellion*. August 4, 2021. Retrieved August 12, 2021, from https://www.baconsrebellion.com/wp/the-left-is-lying-crt-is-peddling-hate-in-our-schools/.
- Jake Dima. "Oregon promoting teacher course on dismantling racism in mathematics." *MSN*. February 12, 2021. Retrieved June 22, 2021, from https://www.msn.com/en-us/news/us/oregon-promoting-teacher-course-on-dismantling-racism-in-mathematics/ar-BB1dDgW8.
- Ryan Mills. "Oklahoma public school district spent $23K on equity training ahead of big budget cut." *National Review*. May 14, 2021. Retrieved June 17, 2021, from https://www.nationalreview.com/news/oklahoma-public-school-district-spent-23k-on-equity-training-ahead-of-big-budget-cut/.
- Tyler O'Neil. "Maryland's most populous county told students there is a double pandemic of COVID and racism." *Fox News*. November 4, 2021. Retrieved November 5, 2021, from https://www.foxnews.com/us/marylands-most-populous-county-told-students-there-is-a-double-pandemic-of-covid-and-racism.
- Staff. "What is CSD's equity plan?" *Equity at City Schools of Decatur*. 2021. Retrieved November 1, 2021, from https://equity.csdecatur.net/what-is-csds-equity-plan.
- Terry Stoops. "CMS to require teachers to attend 1.5 hour race, bias, equity training." *The Locker* Room. May 7, 2021. Retrieved November 1, 2021, from https://lockerroom.johnlocke.org/2021/05/07/cms-to-require-teachers-to-attend-1-5-hour-race-bias-power-equity-training/.

In closing out this chapter, it must be noted that CRT appears to be more than a fad. CRT seems here to stay, and there are new variants being added to its theoretical base, and these are spreading like a psychological virus and infecting students en masse. One thing remains certain. With CRT there has been a radical shift from the days of MLK and his dream about individual character development for his children in schools. One's color is now his or her character, whether black or white.

NOTES

1. Rasool Berry. "Critical [g]race theory: The promise and perils of CRT." *Medium*. August 20, 2020. Retrieved August 8, 2021, from https://rasoolberry.medium.com/critical-g-race-theory-the-promise-perils-of-crt-c5de933d55a1.

2. Jeffrey J. Pyle. "Race, equality, and the rule of law: Critical race theory's attack on the promise of liberalism." *Boston College Law Review* 40, no. 3 (May 1, 1999): 785–827. See p. 788. Retrieved October 22, 2021, from https://lawdigitalcommons.bc.edu/cgi/viewcontent.cgi?article=2124&context=bclr.

3. Stephen Sawchuk. "What is Critical race theory, and why is it under attack." *EdWeek.* May 18, 2021. Retrieved May 20, 2021, from https://www.edweek.org/leadership/what-is-critical-race-theory-and-why-is-it-under-attack/2021/05.

4. Janel George. "A lesson on critical race theory." *American Bar Association.* January 11, 2021. 46(2). Retrieved October 19, 2021, from https://www.americanbar.org/groups/crsj/publications/human_rights_magazine_home/civil-rights-reimagining-policing/a-lesson-on-critical-race-theory/.

5. Carol M. Swain and Christopher J. Schorr. *Black Eye for America: How Critical Race Theory Is Burning Down the House.* Rockville, MD: Be the People Books, 2021, p. 21.

6. Ibram X. Kendi. *Stamped from the Beginning: The Definitive History of Racist Ideas in America.* New York: Bold Type Books, 2016, pp. 443–444. Cf. Kimberlê Crenshaw. "Mapping the margins of intersectionality, identity politics, and violence against women of color." *Stanford Law Review* 43, no. 6 (1991): 1242.

7. Helen Pluckrose and James Lindsay. *Cynical Theories: How Activist Scholarship Made Everything about Race, Gender, and Identity and Why This Harms Everybody.* Durham, NC: Pitchstone Publishing, 2020, pp. 111, 114.

8. George. "A lesson on critical race theory." *American Bar Association.*

9. Gloria Ladson-Billings. *Critical Race Theory in Education.* New York: Teachers College, Columbia University, 2021, p. 108.

10. Matt McManus. "The Frankfurt School and postmodern philosophy." *Quillette.* January 3, 2019. Retrieved August 20, 2021, from https://quillette.com/2019/01/03/the-frankfurt-school-and-postmodern-philosophy/.

11. Ibid.

12. James Bohman. "Critical theory." *Stanford Encyclopedia of Philosophy*, 2005, p. 1.

13. Mark R. Levin. *American Marxism.* New York: Simon & Schuster, Inc., 2021, p. 82.

14. Ibid, p. 86.

15. Bohman. "Critical theory." *Stanford Encyclopedia of Philosophy*, 2005, p. 1.

16. Ibid. Cf. Max Horkheimer. *Critical Theory: Selected Essays.* Trans. by Matthew J. O'Connell, et al. New York: Seabury Press, 1992, p. 246.

17. Bohman. "Critical theory." *Stanford Encyclopedia of Philosophy*, 2005, p. 1.

18. Gloria Ladson-Billings. *Critical Race Theory in Education.* New York: Teachers College, Columbia University, 2021, p. 108.

19. Pluckrose and Lindsay. *Cynical Theories*, p. 19.

20. Ibid., p. 21.

21. Ibid.

22. Ibid.

23. Swain and Schorr. *Black Eye for America*, p. 23.

24. Ibid., p. 24.

25. Richard Delgado and Jean Stefancic. *Critical Race Theory: An Introduction*, 2nd edition. New York: New York University Press, 2012, p. 2.

26. Lindsay Perez Huber and Daniel G. Solorzano. "Racial microaggressions as a tool for critical race research." *Race, Ethnicity, and Education* 18, no. 3 (2015): 297–320.

27. Richard Delgado and Jean Stefancic. *Critical Race Theory: An Introduction*, p. 62.

28. Ibid.

29. Pluckrose and Lindsay. *Cynical Theories*, pp. 56–57.

30. Ange-Marie Hancock. *Intersectionality: An Intellectual History*. New York: Oxford University Press, 2016, pp. 5–6.

31. Pluckrose and Lindsay. *Cynical Theories*, p. 130.

32. Ijeoma Oluo. *So You Want to Talk About Race*. New York: Seal Press, 2019, p. 81.

33. Delgado and Stefancic. *Critical Race Theory*, p. 62.

34. Ibid., p. 67.

35. Ibid.

36. Ibid.

37. Ibid., p. 68.

38. Ibid., pp. 62–63.

39. Pluckrose and Lindsay. *Cynical Theories*, pp. 111–112.

40. Nicholas C. DiDonato. "Theology as queen of science reconsidered: A basis for scientific realism." *Theology and Science* 13, no. 4 (October 12, 2015): 409–424. Retrieved November 1, 2021, from https://doi.org/10.1080/14746700.2015.1082874.

41. Ibid., pp. 57–58. Cf. Kimberlê Crenshaw. "Mapping the margins: Intersectionality, identity politics, and violence against women of color." *Stanford Law Review* 43, no. 6 (1991): 1297.

42. Pluckrose and Lindsay. *Cynical Theories*, p. 123.

43. Ibid.

44. Staff. "Critical race theory." *The Bridge*. 2020. Retrieved October 11, 2021, from https://cyber.harvard.edu/bridge/CriticalTheory/critical4.htm.

45. Pluckrose and Lindsay. *Cynical Theories*, p. 130.

46. Swain and Schorr. *Black Eye for America*, p. 3. Cf. Crenshaw, "Mapping the margins," pp. 1241–1299.

47. Swain and Schorr. *Black Eye for America*, p. 9.

48. Stephen Sawchuk. "What is critical race theory, and why is it under attack." *EdWeek*, p. 3.

49. Ibid.

50. Dorian S. Abbot and Ivan Marinovic. "The diversity problem on campus." *Newsweek*. August 12, 2021. Retrieved August 25, 2021, from https://www.newsweek.com/diversity-problem-campus-opinion-1618419.

51. Ryan Mills. "Massachusetts public school district encourages students to report peers, teachers, for bias violation." *National Review*. June 15, 2021. Retrieved June 15, 2021, from https://www.nationalreview.com/news/massachusetts-public-school-district-encourages-students-to-report-peers-teachers-for-bias-violations/.

52. Ibid.

53. Ibid.

54. Abigail Shrier. "Gender ideology run amok." *Imprimis*. June/July 2021. (50):6–7.

55. M. K. Sprinkle. "Racist mathematics of racism propounded as antiracism? Commentary." *Baltimore Sun*. March 13, 2021. Retrieved August 8, 2021, from https://www.baltimoresun.com/maryland/carroll/opinion/cc-op-sprinkle-031321-20210313-m2lg4tomcndolfj5kebf6asike-story.html0.

56. Ibid.

57. Stephen Sawchuk. "What is critical race theory, and why is it under attack." *EdWeek*, p. 5.

58. Sprinkle. "Racist mathematics of racism propounded as antiracism?" *Baltimore Sun*.

59. Ethan Barton. "Trump OMB chief Russ Vought investigating Biden administration ties to CRT group." *Fox News*. July 28, 2021. Retrieved July 28, from https://www.foxnews.com/us/critical-race-theory-biden-administration-russ-vought-investigation.

60. Ibid. Cf. Bettina L. Love. *We Want to More Than Survive: Abolitionist Teaching and the Pursuit of Educational Freedom*. See chapter 5, 2020. Boston, MA: Beacon Press.

61. Patricia Williams. "Spirit-murdering the messenger: The discourse of finger pointing as the law's response to racism." *University of Miami Law Review*. 1987. Retrieved August 22, 2021, from https://www.semanticscholar.org/paper/Spirit-Murdering-the-Messenger%3A-The-Discourse-of-as-Williams/0dd8b695e4120168f98e5c07ddd1d1ea19fae083?p2df.

62. Khristy Nicholas. "'It keeps us all safe,' and other lies to spirit murder black and brown children." *Education Elements*. Retrieved August 22, 2021, from https://www.edelements.com/blog/lies-used-to-spirit-murder-black-and-brown-children, Cf. Patricia Williams. "Spirit-murdering the messenger: The discourse of finger pointing as the law's response to racism." *University of Miami Law Review*.

63. Robin Givhan. "Blackface is white supremacy as fashion—and it's always been in season." *The Washington Post*. February 7, 2019. Retrieved October 14, 2021, from https://www.washingtonpost.com/lifestyle/blackface-is-white-supremacy-as-fashion--and-its-always-been-in-season/2019/02/07/fdb60c06-2b1e-11e9-b2fc-721718903bfc_story.html. Cf. Charles Hurt. "How Larry Elder became the new black face of white supremacy." *The Washington Times*. September 2, 2021. Retrieved September 4, 2021, from https://www.washingtontimes.com/news/2021/sep/2/how-larry-elder-became-the-new-black-face-of-white/.

64. Delgado and Stefancic. *Critical Race Theory*, p. 7. Cf. Gloria Ladson-Billings. *Critical Race Theory in Education*. New York: Teachers College, Columbia University, 2021, p. 108.

65. R. R. Reno. "Antiracist hysteria." *First Things*. December 2020. Retrieved April 23, 2021, from https://www.firstthings.com/article/2020/12/antiracist-hysteria.

66. Delgado and Stefancic. *Critical Race Theory*, p. 7.

67. Ibid.

68. Janel George. "A lesson on critical race theory." *American Bar Association.*

69. Gloria Ladson-Billings. *Critical Race Theory in Education.* New York: Teachers College, Columbia University, 2021, p. 43.

70. Delgado and Stefancic. *Critical Race Theory*, pp. 8, 26.

71. Ibram X. Kendi. *How to Be an Antiracist.* New York: One World Publishers, 2019, p. 19.

72. Delgado and Stefancic. *Critical Race Theory*, pp. 9–10.

73. Joel Kotkin and Edward Heyman. "Critical race theory ignores anti-Semitism." *UnHerd.* August 9, 2021. Retrieved August 10, 2021, from https://unherd.com/2021/08/critical-race-theory-rewrites-history/.

74. Delgado and Stefancic. *Critical Race Theory*, p. 9. Cf. George. "A lesson on critical race theory." *American Bar Association.*

75. George. "A lesson on critical race theory." *American Bar Association.* Cf. Christine Sleeter. "Critical race theory." *Personal Blog.* May 15, 2021. Retrieved May 27, 2021, from https://www.christinesleeter.org/critical-race-theory.

76. Swain and Schorr. *Black Eye for America*, p. 11.

77. Isabel Funk. "Educational merit of critical race theory sparks heated debate." *Kent Reporter.* August 2, 2021. Retrieved September 4, 2021, from https://www.kentreporter.com/news/educational-merit-of-critical-race-theory-sparks-heated-debate/. Cf. Kimberlé Crenshaw, Neil Gotanda, Gary Feller, and Kendall Thomas (Eds.). *Critical Race Theory: The Key Writings that Formed the Movement.* New York: The New Press, 1995. See Introduction.

78. Carol Anderson. *White Rage: The Unspoken Truth of Our Racial Divide.* New York: Bloomsbury Publishing, 2017, p. 178.

79. Jack D. Warren Jr. "The fatal flaw of the 1619 project." *The American Revolution Institute.* August 14, 2020. Retrieved May 25, 2021, from https://www.americanrevolutioninstitute.org/fatal-flaw-of-the-1619-project-curriculum/.

80. Libby Emmons. "Watch: CNN analyst says all white people have a 'virus' of racism." *The Post Millennial.* May 30, 2020. Retrieved May 23, 2021, from https://thepostmillennial.com/watch-cnn-analyst-says-all-white-people-have-virus-of-racism.

81. Katy Waldman. "A sociologist examines the white fragility that prevents white Americans from confronting racism." *The New Yorker.* July 23, 2018. Retrieved May 1, 2021, from https://www.newyorker.com/books/page-turner/a-sociologist-examines-the-white-fragility-that-prevents-white-americans-from-confronting-racism.

82. Kenneth R. Ginsburg (ed.) and Zachary Brett Ramirez McClain (Assoc. Ed). "Reaching Teens: The traumatic impact of racism and discrimination on young people and how to talk about it." 2nd edition. *American Academy of Pediatrics.* See Chapter 42. June 29, 2020. Retrieved November 1, 2021, from https://www.seattlechildrens.org/globalassets/documents/clinics/diversity/the-traumatic-impact-of-racism-and-discrimination-on-young-people-and-how-to-talk-about-it.pdf.

83. Adrienne Dixson, Celia Rousseau Anderson, and Jamel Donnor. *Critical Race Theory in Education.* New York: Routledge, 2016, p. 83.

84. Roudabeh Kishin and Sam Jones. "Demonstrations and political violence in America: New data for summer 2020." *Armed Conflict Location & Event Data* (ACLED) 2021. Retrieved October 14, 2021, from https://acleddata.com/2020/09/03/demonstrations-political-violence-in-america-new-data-for-summer-2020/.

85. Dana Brownlee. "Dear White people: Here are 5 uncomfortable truths Black colleagues need you to know." *Forbes*. June 16, 2020. Retrieved May 30, 2021, from https://www.forbes.com/sites/danabrownlee/2020/06/16/dear-white-people-here-are-5-uncomfortable-truths-black-colleagues-need-you-to-know/?sh=2bc68646624e.

86. George. "A lesson on critical race theory." *American Bar Association*.

87. Anderson. *White Rage*, pp. 3, 6.

88. Caitlin Bird. "Charleston unveiled its plan to address systemic racism. Will three words derail it?" *The State*. August 6, 2021. Retrieved August 24, 2021, from https://www.thestate.com/news/charleston/article253284808.html.

89. Christopher F. Rufo. "Critical race theory: What is it and how to fight it?" *Imprimis* 50, no. 3 (March 2021): 2.

90. Ibid.

91. Pluckrose and Lindsay. *Cynical Theories*, pp. 13–14.

92. Janel George. Critical race theory isn't a curriculum. It's a practice." *EdWeek*. May 26, 2021. Retrieved August 4, 2021, from https://www.edweek.org/leadership/opinion-critical-race-theory-isnt-a-curriculum-its-a-practice/2021/05.

93. Ibid.

94. Staff. "Advancing health equity: Guide to language, narrative and concepts." *American Medical Association; Center for Health Justice*. 2021. Retrieved November 10, 2021, from https://www.ama-assn.org/system/files/ama-aamc-equity-guide.pdf.

95. Ibid.

96. Matt McManus. "The Frankfurt School and postmodern philosophy." *Quillette*. January 3, 2019. Retrieved August 20, 2021, from https://quillette.com/2019/01/03/the-frankfurt-school-and-postmodern-philosophy/.

97. Ibid.

98. Ibid.

99. Pluckrose and Lindsay. *Cynical Theories*, p. 15.

100. Ibid.

101. Ibid.

102. Ibid., p. 79.

103. Janel George. "A lesson on critical race theory." *American Bar Association*.

104. Rufo. "Critical race theory," p. 2.

105. Ibid., pp. 2–3.

106. Pluckrose and Lindsay. *Cynical Theories*, p. 116.

107. Ibid. Cf. Derrick A. Bell, J. "*Brown v. Board of Education* and the interest-convergence dilemma." *Harvard Law Review* 93, no. 3 (1980): 530–533. Cf. also, Janel George. "A lesson on critical race theory." *American Bar Association*.

108. Gloria Ladson-Billings. *Critical Race Theory in Education*. New York: Teachers College, Columbia University, 2021, p. 43.

109. George. "A lesson on critical race theory." *American Bar Association*.

110. Ibid.

111. Karl Quinn. "Are all white people racist? Why critical race theory has us rattled." *The Sydney Morning Herald*. November 7, 2020. Retrieved September 4, 2021, from https://www.smh.com.au/culture/books/are-all-white-people-racist-why-critical-race-theory-has-us-rattled-20201105-p56bwv.html.

112. Anderson. *White Rage*, p. 43.

113. Ibid.

114. Liv Finne. "Washington public school officials lower academic standards as they implement Critical Race Theory." *Washington Policy Center*. September 21, 2021. Retrieved September 2021, from https://www.washingtonpolicy.org/publications/detail/washington-public-school-officials-lower-academic-standards-as-they-implement-critical-race-theory.

115. Ibid.

116. Ibid.

117. Ibid.

118. Ibid.

119. Ibid.

120. Anderson. *White Rage*, p. 91.

121. Ibid.

122. Ibid, p. 96.

123. Ibid, p. 175.

124. Ibid, pp. 175–176.

125. Ben Shapiro. "The movement against critical race theory is deeply necessary." *Inside Scoop Politics*. June 23, 2021. Retrieved June 24, 2021, from https://insidescooppolitics.com/archives/3657.

126. George. "A lesson on critical race theory." *American Bar Association*.

127. Ibid.

128. Ibid.

129. Cady Lang. "President Trump has attacked critical race theory. Here's what to know about the intellectual movement." *Time*. September 29, 2020. Retrieved July 12, 2021, from https://time.com/5891138/critical-race-theory-explained/.

130. Matthew Lynch. "10 reasons why critical race theory is perfect for confronting racism." *The Edvocate*. August 30, 2021. Retrieved October 14, 2021, from https://www.theedadvocate.org/10-reasons-why-critical-race-theory-is-perfect-for-confronting-racism/.

131. Staff. "Progressives spent decades radicalizing college students. Their new target: Grade schoolers." *Association of Mature American Citizens*. September 14, 2021. Retrieved September 15, 2021, from https://amac.us/progressives-spent-decades-radicalizing-college-students-their-new-target-grade-schoolers/.

132. Tyler Kingkade, Brandy Zadrozny, and Ben Collins. "Is critical race theory taking over your school board? A national organization could be why." *NBC News*. June 15, 2021. Retrieved June 15, 2021, from https://www.nbcnews.com/news/us-news/critical-race-theory-invades-school-boards-help-conservative-groups-n1270794.

133. Ibid.

Chapter 2

What's the Matter with Melanin?

> As a Black woman, race has always been a prominent part of my life. I have never been able to escape the fact that I am a black woman in a white supremacist country. My blackness is woven into how I dress each morning, what bars I feel comfortable going to, what music I enjoy, [and] what neighborhoods I hang out in. The realities of race have not always been welcome in my life, but they have always been there.[1]

> There's a pseudoscientific idea floating around . . . that if you have lots of melanin . . . you will be smart . . . have a warm, outgoing personality . . . and more talented than people with less melanin—that is, white people. . . . But from a scientific standpoint it is just wrong. There's no evidence for melanist claims of black superiority, just as there's no evidence for the pseudoscientific claims of white superiority that have been made for centuries.[2]

The time has come for a bit of honesty about race. More people should just admit the obvious. The United States is not *colorblind*.[3] Even with laws enacted to counter racism, the nation has never been colorblind. The idea that legislation can create a colorblind society just belies the fact that color is an important enough focal point that it garners legal and moral attention. This attention spans all racial demographics and it has been this way for centuries.

If there was a true colorblind society, would whites be the focus of privilege, rage, supremacy, nationalism, and implicit bias? Would black African Americans have had to endure slavery and Jim Crow? Likewise, would people join groups based on skin color and draw conclusions about others from their births? Would there be poverty across racial demographics? The truth is that focusing on character does not reduce the emphasis on race. Skin color is just not the primary focus in teaching and training children in schools,[4] nor should it be.

As long as there are people who view the world differently—and whose primary lens through which they view the world is skin color—each person will see what they choose to see.[5] Laws to change behaviors might work for a while. But these are temporary and behavioral. Those enacting laws about race are hardly able to follow the laws they enact.

Human-derived laws cannot change human hearts. Neither can they change the reality of human nature. Yet, through it all, this does not mean that humans are incapable of viewing human character and traits as actual first-level important features. All humans are, after all, individuals with a variety of needs and one of these needs is to belong.

DOES MELANIN MATTER?

Colorblindness was an ideal under Martin Luther King Jr., and it was noteworthy, biblically conceived, and morally right position to take.[6] However, it remains farfetched to consider such a goal as realistic in this third decade of the twenty-first century—especially given the current political climate and the inordinate focus on race.

There are serious questions that arise within every generation when addressing race. In this case, it seems under the headings of identity politics and cultural appropriation that one's color has become more than an external. Color seems to have become one's character and point of identity. Those who argue for not seeing this color character and resort to the alternative of colorblindness are criticized as racists. By today's standards and racial assumptions, Black progressive leaders would have to relegate MLK to the wrong side of history and as another black face of white supremacy. But they would be wrong to do so.

The reality is that King was right, and the political left that maintains an anti-King posture is eschewing reality. Humans have the capacity to change. Therefore, it is in this sense that those who see color as their identity have reverted backward in history. If the past is prologue, then they are reliving a time when color was an empowered identity, and those empowered by color were the racists. The script has been flipped as the previously oppressed are realizing social and political empowerment.

Certainly, the United States made progress toward eradicating racism. But this was not enough. There is another reason why colorblindness is implausible, and this is because humans are generally not blind to self. There is great difficulty in overlooking color when being ridiculed and diminished by opposing forces. These actions only lead to the sacrifice and diminishing of King's call for character. Focusing on skin color is all to the vexation of the work of Martin Luther King Jr. This leaves American society with the question, "Does melanin really matter?"

What We See, or What We Do?

Americans of all races see color and our view is quite kaleidoscopic. But this is no longer the case. Color is now divergent and dichotomized. There are either Blacks, Indigenous, and People of Color (BIPOC), or not. People see themselves, and others, through group perspective and dynamics. In America, the controversy and challenge surround what and how people are expected to envision.

Colorblindness was not meant to rest alone on what people see. The actual nature of colorblindness in American culture was to be revealed in what people do. How people are treated is actually what is most visible. If there is a colorblind society anywhere in the United States, it could be argued that it exists in cities where lawlessness is tolerated. Does it exist where police are reluctant to enter places infested with gangs, where people are allowed to loot with impunity during riots, or in the focus on social justice in schools and the legal system?

The application and practice of the ideal golden rule is a good example of the true ideal of colorblindness in action. Yet, if Christians find they have a difficult time living by the golden rule, then how much more difficult is it to truly place self aside and to consider others as oneself—especially for others who refrain from the recognition that such a rule exists? On the extremes, there is either the consideration of others as one would consider oneself, or there is the consideration of self over all others. A middle ground is often difficult to achieve. Could one reason be because skin color is in the way?

Race Is Skin Deep

Melanin does matter to some people more than others. Some find that melanin matters in their struggles against what they perceive as power. For example, Lex Scott, the former founder of the Utah BLM group, made national headlines when she stated in public "that people who fly the U.S flag are hostile toward people of color."[7] Scott continued,

> When we Black Americans see this flag we know the person flying it is a racist. When we see the flag we know that the person flying it lives in a different America than we do. When we see this flag we question your intelligence. We know to avoid you. It is a symbol of hatred.[8]

Scott's posting forced her resignation from her position as Utah BLM chapter leader and also from her post at the Utah Black History Museum.

Scott's hatred of the symbols she associates with racism probably will not cause her concern in the new community in which she decided to move her family. She relocated her family to a community outside Utah, one which "she cheerfully described as all Black."[9] Scott presumes to speak for all blacks and this is simply not the case.

Separatist Space for Race

Nikole Hannah-Jones, "Pulitzer prize-winning journalist"[10] and an Iowa native, is launching a free "community-based after school program."[11] The name of the after-school program is the *1619 Freedom School*, and it will be based in Waterloo, Iowa. The program will even incorporate an emphasis on three colors that represent the "Black Nationalist Flag so that students can evoke a sense of pride in their culture."[12]

The after-school program obviously is not a welcome place for students who are not black or feel their patriotism runs red, white, and blue. The latter might have negative effects on funding for the school, which intends to rely on contributions from donors. According to Hannah-Jones, these contributions would enable students to attend the 1619 Freedom School program at no cost.

Hannah-Jones admits that the controversy surrounding CRT and her *1619 Project* has had "a chilling effect on potential partnerships and funding opportunities for the program."[13] Separatism may not be as popular as some wish it to be. Setting up of spaces for those of color is evidence that color-blindness is a façade. The concept is supposed to apply to all.

Consider Ijoema Oluo's declaration about the perception of racism: "It is about race if a person of color thinks it's about race. . . . Our lived experiences shape us, how we interact with the world, and how we live in the world."[14] Oluo illustrates why there ought to be more lobbying for the development of traits of the human and his or her character. Character is as much about individual development as it is about how people act from the basis of this development—especially when others are not around to see the actions.

The reliance on melanin will ultimately result in the success or failure of persons who are either considered black enough or as too white. Caught in the middle are those adjacent to one race or another and uncertain as to their cultural status, which is often determined by a cabal of self-righteous ideologues. Oluo's perception is that "race has . . . become alive. Race was not only created to justify a racially exploitative economic system, it was invented to lock people of color into the bottom of it."[15] This is another example of an ideology that emphasizes race from only one perspective. In Oluo's mind,

"Racism in America exists to exclude people of color from opportunity and progress so that there is more profit for others deemed superior."[16]

Racism at the Birthplace of CRT?

Harvard University is the birthplace of CRT. Sadly,

> Asians now face official discrimination much as Jews in the last century. In the same vein, when violence is inflicted on Asians, advocates of CRT even suggest that it is somehow the product of white nationalism. Meanwhile, some race theorists, like Robin DiAngelo, accuse Asians of being *white adjacent.*[17]

DiAngelo defines white adjacency this way:

> "The closer you are to whiteness . . . you're still going to experience racism, but there are going to be some benefits dues to your perceived proximity to whiteness. The further away you are, the more intense the oppression's going to be. According to CRT advocates, Asian Americans are the most white-adjacent minority."[18]

DiAngelo's standard used to judge white adjacency is racist, through-and-through. Strangely, it is Asians bearing the brunt of this application of racist judgment because they are considered as Caucasians. However, the same label is applied to successful blacks who do not ascribe to the privilege rhetoric.

All things considered,

> perhaps no group has been more forgotten in the broad assault on whiteness than the Jews. CRT, notes David Suissa, publisher of the *Los Angeles Jewish Journal*, forces people of whatever background to allow themselves to be defined by their peculiar *systemic ethos*. This means that Jews are whites like any other, despite millennia of persecution in virtually every country where they have settled. Their right to a separate identity is denied; their unique history obliterated.[19]

Rabbi Meir Y. Soloveichik points to CRT and observes that it

> represents an increasingly secular America: A strange form of moral Puritanism without faith, and therefore without forgiveness. Its functionaries on campuses and in the street often embrace their dogma like the sometimes hysterical Chinese Red Guards, who demonized their own country's rich history to create a totally new one. Mao would certainly have understood such things as

> dismantling the *systems of hegemonic power* and introducing *compulsory anti-racism training*, throughout education, business, and government.[20]

The reader should note that objectionists like Oluo have difficulties coming up with good definitions for the term *racism*.[21] What is interesting at this point is that efforts to try to pin down colorblindness, on the one hand, and the surety of racism, on the other hand, yield a peculiar point of intersection between the two. Pointing to events that demonstrate both colorblindness and racism, while admitting uncertainty as to specific definitions of both, is quite telling. Using events to help to flesh out racism means anything can then be racist if a person deems it so. Others can claim any actions deemed as colorblind can be demonstrated by having friends of color.

In order to attempt to avoid implicating all races as racists, Oluo encourages people of color to view individual actions they label as racist as "part of a larger system."[22] Essentially, this comes down to the admission by Oluo that "we inaccurately reduce issues of race in America to a battle for the hearts and minds of individual racists, instead of seeing racists, racist behaviors, and racial oppression"[23] connected to something more grand and comprehensive.

Oluo incisively leans on personal experiences to attempt to prove racism is pervasive and systemic in America. The rights activist makes sweeping generalization, such as "over four hundred years of system oppression have set large groups of racial minorities at a distinct power disadvantage,"[24] among others. Thus Oluo reveals exactly the problems associated with determining what is racist in America. The inability to define racism leaves it wide open for anything to be considered racist if someone thinks it is racist. Accordingly, Oluo admits, "How we define racism also determines how we battle it."[25]

The Matter with Melanin

The matter with melanin is that melanin matters. The attachment of actions with melanin, and then drawing emotionally fuzzy conclusions, is to reveal the weakness in relying on an external trait to assist in decision-making. Oluo reveals this weakness when she stipulates that

> racial oppression should always be an emotional topic to discuss. It should always be anger-inducing. As long as racism exists to ruin the lives of countless people of color, it should be something that upsets us. But it upsets us because it exists, not because we talk about it. And if you are white, and you don't want to feel any of that pain by having these conversations, then you are asking people of color to continue to bear the entire burden of racism alone.[26]

When melanin matters as one's identity, it becomes a point of self-confliction. For example, "Often, being a person of color in white-dominated society is like being in an abusive relationship with the world."[27] There is no disagreement with the average person that labeling of a group's superiority or inferiority, based on race, is certainly morally wrong and a terrible idea. When it comes to students, the application of labels can also have scarring effects. Students have not yet developed any sophisticated system of realizing oppression or victimization, given most of their ages. As a result, they rely on adults to shape this system. Here is where schools step in and cause parents some concerns.

Even in the face of a psychological or emotional effect upon students, there is an assumption taught that

> if you are a person of color, know this: the world will try to tell you that what you are seeing, hearing, thinking, and feeling is wrong. The world will tell you that you do not know how to interpret what is happening to you and to your community. But you are not wrong, and you have just as much right to be heard and believed as anybody else. If you think it's about race you are right.[28]

If a person of color does not think it is about race, is that person also right or is such a person dismissed, labeled, or canceled? There are so very many people of color who have come out and stated that race is not the primary factor in their lives and that their success is not predicated on their melanin. Rather than laying claim to victimhood, they focus on taking advantage of the opportunities which have served others well, in order to realize varying measures of success.

PROBLEMS WITH CONSIDERING COLOR OVER CHARACTER

In America today, skin color is now one's brand. In some quarters, skin color is one's ticket to near-exclusive control over conversations and an icon to be feared if not acknowledged correctly. It is a comparative measure of value that becomes an empowerment for the "haves."

This color-branding should raise some serious red flags. The media is replete with examples of arguments and even violence that depicts color controversies in society. Disagreement with the owners of the *melanin power property brokers* brings disparagement. In a strange twist, such calumnies are even applied to BIPOC which are not in agreement with the expectations of racial status empowerment.

Frederick Douglass understood that the values that helped to forge America would eventually lead to the undoing of slavery. In fact, as Swain and Schorr assert, "Far from a fig leaf for white supremacy, American values are the reason why *true* systemic racism—slavery and Jim Crow—was ultimately unsustainable in the United States."[29]

Douglass is credited with quite a number of wonderful achievements. He was known to be provocative and in astute fashion he

> weaponized the contradiction between American values and chattel slavery by calling whites to task for failing to live up to their nation's founding and purpose. Martin Luther King did the same while also emphasizing the contradiction between racial oppression and America's Judeo-Christian inheritance.[30]

Actions that get results, without destroying all the good achieved in the past, should be the goal.

Taking Action

Recently, a private school student and his classmates wrote a letter to the administrator of the school. The letter was a petition to change Columbus Day to Native People's Day. The school obliged the students' request. The parents of the student who led the way were mildly surprised at how their child stepped forward to pursue an antiracist activism on his own. However, the truth of the matter is the parents chose the school for its antiracist curriculum and encouragement toward antiracist activism. When antiracism manifests itself in action, then activism is the result.[31]

Parents will find schools that reflect their own personal values and should not be surprised when the students demonstrate their training. The private school in question did not consider dissenting parents in their decision but encouraged the students in their pursuit of antiracism. As one of the parents stated, "One of our ongoing societal challenges will be figuring out ways to move beyond individual education and address the root issues of inequality—and our role in upholding them."[32]

Noah Berlatsky recently reviewed a book by Mississippi State University sociologist Margaret Hagerman. Hagerman spent two years researching thirty families in a mid-western city. Berlatsky wrote that the professor observed only white-affluent parents and their children and interviewed them about race and racism. What she discovered is what could be expected.

Certain stereotypes were persistent about students of color and some students and parents reinforced these stereotypes, while others challenged them. Hagerman found "important differences in the ways that parents talked to their children about race, and important differences in the ways that kids responded. But she also found that white parents—even anti-racist white parents—actively reproduce inequality,"[33] and that "the spectacle of well-intentioned people working, half-consciously, to solidify and perpetuate their own power is not an encouraging one."[34]

Thus, the real message for any and all who seek an unbiased, antiracist, and deconstructed white society in America is that people will generally default to their own self-interests, even as they talk a good game to the contrary—regardless of one's color. Again, is there any such thing as a colorblind society?

Berlatsky seems not to understand human nature and the nature of parenting itself. What person of any race would not seek to prop up their own children and step in to set up successful pathways, if they could? A major problem arises when race is the reason for this success. When color is considered over character, particularly when black students use the so-called *white system* to their advantage to displace others, those that lose out do not consider it as fair.

When people of any race or ethnicity succeed, one must consider that it is not the system that keeps them down. Instead, racist assumptions about the system are probably the culprits. How can people be faulted for discovering that a system is not as systemically racist as activists claim it to be? In fact, many public figures of color are themselves doing quite well economically. Is this because of favoritism over skin color or the brand of work ethic they apply? What this should demonstrate is that melanin does not matter as much as some people think. What matters are hard work, merit, and the development of individual character. Booker T. Washington said it best, when he wrote, "Character, not circumstances make the man [or woman]."[35]

RACISM AND CRT AFFECTING MAINSTREAM AMERICA

Sawchuk understands that CRT is all about the product, the final analysis, or, as is referred to in education, "an emphasis on outcomes, not merely on individuals' own beliefs."[36]

In real terms, there are people who know precisely the advantages of using skin color and ways to issue claims of oppression and systemic racism to their advantage. CRT, as it currently stands, was the result of a conscious pivot by groups such as BLM. The link to a tragedy, continuing inner-city destruction, and the demonization of police and whites created a perfect storm.

CRT was able, until recently, to operate below the radar. When it began to be noticed, people realized that the theory exuded skepticism "of the idea of universal values, objective knowledge, individual merit, Enlightenment rationalism, and liberalism—tenets that conservatives tend to hold dear."[37] CRT has now infected government, corporate America, the military, journalism, law, K-16 education, teacher training programs, and local civic community programs such as scouting.

Politicians are also heavily invested in CRT. Elections have consequences and the election of President Biden accelerated the push for CRT and his administration. As with most political policy shifts involving race, previous administrations get blamed for perceived failures. In the case of Biden administration, white nationalism and former president Trump were saddled with the responsibility of many of America's current racial problems.[38]

CRT and Thee

For a theory that was supposed to be moored in legal issues pertaining to housing inequities and race, law school classes, and academe, CRT is now on the lips of a vast number of Americans. White children are feeling the tension to be accepting but not feeling quite right about what they are accepting. They also are being told by BIPOC that they are not welcome to join their groups or violate their designated safe spaces. Once a generation has been indoctrinated by race, the ideology is with them for a long time.[39]

The effects of being indoctrinated, without the freedom to question what is taught, stunt human growth and limit the search for truth. The example that hits home, in terms of parental concern over the impact of CRT upon their children, is illustrated throughout the following *SLATE* letter. A parent wrote to the website's advice editor. *SLATE*'s reply is equally as telling and indicative of the continuing racial divide in America.

> Dear Care and Feeding:
>
> I am a liberal, White, upper-middle-class parent, and we live in a mixed-income, racially integrated urban neighborhood. When it came time to enroll our daughter in high school, we selected a school that was majority Black because it was close by, and we rejected the notion of getting caught up in which magnet school was most prestigious.
>
> Our daughter had a horrible time there—she was harassed so much that we had to pull her out, and other non-Black students there were victimized because of their race. I am struggling to make sense of the experience. I think she's managed it well and hasn't let it affect her general views on race, and I believe I'm doing the same, but mostly I am just so angry that our daughter had to endure this, and I feel guilty that I put her in this position.
>
> I also feel caught between friends who seem to want to say, "I told you so," and those who seem to think that saying that she was the victim of racial harassment somehow makes me seem racist since it was at the hands of Black students. Maybe I should just chalk it up to bad luck, but how can I let go of the guilt and anger and all the other awful reactions I'm having to this?[40]

> The response:
>
> Your daughter might not have done anything deliberately to harm anyone or to invite mistreatment, but her presence disrupts something truly fragile: the feeling of safety Black kids get from being with other Black kids. Those kids see their parents struggling to afford to live in an area that is changing to better reflect people like you. They think of how they and the adults they love have been treated by White folks in positions of authority their entire lives (perhaps including some of the teachers at this Black school). They know the world is kinder to your child than it is to them. The combination of that knowledge, that pain, and their youth can be very volatile.[41]
>
> Imagine if your daughter had been very popular at this school, well-liked and embraced by her peers. What if her *Whiteness* had made her a celebrity of sorts, accepted and celebrated by students and teachers alike because of the ways that society typically privileges White girlhood? How might you have reacted to that? Would you have been concerned about how this could affect the Black girls in her class? What if she were the valedictorian in that all-*Black* school? Would that have been a problem to you?[42]

Recently, Robert Woodson, founder of the Woodson Center, was interviewed by best-selling author Mark Levin. Woodson reiterated what many successful blacks are saying. Woodson stated that a victim's mentality is keeping blacks down and that as long as they follow those who victimize them, they will remain as such. In the interview, Woodson vehemently "blasted those who keep telling Black people they are oppressed and are powerless to change their lives."[43] Woodson added, it is the character of a person that serves as the "foundation that has caused people to propel and move from poverty to prosperity. And so we must elevate them and make them the spokesperson against these naysayers who are profiting from the death of Blacks in these cities and their despair."[44]

Woodson refers to the naysayers as "prophets of despair."[45] Focusing on what one cannot do because of skin color is not an optimistic message. It results in a pessimism that draws on the lesser aspects of psychology, human motivation, and soulful character development.

CRT IS EXCLUSIONARY AND RELATIVISTIC

The mainstream critical race theorist is not in step with Woodson, because of his age and his push for equality of opportunity. Although Woodson is black, CRTs also deem white scholars just as ill-suited to address issues dealing with CRT. The issue comes down to standing and, as Delgado and Stefancic explain, standing

> usually comes into play when white scholars talk and write about racial encounters or other subjects outside their experience. Critical race theorists believe that, while white scholars should not be excluded from writing about such subjects, they are often better addressed by minorities.[46]

With respect to Woodson and other scholars with whom theorists disagree, they are simply not considered black enough to have standing, either.[47] Furthermore, Woodson's reliance on objective truth places him out of touch with the narrative-driven, subjective modern theorists. Delgado and Stefancic explain this separation, "For the critical race theorist, objective truth, like merit, does not exist, at least in social science and politics. In these realms, truth is a social construct created to suit the purposes of the dominant group."[48]

The battle over race continues and the impact upon education is having a chilling effect. As an offering toward optimism, Woodson is adamant that if a person strived to develop his or her character, rather than adopting a tribal character assigned by others in power, then achievement as an individual would no longer be in the realm of the impossible.[49] As it stands now, there are cultural fragmentations in American society and CRT distracts from the reality of widespread underachievement.[50]

CRT and Cultural Fragmentations

The election of Joseph Biden and Kamala Harris to the Executive Branch in 2020 brought with it hope and promise. President Biden stated he was going to be the president of all Americans. His plan was to rally Americans to unity and diminish the marginalization politically, by working *across the aisle*.[51] However, his rhetoric has not yet panned out and seems to have created an environment that is making racial harmony more difficult. Biden's goal has remained unrealized as the nation remains fragmented by race. There are several policy reasons for this fragmentation and one of them is what is taking place in America's institutions of learning, by supporting equity and cultural neo-Marxism.

Many Americans are waking up to the fact that neo-Marxism has made significant inroads into K-16 schooling in America.[52] Many people—and not just whites—take offense to this movement and it is causing its own serious rifts in American education. The battle is also over the tenets and practices that accompany CRT and its overlap with Marxist ideology. The theory pits power structures against one another based on skin color. The CRT found swarming American society at all levels implicates whites and their whiteness as the fundamental basis of most racial problems in American and other nation's institutions.[53]

Dr. Ben Carson, in the Foreword to the book *Black Eye for America*, writes,

> Our country is fractured and in danger of coming apart at the seams. The misguided ideology of Critical Race Theory is corrupting our institutions, dividing Americans by race, and pitting them against one another based on that arbitrary characteristic. . . . There is only one just outcome in this fight. Our only option is to treat people like individuals, with their race being only one characteristic of the complex web of traits that makes up who they are. . . . But Critical Race Theory does not allow this, in fact, it requires the opposite. For Critical Race Theory, the only thing that matters is a person's race.[54]

Those in favor of CRT "have jettisoned the quest for racial reconciliation and a colorblind society where individuals are free to pursue their dreams for a better life. In place of equal opportunity, CRT demands equity—equal outcomes by groups."[55] Parents who have taught their children to develop their talent, knowledge, and skills to compete are finding themselves increasingly frustrated by learning institutions that preach a contradictory message.

For example, the impact of CRT is that it draws contrasts between groups and individuals.

> Individual behavior is insignificant because everyone in America functions within a society of systemic racism, structural racism, and institutional racism. CRT affirms this perspective by pointing to various existing racial disparities, which it claims are the result of racist discrimination. . . . CRT offers two responses to this situation. First, all whites must admit their culpability by confessing the advantages white supremacy confers on them.[56]

Failure to admit culpability "reflects white fragility—an instinctive defensiveness that whites are said to display after they have been enlightened as to their investment in racism."[57]

Second, "Individual whites cannot hide behind any personal history of non-discrimination or the desirability of race-neutral laws or policies because the collective action of their race has been oppressive."[58] George R. La Noue explains that

> whites, therefore, must support *anti-racist* policies that require various forms of race preferences for non-whites across a variety of fields for an indefinite period. This is required even where whites are a local minority and power structures are controlled by non-whites or Blacks, Indigenous, and People of Color—BIPOCs in the current terminology.[59]

As an example, some Portland teachers revealed to Christopher Rufo, they were warned

> from the beginning . . . that we couldn't question [the anti-racism program] . . . teachers needed to support . . . CRT, or at least profess support . . . and . . . one teacher was informed she could lose her job if she did not "teach that way."[60]

It is clear that "the ideology of 'anti-racism' has permeated every department" of the Portland school district—and they are not alone.[61]

According to Rufo, and others, Portland Public Schools have "adopted a pedagogy of the oppressed."[62] This pedagogy comprises the fundamental idea behind the demonstrations of activism and serves as the catalyst for lashing out on the streets. The fundamental *truth* that encourages the mobilization of cohorts of young Americans toward physical violence and revolution is found in the basic premises of neo-Marxism and exacerbated by CRT.

INFLUENCE OF PAULO FREIRE

One of the "most influential philosophers of education of the twentieth century," Paulo Freire,[63] has had tremendous impact on the formation of the argument favoring the oppressed. Freire frames the argument in terms of pedagogy:

> The pedagogy of the oppressed, which is the pedagogy of the people engaged in the fight for their own liberation, has its roots here. And those who recognize or begin to recognize themselves as oppressed must be among the developers of this pedagogy. No pedagogy which is truly liberating can remain distant from the oppressed by treating them as unfortunates and by presenting for their emulation models from among the oppressor. The oppressed must be their own example in the struggle for their redemption.[64]

Freire adds,

> The pedagogy of the oppressed, animated by authentic, humanist . . . generosity, presents itself as a pedagogy of humankind. Pedagogy which begins with the egoistic interests of the oppressors. . . . This is why . . . the pedagogy of the oppressed cannot be developed or practiced by the oppressors[65]

The practice then becomes the activism.

The oppressed are said to possess at least two distinct pedagogical devices. Freire explains:

> In the first, the oppressed unveil the world of oppression and through the praxis commit themselves to its transformation. In the second stage, in which the

> reality of oppression has already been transformed, this pedagogy ceases to belong to the oppressed and becomes a pedagogy of all people in the process of permanent liberation.[66]

Adrienne Dixson, Celia Rousseau Anderson, and Jamel Donnor echo Freire in their statement,

> It is also important to note where other roads or offshoots have developed as CRT has been applied in different ways related to education. One of the way that scholars in education have begun to think about CRT is through a specific focus on pedagogy. In particular, scholars have begun to explore the question: What would a critical race pedagogy look like.[67]

Freire believed that violence can be an expression of love, after which he implies

> it is paradoxical though it may seem—precisely in the response of the oppressed to the violence of their oppressors that a gesture of love may be found. Consciously or unconsciously, the act of rebellion by the oppressed (an act which is always, or nearly always, as violent as the initial violence of the oppressors) can initiate love.[68]

Only by the use of irrational thinking, can it be that violent acts committed upon others would be hailed as expressions of love. If this is love, then anyone claiming to be oppressed can use as their defense for violence a concept of love-in-action.

To phrase it another way and borrowing from Freire, BIPOC have to rise up and show how much they love by their actions. Only by this can the *oppressed lovers* put those who are the oppressors in their rightful, humanized places.

Some people have already been convinced that violence can sometimes be the most loving thing a person can do for an oppressor. Traumatizing another human by loving them in this way is quite bizarre and illogical. There is nothing to be gained by such actions except to misplace anger and cause harm to another human being. At such a point there are two oppressors, and only one feels better about it.

Violence begets violence. When violence is added to vengeance, theories become practice. America is still reeling[69] from the 2020 *summer of love* in Seattle[70] and the *riots of love* in Portland. Cheryl Matias and Ricky Allen explain further, "Critical humanizing love is an essential emotional, motivational force for creating the kind of social bonds and human organization that will replace oppression with humanization."[71] How is this meant to be interpreted? If White oppressors are to become humanized, critical humanizing loving actions are necessary. Adding CRT in schools to further divide students and families is certainly not a loving thing to do.

CRT and Neo-Marxism

The neo-Marxist underpinnings of CRT bring with them the idea that all whites are racists, whether they are aware of their racism or not.[72] The labeling of a group based on race is certainly an erroneous idea—and even worse reality—the world had previously endured.[73] Critical race theorists "are typically Marxists in orientation and mostly consider their theory for transitioning society as blending with the Marxist agenda."[74] This has serious implications for schools and colleges.

The K-16 educational system is now almost completely infected with CRT. The creation of indoctrinated activists and revolutionaries is the main goal of CRT. Civics knowledge has turned to civic action. Capitalism is seen as evil and equity has become status quo for predetermined outcomes for select groups. Students are told that they are either oppressed or oppressors. Levin concurs, "Clearly academe is not merely about teaching students how to think—or, in the case of Marxism and CRT, what to think through repetition and indoctrination—but to develop and army of activist revolutionaries."[75] One of the results of these educational changes is the loss of millions of students to indoctrination in public schools.[76]

Since the COVID pandemic, parents have seen enough examples first hand and observed the indoctrination that occurs in some of their children's classrooms. The CRT reality is that Americans are told to choose sides. Either they are to adopt the package of neo-Marxist CRT and antiracism or they will remain sympathetic as racists and assumed as capitalist oppressors.

CRT TURMOIL AND DOUBLE STANDARDS

Critical race theorists have "stoked racial turmoil and helped to spawn cancel culture, safe spaces, trigger warnings, racially segregated dorms and graduations, and, on some campuses, separate course sections by race."[77] The reality in America is that

> White people who claim to be innocent of the charge of racism and discrimination are deemed guilty of harboring hidden racial biases. It does not matter if the white person is a descendant of abolitionists, including those who risked their lives sheltering runaway slaves in the Underground Railroad.[78]

Furthermore, the Christian faith and the Western world are categorized as oppressive. As a result, "CRT thus harms its intended beneficiaries by creating a sense of hopelessness while eroding decades of goodwill."[79]

Supporters of anti-Western civilization ideologies practice relativism and double standards. This is especially true among those described as *woke*. Within the *woke*, there is a "radical relativism in the form of double standards, such as assertions that only men can be sexist and only white people can be racist."[80] The action side of this double standard is mirrored in positions taken by American media and leftist politicians.

The *Los Angeles Times* editorial board takes the position that CRT belongs in schools in the United States. The position of the board is as follows:

> What many of its detractors do realize—and what they can't stand—is that critical race theory challenges the notion that this is a land of equal opportunity for all, regardless of race, ethnicity or background. This is land of equal opportunity—but only for some people. . . . One of the main tenets of critical race theory is to point out this reality and make students of all backgrounds aware of the impact it has on their lives every day.[81]

This is their position, but holding leaders accountable when BLM violence occurs, or when their favored political party does not abide by the rules established, is often outside their attention.

A specific example of the turmoil created by CRT, and how this turmoil affects schools, is found in the Buffalo Public Schools (BPS). In addition to adopting new methods of instruction, the school administrators of BPS decided to include coursework and pedagogy focused on buzzwords generated from the tenets in CRT. Four of these new instructional strategies and curricular additions include "(1) culturally responsive teaching, (2) pedagogy of liberation, (3) equity-based instructional strategies, and (4) emancipatory curriculum."[82] In addition, for professional development, teachers were subjected to a BLM "antiracist training program."[83] The results of these trainings, which were designed and set up by Fatima Morrell, the BPS diversity administrator, included antiracist training for educators and self-loathing exercises meant to induce shame, but only within the consciences of whites.

Rufo discovered that in kindergarten, teachers asked the students "to compare their skin color with an arrangement of crayons and watch a video that dramatizes dead black children speaking to them from beyond the grave about being killed by racist police and state-sanctioned violence."[84] None of the exercises are presented with photos of criminals arrested by police in the inner cities.

Furthermore, by grade 5, Rufo found that students are told that America has created a "school-to-grave pipeline for black children"[85] and that as incarcerated adults, "one million Black people are locked in cages."[86] The double standard of CRT that impacts education is that America is systemically racist and that white people are rich only because they have taken advantage of blacks. The successes and attainment of wealth and power by blacks are left unaddressed. The standards are different based on the application of CRT and the effects upon school children will be chilling.

CRT AND LOWERED STANDARDS

According to CRT protagonists, racism is inescapable and ingrained in society. Moreover, CRT infers that there is certain blindness that whites possess, which inhibits their ability to fathom that racism actually exists. Many would agree that this is the way it has always been. Carol Anderson is counted among those that agree. She writes, "Ambition was forbidden"[87] for blacks and they were acutely aware of the "Dixie limit, which made certain not to allow Blacks to advance in society."[88] Few would disagree that today, there are disincentives for black advancement. But is this the result of racism, or are there also cultural issues at play?

Beginning with public schools, poorly performing teachers and students are not promoting the academic bar of achievement to be raised. Instead, the bar is lowered to meet a new definition of educational fairness based on equity. In addition to these predetermined educational outcomes, there exists a bevy of social safety net programs that compete economically and financially as goodwill alternatives to full-time employment. If ambition was forbidden, advancement is discouraged.

An example of this is found in the state of Washington. The state has been a leader in forging ahead with CRT. In order to assure that there is a positive impact upon students, the teaching of CRT is coupled with the lowering of academic standards. This lowering is meant to achieve positive outcomes with CRT. To this end, Washington's new learning standards have been released in the five core areas of study, which include "English language-arts, history, social studies, math and science."[89]

These standards are "disguised by the label Ethnic Studies"[90] standards and "will replace Washington's academic learning standards with controversial Critical Race Theory content."[91]

Furthermore, the new set of Washington State standards presents "academic material according to four CRT domains: Identity, Power and Oppression, History of Resistance and Liberation, and Reflection and Action."[92]

In another example, "instead of teaching English grammar, Washington State standards require teaching the concepts of White supremacy, Institutional racism, Structural racism, and White privilege."[93] The demonstration of the learning of these new standards is accompanied by encouraging and influencing "students to take action."[94] This call to action is found in the literature of CRT that requires such action on behalf CRT and elements of social justice.

Washington's governor signed "SB 5044 . . . to require the implantation of mandatory Critical Race Theory training for all teachers and staff at K-12 schools"[95] so that all the teachers could be ready to apply CRT in their curriculum. Apparently, "Politicians, educators, and pundits all [were] . . . arguing that the hundreds of thousands of students who did not go on to college were being *lost* to the nation."[96] Pertinent to this concern are the words of the late Alabama congressman Carl Elliott. He warned the nation that what is taught in America's public schools will be what America will "face a nation."[97] CRT is a fulfillment of Elliott's prediction.

CRT AND ANTIRACISM

Anderson provides insight into the historical mindsets and emphases blacks placed on gaining education.

> Since the days of enslavement, African Americans have fought to gain access to quality education. Education can be transformative. It reshapes the health outcomes of a people; it breaks the cycle of poverty; it improves housing conditions; it raises the standard of living. . . . In short, education strengthens a democracy.[98]

Americans must stand up and proclaim the vision for the nation they wish to imagine. Anderson believes this can be best accomplished as people work to

> defuse the power of white rage. It is time to move into that future. It is a future where the right to vote is unfettered by discriminatory restrictions that prevent millions of American citizens from having any say in their own government.[99]

She adds, "It's time to rethink America."[100]

Ibram X. Kendi, director for Center for Antiracist Research at Boston University, is in support of rethinking and remaking America. Toward these ends, he

> has proposed the creation of a federal Department of Antiracism. This department would be independent of . . . the elected branches of government, and would have the power to mollify, veto, or abolish any law at any level of

> government and curtail the speech of political leaders who are deemed insufficiently *antiracist*.[101]

Kendi would reimagine America by using the proposed department for the "overthrow of capitalism."[102] To Kendi, there is only one acceptable dichotomy that exists. One is either antiracist, or he is not. Furthermore, "*in order to be truly antiracist, you also have to be anti-capitalist*. In other words, identity is the means and Marxism is the end."[103] One could add that melanin is the bridge for BIPOC toward achieving this end.

Kendi's proposal would not pass constitutional muster.

> The 1972 Education Amendments to the Civil Rights Act of 1964 state that *no person in the United States shall, on the ground of race, color, or natural origin* (Title VI) or *on the basis of sex* (Title IX) *be subjected to discrimination under any program or activity receiving federal financial assistance*.[104]

However, with the proliferation of neo-Marxism in American politics, and the tendency for the Executive Branch to challenge the Constitution, one never knows!

A radical reordering of America is being visited upon schools across America. As CRT cements itself into the curriculum and is ingrained into educational philosophies in higher education, the impetus for change will continue to increase. In adding to already foreboding future, there is another movement-gaining traction. This movement is in conjunction with the Zinn Educational Project (ZEP) and is calling for rebellion.

The aim of the ZEP movement is to collect as many public school educators as possible who would be inclined to break the laws of states, as well as policies of districts, that forbid the teaching of CRT. The goal of the project is for large numbers of teachers to break the laws and policies and teach CRT anyway. These are the types of rebellion and activism that are beyond civil disobedience. These are also the types that radical professors and supportive secondary teachers encourage students to pursue.[105]

CRT AND POVERTY

Many politicians on the left use poverty as the main evidence of racism and racial disparity in America.

> If racism is largely economic in nature—a search for profits—and hypercapitalism is increasingly showing itself as a flawed system, what follows for a theory of civil rights? A further concern that some crits raise is that the movement has

> become excessively preoccupied with issues of identity, as opposed to hard-nosed social analysis.[106]

At this juncture, it is appropriate to consider why rights for anyone would mean anything if these rights were not allowed to be expressed in a capitalist system. What would there be, in terms of protest, without freedom enough to express such a right?

Delgado and Stefancic contrast the differences between black and white poverty. They agree that

> White poverty usually lasts for only a generation or two (even for white immigrant families); not so for the black or brown variety—it is apt to last forever. By the same token, middle-class or professional status for blacks, browns, or American Indians is less secure than for others . . . the recipients of welfare [have] black or brown faces—even though more whites receive welfare than do people of color.[107]

That being said, there does appear to exist a racial divide when examining poverty among blacks and whites. Although black children in 2014 were "three times more likely to be in poverty than a white child,"[108] the data do demonstrate that overall poverty rates remained steady from 1974 to 2014. However, from 2015 to early 2020, the poverty rates for blacks and whites dropped, while the poverty gap remained between two and three times the rate for blacks, when compared to whites.[109]

One of the main factors for the rise in poverty in late 2020, and into 2021, was the COVID-19 pandemic.[110] However, even with poverty rates as they are, the conclusion drawn from the data from the *Urban Institute* in 2016 was that "childhood poverty has little bearing on whether Black adults become poor."[111]

In the final analysis, it is quite clear that melanin matters much—but not as much as money. Whether rich or poor, the immutable characteristic of skin color remains the same. As the leaders of the CRT movement gain wealth, the question remains how their wealth has helped their followers and especially the children who sit floundering in failing schools[112] or risk their lives daily in crime-ridden cities like Chicago.[113]

In 1988, the late pop singer Michael Jackson released the song "Man in the mirror." The lyrics are hauntingly relevant at this critical juncture, as America continues to struggle with racial issues that are fraying the fabric of American society. A few lines of Jackson's tune are a stark reminder that everyone lives as individuals and accountability eventually comes knocking on everyone's door. Jackson sings,

> I'm gonna make a change for once in my life. Gonna feel real good. Gonna make a difference. Gonna make it right. . . . I'm starting with the man in the

> mirror. I'm asking him to change his ways. And no message could have been any clearer. If you want to make the world a better place. Take a look at yourself, and then make a change.[114]

The promise of CRT is that it can be deployed as a change agent for uncovering many types of inequity and social injustice—not just racial inequity and injustice.[115] The question remains how much does skin color really matter? The traits that lead to ultimate success for people of any color are those based on one's character. MLK's axiom of *content of character* over *color of skin* still resonates as elevated truth. By contrast, the deeper the dive into cultural neo-Marxism and CRT, the clearer the bottom. The unfortunate and likely reality is that the true matter with melanin is that it is not the color green.

NOTES

1. Ijeoma Oluo. *So You Want to Talk About Race*. New York: Seal Press, 2019, p. 1.
2. Christopher Wills. "The skin we're in." *Discover*. October 31, 1994. Retrieved November 7, 2021, from https://www.discovermagazine.com/health/the-skin-were-in.
3. Jesse Washington. "Martin Luther King Jr. content of character quote inspires debate." *MassLive*. January 21, 2013. Retrieved November 6, 2021, from https://www.masslive.com/news/2013/01/martin_luther_king_jr_content.html.
4. Gerard Robinson. "The content of their character: King's theme across the years." *American Enterprise Institute*. January 17, 2020. Retrieved November 6, 2021, from https://www.aei.org/articles/the-content-of-their-character-kings-theme-across-the-years/.
5. Fran Wendelboe. "My turn: Democrats are the ones who judge by skin color." *Concord Monitor*. August 28, 2019. Retrieved November 6, 2021, from https://www.concordmonitor.com/Democrats-and-skin-color-27999174.
6. Dennis Prager. "Should we be colorblind?" *PragerU*. November 1, 2021. Retrieved November 2, 2021, from https://www.prageru.com/video/should-we-be-colorblind?utm_source=Iterable&utm_medium=email&utm_campaign=campaign_3117330.
7. Jessica Chasmar. "BLM Utah head called American flag symbol of hatred resigns, citing Utah death threats." *Fox News*. August 12, 2021. Retrieved August 13, 2021, from https://www.foxnews.com/politics/black-lives-matter-utah-american-flag-symbol-hatred-resigns.
8. Ibid.
9. Ibid.
10. Melody Mercado. "Pulitzer-winning journalist Nikole Hannah-Jones opening after-school program, 1619 Freedom School, in Waterloo." *Des Moines Register*. August 31, 2021. Retrieved September 2, 2021, from https://www.desmoinesregister

.com/story/news/education/2021/08/31/nikole-hannah-jones-launching-1619-project-freedom-school-waterloo-iowa-black-history-literacy-crt/5651900001/.

11. Ibid.
12. Ibid.
13. Ibid.
14. Oluo, *So You Want to Talk About Race*, p. 15.
15. Ibid, p. 12.
16. Ibid.
17. Joel Kotkin and Edward Heyman. "Critical race theory ignores anti-Semitism." *UnHerd*. August 9, 2021. Retrieved August 10, 2021, from https://unherd.com/2021/08/critical-race-theory-rewrites-history/.
18. Kenny Xu. "Critical race theory has no idea what to do with Asian Americans." *Newsweek*. July 13, 2021. Retrieved August 3, 2021, from https://www.newsweek.com/critical-race-theory-has-no-idea-what-do-asian-americans-opinion-1608984.
19. Kotkin and Heyman. "Critical race theory ignores anti-Semitism." *UnHerd*.
20. Rabbi Meir Soloveichik. "The power of the mob in an unforgiving age." *SAPIR: A Journal of Jewish Conversations* 2 (Summer 2021). Retrieved August 20, 2021, from https://sapirjournal.org/power/2021/07/the-power-of-the-mob-in-an-unforgiving-age/. Cf. Kotkin and Heyman. "Critical race theory ignores anti-Semitism." *UnHerd*.
21. Oluo. *So You Want to Talk About Race*, p. 26.
22. Ibid, p. 27.
23. Ibid, p. 12.
24. Ibid, p. 28.
25. Ibid, pp. 28–29.
26. Ibid, p. 51.
27. Ibid, p. 19.
28. Ibid, p. 22.
29. Carol M. Swain and Christopher J. Schorr. *Black Eye for America: How Critical Race Theory Is Burning Down the House*. Rockville, MD: Be the People Books, 2021, p. 33.
30. Ibid.
31. Noah Berlatsky. "White kids, racism, and the way privileged parenting props up an unjust system." *NBC News: Think*. January 2, 2019. Retrieved August 3, 2021, from https://www.nbcnews.com/think/opinion/white-kids-racism-way-privileged-parenting-props-unjust-system-ncna953951. Cf. Leighton Woodhouse. "The reality of anti-racism across America." *Substack*. October 21, 2021. Retrieved October 29, 2021, from https://bariweiss.substack.com/p/the-reality-of-anti-racism-across.
32. Berlatsky. "White kids, racism, and the way privileged parenting props up an unjust system." *NBC News: Think*.
33. Ibid.
34. Ibid.
35. Booker T. Washington. *Brainy Quote*. Retrieved September 26, 2021, from https://www.brainyquote.com/quotes/booker_t_washington_132461.

36. Stephen Sawchuk. "What is Critical Race Theory, and why is it Under Attack." *EdWeek*. May 18, 2021, p. 4. Retrieved May 20, 2021, from https://www.edweek.org/leadership/what-is-critical-race-theory-and-why-is-it-under-attack/2021/05.

37. Ibid.

38. Chris Rufo. *Critical Race Theory Briefing Book*. July 2021, pp. 9–11. Retrieved August 1, 2021, from https://christopherrufo.com/crt-briefing-book/.

39. Wendy Hasenkamp. "Can we change racial bias?" *Mind & Life Institute*. July 17, 2020. Retrieved November 8, 2021, from https://www.mindandlife.org/insight/can-change-racial-bias/. Cf. Leah Donnella. "Will racism end when old bigots die?" *NPR*. January 14, 2017. Retrieved November 8, 2021, from https://www.npr.org/sections/codeswitch/2017/01/14/505266448/will-racism-end-when-old-bigots-die.

40. Jamilah Lemieux. "My White daughter was bullied out of her Majority-Black school." *SLATE*. March 19, 2021. Retrieved August 12, 2021, from https://slate.com/human-interest/2021/03/racialized-bullying-school-care-and-feeding.html.

41. Ibid.

42. Ibid.

43. Robert Woodson. "Character is what moves people from poverty to prosperity." *Life, Liberty, and Levin*. July 12, 2021. Retrieved August 29, 2021, from https://video.foxnews.com/v/6263312559001#sp=show-clips.

44. Ibid.

45. Ibid.

46. Richard Delgado and Jean Stefancic. *Critical Race Theory: An Introduction*, 2nd edition. New York: New York University Press, 2012, p. 104.

47. Lindsay Kornick. "MSNBC host Tiffany Cross claims some Black media faces are not necessarily Black voices" *Fox News*. October 11, 2021. Retrieved October 11, 2021, from https://www.foxnews.com/media/msnbcs-tiffany-cross-some-black-media-faces-not-black-voices.

48. Delgado and Stefancic. *Critical Race Theory*, p. 104.

49. Woodson. "Character is what moves people from poverty to prosperity." *Life, Liberty, and Levin*.

50. Bob Woodson and Ian Rowe. "Critical race theory distracts from widespread academic underachievement." *Newsweek*. September 17, 2021. Retrieved September 18, 2021, from https://www.newsweek.com/critical-race-theory-distracts-widespread-academic-underachievement-opinion-1629028.

51. David Smith. "Biden plans to reach across the aisle—but is he walking into a Republican trap?" *The Guardian*. November 14, 2020. Retrieved November 8, 2021, from https://www.theguardian.com/us-news/2020/nov/14/joe-biden-president-republicans-democrats.

52. Mark Levin. *American Marxism*. New York: Simon and Schuster, 2021. See Chapter 11.

53. Karl Quinn. "Are all white people racist? Why critical race theory has us rattled. *The Sydney Morning Herald*. November 7, 2020. Retrieved November 8, 2021, from https://www.smh.com.au/culture/books/are-all-white-people-racist-why-critical-race-theory-has-us-rattled-20201105-p56bwv.html.

54. Swain and Schorr. *Black Eye for America*, p. xv.

55. Ibid, p. 10.

56. Christopher F. Rufo. "The child soldiers of Portland." *City Journal*. Spring 2021. Retrieved May 22, 2021, from https://www.city-journal.org/critical-race-theory-portland-public-schools?mc_cid=9ddf5edee7&mc_eid=dd2cd80aa4.

57. Ibid.

58. George R. La Noue. "Critical race training or civil rights law: We can't have both." *Law & Liberty*. November 4, 2020. Retrieved September 11, 2021, from https://lawliberty.org/critical-race-theory-or-civil-rights-law-we-cant-have-both/. Cf. Mark R. Levin. *American Marxism*. 2021. New York: Simon & Schuster, Inc., p. 87.

59. Ibid.

60. Christopher F. Rufo. "The child soldiers of Portland." *City Journal*.

61. Ibid.

62. Ibid.

63. Kim Diaz. "Paulo Freire (1921-1997)." *Internet Encyclopedia of Philosophy*. 2021. Retrieved October 22, 2021, from https://iep.utm.edu/freire/.

64. Paulo Freire. *Pedagogy of the Oppressed*. Translated by Myra Bergman Ramos. New York: Continuum International Publishing Group, 1993 (1970), p. 54.

65. Ibid.

66. Ibid, pp. 54–55.

67. Adrienne Dixson, Celia Rousseau Anderson, and Jamel Donnor. *Critical Race Theory in Education*. New York: Routledge, p. 45.

68. Paulo Freire. *Pedagogy of the Oppressed*. 1993 (1970), p. 56.

69. *Gee* Scott and *Ursula* Reutin. "Gee and Ursula: Durkan never recovered from CHOP summer of love remark." *MYNorthwest*. December 8, 2020. Retrieved October 22, 2021, from https://mynorthwest.com/2352051/mayor-durkan-reelection-chop/.

70. Ian Schwartz. "Seattle Mayor Durkan: CHAZ has a block party atmosphere, could turn into a summer of love." *RealClear Politics*. June 12, 2020. Retrieved October 22, 2021, from https://www.realclearpolitics.com/video/2020/06/12/seattle_mayor_durkan_chaz_has_a_block_party_atmosphere_could_turn_into_summer_of_love.html.

71. Cheryl E. Matias and Ricky Lee Allen. "Do you feel me? Amplifying messages of love in critical race theory." *Journal of Education Foundations*. 2016. 29(4): 5. Retrieved August 23, 2021, from https://www.proquest.com/docview/2043654218. Cf. Tracy Lachica Buenavista, Stephanie Cariaga, Edward R. Curammeng, et al. "A praxis of critical race love: Toward the abolition of Cisheteropatriarchy and toxic masculinity in educational justice." *Educational Studies* 57, no. 3 (May 26, 2021): 238–249. Retrieved August 19, 2021, from https://www.tandfonline.com/doi/abs/10.1080/00131946.2021.1892683.

72. Karl Quinn. "Are all white people racist? Why critical race theory has us rattled." *The Sydney Morning Herald*.

73. Sawchuk. "What is critical race theory, and why is it under attack." *EdWeek*, p. 3.

74. Levin. *American Marxism*, p. 91.

75. Ibid, p. 95.

76. Carter Evans. "Public schools have seen a massive drop in enrollment since the start of the pandemic." *CBS News*. August 25, 2021. Retrieved August 26, 2021, from https://www.cbsnews.com/news/public-schools-enrollment-drop-pandemic/. Cf. Essha Pendharkar. "More than 1 million students didn't enroll during the pandemic. Will they come back?" *Education Week*. July 22, 2021. Retrieved July 24, 2021, from https://www.edweek.org/leadership/more-than-1-million-students-didnt-enroll-during-the-pandemic-will-they-come-back/2021/06.

77. Swain and Schorr. *Black Eye for America*. p. 1.

78. Ibid, p. 10.

79. Ibid, pp. 10–11.

80. Helen Pluckrose and James Lindsay. *Cynical Theories: How Activist Scholarship Made Everything about Race, Gender, and Identity and Why This Harms Everybody*. Durham, NC: Pitchstone Publishing, 2020, p. 18.

81. Staff. "What critical race theory is—and isn't—and why it belongs in schools." *Los Angeles Times*. August 8, 2021. Retrieved August 21, 2021, from https://www.latimes.com/opinion/story/2021-08-08/editorial-what-critical-race-theory-is-and-isnt-and-why-it-belongs-in-schools.

82. Christopher F. Rufo. "Buffalo students told all white people play a part in perpetuating systemic racism." *New York Post*. February 24, 2021. Retrieved August 13, 2021, from https://nypost.com/2021/02/24/buffalo-students-told-all-white-people-play-a-part-in-systemic-racism/.

83. Ibid.

84. Ibid.

85. Ibid.

86. Ibid.

87. Carol Anderson. *White Rage: The Unspoken Truth of Our Racial Divide*. New York: Bloomsbury Publishing, 2017, p. 43.

88. Ibid.

89. Liv Finne. "Washington public school officials lower academic standards as they implement Critical Race Theory." *Washington Policy Center*. September 21, 2021. Retrieved September 2021, from https://www.washingtonpolicy.org/publications/detail/washington-public-school-officials-lower-academic-standards-as-they-implement-critical-race-theory.

90. Ibid.

91. Ibid.

92. Ibid.

93. Ibid.

94. Ibid.

95. Ibid.

96. Anderson. *White Rage*, p. 91.

97. Ibid.

98. Ibid, p. 96.

99. Ibid, p. 175.

100. Ibid, pp. 175–176.

101. Christopher F. Rufo. "Critical race theory: What is it and how to fight it?" *Imprimis*. March 2021. 50(3): p. 3.

102. Ibid.

103. Ibid.

104. Swain and Schorr. *Black Eye for America*, p. 52. Cf. Staff. "Civil Rights Act of 1964." *History Channel*. January 25, 2021. Retrieved September 30, 2021, https://www.history.com/topics/black-history/civil-rights-act. Cf. also, Staff. "Title IX and sex discrimination." *U.S. Department of Education Office for Civil Rights*. August 2021. Retrieved September 30, 2021, from https://www2.ed.gov/about/offices/list/ocr/docs/tix_dis.html.

105. Molly Pulda. "More students are becoming activists. Teachers can help strengthen their voice." *EdSurge*. January 21, 2019. Retrieved July 6, 2021, from https://www.edsurge.com/news/2019-01-21-more-students-are-becoming-activists-teachers-can-help-strengthen-their-voice.

106. Delgado and Stefancic. *Critical Race Theory*, p. 107.

107. Ibid, p. 123.

108. Diana Elliott. "Two American experiences: The racial divide of poverty." *Urban Institute*. July 21, 2016. Retrieved September 6, 2021, from https://www.urban.org/urban-wire/two-american-experiences-racial-divide-poverty.

109. Joint Economic Committee. "The economic state of Black America in 2020." *United States Senate*. February 14, 2020. Retrieved September 6, 2021, from https://www.jec.senate.gov/public/_cache/files/ccf4dbe2-810a-44f8-b3e7-14f7e5143ba6/economic-state-of-black-america-2020.pdf.

110. Alexandre Tanzi and Catarina Saraiva. "U.S. suffers sharpest rise in poverty rate in more than 50 years." *Bloomberg News*. January 25, 2021. Retrieved September 6, 2021, from https://www.bloomberg.com/news/articles/2021-01-25/u-s-suffers-sharpest-rise-in-poverty-rate-in-more-than-50-years.

111. Elliott. "Two American experiences: The racial divide of poverty." *Urban Institute*.

112. Auguste Meyrat. "Critical race theory is just another faddish attempt to hide public school failures." *The Federalist*. April 6, 2021. Retrieved November 1, 2021, from https://thefederalist.com/2021/04/08/critical-race-theory-is-just-another-faddish-attempt-to-hide-public-school-failures/.

113. Tom Schuba, David Struett, Madeline Kenney, et al. "Our kids are becoming extinct: Chicago children are being killed by guns at far faster rate than years past." *The Chicago Sun Times*. June 8, 2021. Retrieved November 8, 2021, from https://chicago.suntimes.com/crime/2021/6/8/22523157/chicago-gun-violence-children-kids-killed-shootings.

114. Michael Jackson. "Man in the mirror." *Epic Records*. February 6, 1988. Retrieved November 7, 2021, from https://genius.com/Michael-jackson-man-in-the-mirror-lyrics.

115. Gloria Ladson-Billings. *Critical Race Theory in Education*. New York: Teachers College, Columbia University, 2021, p. 114.

Chapter 3

Critical Race and Common Grace

> A lie doesn't become truth, wrong doesn't become right, and evil doesn't become good, just because it's accepted by a majority.[1]
>
> – Booker T. Washington

> Grace is what the Franciscan priest and writer Richard Rohr calls the x-factor. It knits families back together after betrayal, hurt, and even violence. It's the father running to embrace the prodigal son . . . True grace is otherworldly. It goes against every instinct we have to seek revenge for wrongs or to shame and humiliate people who have acted immorally or unethically.[2]

After reading chapters 1 and 2, the reader may have come away with the sense that the terms *America* and *beautiful* are probably not best suited to appear in the same sentence. But it would be a mistake to draw such a conclusion. Although the history of America is marked with some serious blemishes, the nation has also been truly blessed. Even with all the problems associated with a country's past, what is it about a nation's people that brings them to pen songs extolling its beauty?

One of America's national treasures is the song *America the Beautiful*. Penned by Wellesley professor Katherine Lee Bates as a poem in 1895, and then adapted to an already existing musical tune, *Materna*, by Samuel A. Ward in 1903, *America the Beautiful* became popular in short order.[3]

Music lovers will always remember the first moment they heard Ray Charles proudly singing his rendition of Bates' and Ward's song. Emotions are easy for so many Americans when America's national songs are played and sung. "America, America . . . God shed His grace on thee. And crown thy good, with brotherhood. From sea to shining sea." Unfortunately, it is not this way for some others whose history and current living situations prevent them from celebrating America's blessed grandeur.

Politicians are acutely aware of these two disparate realities and that emotions flow easily for those whose experience and understanding are that America is a land blessed by God. Conversely, emotions are also deeply expressed, for those who continue to feel disenfranchised from a nation that remains in their minds a place systemically racist and unchanged.

GOD AND GRACE

Referring to God's action of shedding grace upon America implies something personal about America. Certainly, America is not the only nation upon which grace has been shed. It is with these things in mind, and in this spirit, that the reader will be offered a conceptual understanding of common grace according to (1) the application of grace to America's history its people and (2) application of grace to the nation's present racial tensions, including those that arise from the controversial CRT. This chapter is meant as a conversation starter on a topic that many are unwilling to address, especially for the churches and Christians in America.

When it comes to interpersonal human relationships, there appears a correlation between the level of human grace that exists between people and groups, and the depth of the relationships manifested. As relationships grow, the measures of grace also grow with them. In fact, the more personal the relationships, the greater the probability acts of grace and forgiveness may be extended to the parties involved.

All humans are imperfect and so is their history. Americans are souls just as desperate for God's grace as souls of any other nation—and this raises an interesting consideration. The United States of America still claims a majority with a belief in God and Jesus Christ. Even so, something is lacking[4] among the people.

The expressions of faith may be messy at times, as beliefs are lived out. But the beliefs are there and so are remnants of the character of a nation based on Christian principles. The question is whether Americans can dig deep enough to see beyond sins of the past and differences in the present to begin a healing process and demonstrate some measures of grace.

HUMANS AND SYSTEMIC CORRUPTION

Most Americans understand forgiveness and find it easier to offer it to individuals they know, rather than offering it to governments and elected officials they do not know. There is a relationship between forgiveness and common grace, in that one need not be religious to understand, or even to practice, each.

There are various reasons why people are assailed today. Some are held to a tight standard regarding their beliefs. Others hold grudges against nations and people who claim to be part of those nations. Still others are holding grudges against their nation because of its past. These grudges often mean holding bitterness against history and the people who may or may not have had any past connection to that history.[5]

When these grudges manifest themselves by extreme actions, corrections that may be better served are lost by the taking of sides. Thus, bad memories are kept alive, and people segregate from those deemed responsible for transgressions. Incidentally, this seems to characterize where marginalized groups are today in America.

A Lack of Grace

There is a general lack of grace in American culture and the nation is embroiled in political battles over differences between parties. One of these differences pertains to public education and the specific issue with which the nation is struggling is CRT.

When it comes to grudges over things like CRT, group grievances are more impersonal than telling a neighbor's five-year-old that she is a racist for being white, or admonishing a child's teacher in a social media post for exercising white privilege. When it comes to individual students and families, the dynamics of the expressions of concerns change.

Most Americans who understand grace have this understanding because they have experienced it in their own personal lives. This grace may have come into their lives, despite appearance and association. Admittedly, critical race theorists are correct in their understanding of some historical elements of group-level systemic issues and that remnants of these elements persist today. Although historical events have their own contexts, the context of events today is vastly different.

For example, CRTs are not correct in assigning guilt to whites or to a group's whiteness, because of past sins. If institutions are systemically corrupt, yet built by humans, it is people that have caused that corruption, not their skin color. Individuals comprise groups, and not the other way around. If corruption was only a white issue, no other member of another racial group could be blamed for corruption. World history and world events easily demonstrate this is not the case.

There has never been a utopian society. Furthermore, even the notion of one built by imperfect humans is a ridiculous idea given any view of human nature. Even those who claim to be woke politically and spiritually reborn, with a renewed sense of secular-spiritual identity, are as human as everyone else. So this, then, is the starting point for understanding this chapter. *It is by grace that we are saved and not by race.* Believers in grace comprehend that it is the color of shed blood that unites all *believers* in grace and not the color of skin. They also are aware that the color of blood runs red on any shade of melanin. Grace should be applied with this in mind as well.

Corruption of Grace

One of the concerns that arises in discussions on race is whether people can avoid incorporating politics into these discussions. Politics as a system is corrupt, and it tends to corrupt those within it. Anyone entering the fray with a somewhat clear set of values of right and wrong will find that the system has built into it a series of compromises—sometimes requiring choices to appear hypocritical.

Finding grace in politics is like discovering humility by filtering through arrogance. Adding color to the mix does not bring unity or clarity. Political parties as groups are working overtime to prove which can be considered as more corrupt, and melanin makes no difference in that respect. In fact, skin color sometimes stultifies individual relationships and group agreements, especially in politics.

Bludgeoning of character has become acceptable as blood sport and is certainly not considered gracious. Betrayal of one's melanin is equally unacceptable in American society. Assaulting of reputations by means of social media hit mobs and stalking of politicians and their families are becoming commonplace tactics. Bullying and threats now rule behind the scenes in efforts to thwart anyone who dares to counter the system of corruption. Although politics is a good example of grudges and vitriol, religion is a close second. What has corrupted both of them is what they both share: people.

The reader may now be questioning the reason for addressing corruption, skin color, and bad behaviors in a chapter on *grace*. The answer lies in the fact that the message of grace that many religious people consider as critically important has been ceded to another religion—one that is secular and seeks to deconstruct status quo believes in long-term grudges and is based on race.[6]

Within the teachings of this new religion, any person born as white is automatically classified as a potential oppressor. Within this racial religion, wrongdoings committed by Americans of the past are imputed to Americans of the present. Continuous vengeance over forgiveness is acceptable as atonement for the past. In contrast, with the practice of common grace, skin color is not one's primary identity.

Anytime a theory explodes in popularity and grips the nation's attention as CRT has[7] people should take a step back to consider its tenets, and what it asks of them. On one hand, in this case, people are asked to give themselves over to a greater awakening espoused within the tenets of the CRT belief system. Enlightenment is promised if they *do the work*[8] required to achieve it. On the other hand, choosing not to delve into the tenets of the theory runs the risk of being labeled as part of the oppressor class.

When people dig more deeply into the religious tenets posted by advocates of *CRT*, they will come away as either *woke to oppression* or be *lost to the system of oppressors*. What seekers will find as they examine CRT is a tenet for practitioners that "involves deconstructing . . . to discover systemic racism beneath the surface."[9]

A CLOSER LOOK AT CHARACTER AND GRACE

Zig Ziglar, the late motivational speaker, wrote, "Check the records. All great failures in life are character failures, and all complete successes are character based. The need for character education is irrefutable."[10] Should Ziglar be dismissed out-of-hand because he was white? Character is a part of everything we say and do in life and most parents are keenly aware of this.

When MLK called for his children to be judged by the content of their character, he was calling for people to examine the package that comprised his children's complete *being* as unique human persons, created by God. There are still many who believe King's clarion call has not yet to have achieved,[11] and, therefore, the call has remained and is largely supported by conservative Americans.[12] Liberals, on the other hand, have moved from content of character to color of skin. In other words, the movement away from equality of humanity has been usurped by guaranteed equity by government.

What Is Character?

Kevin Ryan and Karen Bohlin define character as "the sum of . . . intellectual and moral habits . . . the composite of . . . good habits, or virtues, and out bad habits, or vices, the habits that make us the kind of person we are."[13] The authors continue and include that "good character is about *knowing the good, loving the good, and doing the good*."[14]

One might ask, then, what is *the good*, and how can it be known, loved, and achieved? To begin, knowing the good is what Aristotle called "practical wisdom,"[15] which implies knowing what type of thinking and action a situation would call for. These are often referred to broad, critical thinking skills and even logic.

Loving the good means "developing a full range of moral feelings and emotions, including a love for good and contempt for evil, as well as the capacity to empathize with others."[16] Doing the good implies some form of the golden rule. It means fundamentally "respect for the dignity of others"[17] and the shared values of the good that

> is a cross-cultural composite of moral imperatives and ideals that hold us together both as individuals and as societies. Those ideals that tend to cut across history and cultures and show up most frequently are the Greek cardinal virtues: wisdom, justice, self-mastery, and courage.[18]

One has to wonder whether competing perspectives are beneficial in subjective terms, or whether there is an objective standard of goodness that exists. Such a question cannot be answered by politics, because the best that politicians can muster is a semblance of a bipartisan agreement.

Common grace is not arrived at by common agreement. That is called *compromise*, and it can be both productive as a legislation tool and destructive as a label when values are sacrificed. There is a strong connection between common grace and loving, knowing, and doing what is good. One need not be religious to demonstrate these. Thus, there is an affinity between common grace and character.

MLK AND CHRISTIAN CHARACTER

MLK was quite aware of the doctrines and virtues of the Christian faith, which are found throughout the New Testament. His sermons presented these regularly. Love, grace, and character are hallmarks of the believer and were often repeated themes in MLK's sermons. One example is 1 Corinthians, where the Apostle Paul writes,

> Love is patient, love is kind, it is not jealous; love does not brag, it is not arrogant. It does not act *disgracefully*, it does not seek its own *benefit;* it is not provoked, does not keep an account of a wrong *suffered,* it does not rejoice in unrighteousness, but rejoices with the truth; it keeps every confidence, it believes all things, hopes all things, endures all things.[19]

Christian character acts gracefully and does not keep account of wrongs suffered. For many Americans, these elements alone are enough to disqualify the Baptist pastor with those wishing to hold a moralistic legalism of past wrongdoings to present generations. Grace releases. Legalism ensnares. Positive character builds up. Negative character destroys. Grace is extended to others, so as to edify and to call attention to the One in whom grace exists eternally. Focusing on skin color is temporal, and edifies self, and is exclusive to members of a shared identity group.

When MLK spoke about the content of his children's character, he was addressing all people. Certainly, his dream was a challenge to racist whites at the time. Horrifically, his life was cut short at age thirty-nine by an assassin's bullet. After giving his life for the movement of equality, racial, and social justice for blacks, another generation has now decided to lay down the mantle of the past. The current movement seeks justice as well. However, the ideology and the means by which modern justice movement seeks a radically different approach to that of Dr. King's.

Nevertheless, King's call for character still resonates. It resonates from the annals of history and from the sermons of others in churches across the land. A character without grace is like living a virtuous life absent the understanding of virtues. Justice without being just for all is another form of injustice. The real challenge is practicing grace when one's character is tested.

The real blessing of grace and justice is in a relationship with the eternal personage who grants them.[20] This is echoed in the last portion of 1 Corinthians 13 details what truly lasts: "But now faith, hope, and love remain, these three; but the greatest of these is love."[21] For now, American society appears to have fallen away into a separation from the values that really matter.

Using MLK

When it comes to modern debate as to whether CRT belongs in schools or not, opponents of the theory are quick to insert the name of Martin Luther King Jr. King's name is used in conjunction with several statements he made on character and colorblindness, and none more iconic than his *I Have a Dream* speech at the March on Washington, on August 28, 1963. Critics are quick to point out that people who use MLK's name should not invoke his name, or quote what he taught, and then go to "ignore his real message."[22]

For example, those who use King for their argument of character over color would never quote what King wrote to his wife about his personal views on various political topics. One example, which pertains to economics, King appears to lean in on equity, in his letter stating he was "much more socialistic"[23] in his economic theory than capitalist. He also did not say that because he desires character to be the arbiter for children that using race in other contexts was wrong. King was human like the rest of us.

Others express their opinions on King, as well. Javonte Anderson of *USA Today* celebrates how "Martin Luther King Jr.'s words of unity and truth transcend how they are often twisted,"[24] and Jenne Theoharis of *Time* penned the piece titled "10 historians on what people still don't know about Martin

Luther King Jr."[25] Certainly, as with all people who are larger than life, not all scholars agree on the meanings of their words. MLK is treated no differently.

There is a certain level of exhaustion that seems to be developing over the argument as to whether King meant one thing or another. Wenyuan Wu illustrates this exhaustion by referencing a query from antiracist Ibram X. Kendi, who acts as an arbiter of citations when he asks, "Who has permission to quote MLK?"[26] Wu then quotes Kendi, who asserts, "Those who distort King's dream are now distorting critical race theory, and distorting CRT to distort King."[27] The arbiter does rule himself out from using King's quotes.

During his heyday, King was labeled once as "the most dangerous man in America."[28] Yet, what was the danger? Was there fear of flipping the script and condoning violence against the dominant culture? This would please the modern neo-Marxists, who are trying to reinterpret King's original messaging on character. The danger was that he would lead blacks, primarily in the South, to revolt and gain their rightful standing as citizens and this was a danger to the established hierarchy of the South. The lack of grace toward others was a catalyst of inequality and this was evident in the dominant culture[29] of the South. A lack of grace is again catalyzing America, but with a much different notion of equality.

King's letter from the Birmingham jail was most eloquent and called out the white moderates who supported his message, but not necessarily favored his strategy in the South—even though it focused on nonviolent protests. It is true that King protested peacefully, "but he also pointed his finger at the white majority and asked them to take up the fight."[30] The fight for equality in the 1960s is quite different from the struggle for outcome equity and violent dismantling of the system that preexisted King.

Would King support or discourage the fight today because of the messaging and tactics used against people in canceling them, destruction of property, killing of police, and the seeking to overthrow American society instead of changing it? Would he have favored the 1960s version of the CRT of his day? As a minister of the Gospel, could King have found a commonplace with BLM when they call for the dissolution of the concept of traditional marriage and family and the diminishment of individuals? It would be nearly impossible to look back at the violence that emerged from the death of George Floyd and say that King would have supported the mayhem, murder, and destruction.

King lived through the deaths of President Kennedy (November 22, 1963) and Malcolm X (February 21, 1965) and only when King was assassinated on April 4, 1968, did cities experience major riots and destruction. The rhetoric used by Malcolm X in the 1960s could easily be heard from the lips of today's neo-Marxist race-radicals.[31]

King also understood there was a time to pray, and a time to act, echoing Solomon's words, "There is an appointed time for everything. And there is a time for every matter under heaven."[32] King also knew there would be accountability for the actions and inactions of mankind: "God will bring into judgment both the righteous and the wicked, for there will be a time for every activity, and a time to judge every deed."[33] Trusting in God's grace seems a better bargain than trusting in the plans of mankind.

King as Reclaimed Radical?

MLK is persona non grata within the current groups of CRTs and antiracist scholars. BLM is making every effort to reclaim King and portray him as just as radical as they claim for themselves. As evidence, the Chicago branch of BLM was pushing the hashtag #ReclaimMLK on Twitter.[34] They assert that turning the other cheek was too simplistic as a description of King's radicalism.[35] So the group seeks to reinterpret King for the current generation and its push for equity.

It seems lobbying for character development and seeking legislation that was colorblind is not enough for today's activists. The neo-Marxism in their minds and hearts drives them toward revocation and removal of every mention of American character and any unifying values that connect to the past. Their efforts have their basis in the chants, *no justice, no peace*, and when it comes to killing law enforcement authorities, "*filthy, disgusting animals . . . fry like bacon.*"[36]

Without peace there is violence and destruction—the likes of which MLK decried in his early years.[37] It is true that some of King's positions on race, racism, and peaceful protest were certainly controversial for their time. LaNeysha Campbell, podcaster and entertainer, explains:

> The reality is, what Dr. King believed in—non-violence peaceful protesting—was also considered to be radical at the time. I think some who post his quotes are sugarcoating and misrepresenting the true intention of Dr. King's message to silence protesters who they deem are being too radical.[38]

There is some evidence to this effect, both in the attempts to enlarge the radicalism of King's Gandhian approach to nonviolence protest and the possible changes in his beliefs on the effects of violence, near the end of his life.[39] This is one reason BLM is seeking to transform the image of MLK.

King is remembered largely as a civil rights icon, a man of faith, and a political leader of peaceful protest actions. People showed up to marches wearing their Sunday best clothes and walked the streets. Azie Dungey, the creator of the web series, *Ask a Slave*, elaborates:

> In the '60s we wore our Sunday best, held hands, sang Christian songs, and did not fight back . . . because we were still proving we were as human as the white person . . . we should never have had to prove that. But that was the strategy.[40]

Contrast the riots of more recent days. People today wear helmets, carry weapons, wear body armor, and lift signs with messages that would besmirch the legacy of King. Today's rioters use Molotov cocktails and bring weapons. What the media refer to as protesters, the rest of the nation refers to as revolutionaries.

King's marches had character and honored the First Amendment. Today's groups, such as BLM, Black Panthers, and the Nation of Islam, harass people on the streets, walk into businesses, and taunt and assault those with whom they disagree. Of course, this does not pertain to all members of any one group. Yet, the strategy of overturning society is a joint goal. If a group cannot practice nonviolent protests, while claiming the name of King, then there is only one option. There must be a concerted effort to remake King into someone as radical they are. This is precisely what they are attempting to do.

The modern neo-Marxist movement that is BLM disenfranchised King's message of character some time ago. The current struggle against things like police brutality and law enforcement, in general, supplant the wider-reaching issues that are found in black families, the public schools in inner cities, and so on.

There is no character in failing schools. There is no character in poverty and there is no character in destroying the nuclear family.[41] There is also no character in law enforcement that treats people unjustly and unequally under the law. Last, there is no character in destroying that for which MLK gave his life. The nation could use a revisit of the grace preached by Dr. King.

A Dangerous Character?

The legacies of great leaders live on even beyond interpretation by historians. If Martin Luther King Jr. and his message of character over color made him the most dangerous man in the 1960s, then the sweeping movement to label all Whites as racists by birth and implicit bias is at least an equivalent characterization. In reality, it is much worse.

King's followers were viewed contemptuous during his time. The changing times have led to an entire demographic saddled as racists and considered dangerous nationalists. The most dangerous part of King's message is not in what he accomplished during his time. His danger was his claiming of the name of Christ and understanding of grace. This understanding resonates still and is prominent in today's culture.

Twenty-first-century groups of Americans are wandering as spiritually challenged prodigals, seeking to discover passion and purpose. In the midst of wandering, all prodigals have great difficulty in seeing their choices and how they affect others. But there is grace.

In the text of one of King's sermons, we find a masterful teaching about grace.

> Grace has a very vital place in any life. It has a very vital place in understanding the whole predicament of man and the whole predicament of the universe, for you can never understand life until you understand the meaning of the grace of God. The whole of life hinges on the ever flowing power and ever flowing stream of God's grace. Grace is just that something that God gives us. It's a gift that we don't merit, that we don't deserve, but which we so desperately need. That's grace, and none of us could live without it.

Those words echo as if they were written today.

King illustrates that the father of the prodigal had every right to say to his wayward son, "You deceived me; you disappointed me; you did everything against my will." But instead of doing that, the father said, "Come back home. Come in and be elevated into this home, for you are my son and I still love you." And that's what Jesus is saying; that's what the Gospel is saying; that's the meaning of grace—that no matter how low we sink, no matter how far we go, God still stands there saying, "If you come back home, I'll take you in." Can this prodigal principle be understood as applicable to a nation that has gone astray? If grace is as King eloquently described it, then it is not out of the reach of anyone.

However, when it comes to CRT, there is little if any compatibility with the very principles upon which this nation was founded. There is no authentic overlap between the Christian faith and CRT. Embarrassingly and erroneously, the use of Christianity—or any religion for that matter—to justify America's past of slavery is blasphemous and demonstrates that God's grace is cheapened by human actions. The crafting and enforcement of any policy that uses race to diminish others emanates from hearts in desperate need of King's message of grace.

COMMON GRACE IN ACTION

Common grace is responsible for the shaping of

> the United States in at least four important aspects. The . . . most obvious is the direct influence of Christianity—and of its antecedent Judaism—on American culture through the faith traditions of the American people. . . . Prominent

institutions . . . were founded with the aim of teaching faith and promoting Christian understandings of public virtue.[42]

Common grace refers to

the grace of God that is common to all humankind. It is *common* because its benefits are experienced by the whole human race without distinction between one person and another, believers or unbelievers. It is *grace* because it is undeserved and sovereignly bestowed by God.[43]

Reformed theologian Louis Berkhof writes that

[Common grace] curbs the destructive power of sin, maintains in a measure the moral order of the universe, thus making an orderly life possible, distributes in varying degrees gifts and talents among men, promotes the development of science and art, and showers untold blessings upon the children of men.[44]

Common grace is resident in at least three truth statements, each of which transcends culture. The first is that God cares for the creation. Second, God provides a level of restraint for society with governments, police, and so on. The third aspect of common grace is God's providential restraint of sin. It does not take long to see that many of the struggles in the United States over race stem from the inability to acknowledge that common grace exists, or that it matters. Some people choose to allow past evils to affect the present and obscure common grace.

Common Grace in Higher Education

Historically Black Colleges and Universities were founded on Christian principles and, in most cases, founded by Christian denominations. The Christian faith echoes from the storied halls of colleges the likes of Bethune-Cookman University, Philander Smith College, Clark Atlanta University, Morehouse College, Cheyney University, Lincoln University, and many others. This does not imply that America was established as a Christian nation. However, it does imply that many of the Western Christian values that were found in European culture are embedded in America's documents and systems. These embedded values are not white values. These values are common Christian values preached and practiced also in historic black churches as well.

From the early to mid-nineteenth century, many American institutions of higher education were established by people of faith. Church-oriented foundations and missions were parts of the original colleges of the Original

Thirteen States. Many of these served as seminaries to train men for full-time Christian service. Later, across the South, colleges were segregated. But these first steps led to others and what resulted was a lengthy fight for equality.

A true Christian grace-in-action resulted in

> religious leaders, local churches, missionaries, and denominations . . . descending across the South in the 19th century, believing that it was worth it to spend their time and money and do the right thing when they decided to establish seminaries, classrooms, colleges, and even medical schools for Blacks.[45]

In addition to its contributions to schools and higher education, Christianity impacted the development of the US Constitution and states' constitutions, local laws, the justice system, morality, and rights.

There are testaments to faith engraved all over America's national monuments and the nation's currency. The pivotal document Declaration of Independence, which set America on the path to eventual independence as a nation, recognized God "in four distinct ways." "God was recognized as (1) designer of the universe and source of natural law, (2) source of . . . inalienable rights, (3) Supreme Judge of the world, [and] (4) source of divine providence."[46]

Undeniably, America was a land of changes and grace and, despite the negative overtones over the battle over race in the nation, America is still a land of grace. The acceptance or rejection of common grace is left to the wills of humans and is responsible for both progress and problems in society.

There is just a lot of noise about race and separation being made by certain groups that grace among the average Americans should be preserved for personal relationships and families. In contrast, there is little room for grace among *the woke*. According to "the *woke* version of social justice, every aspect of our lives, [and] even our use of pronouns, must be bent toward political ends. Nothing can be enjoyed for its own sake."[47] Rejection of common grace for political purposes leads only to further separation and social marginalization.

The Challenge for the Church

BLM is

> much bigger, broader and more fluid than the organization. Unlike the previous Civil Rights Movement of the 1960s, it's not based in the Black church and as a result will include ideologies and perspectives that the church finds offensive, false, and even problematic.[48]

This reality has implications for the American church. If grace is to have any lasting impact, it must be shared within the walls of the church and then taken outside by the *ekklesia*, "the called out ones, and applied to make a difference."

CRT "exists because the Church in America ignored the inherent Biblical critique of systemic racism in America."[49] The truth is, "The gospel gives us insight to respond and subversively fulfill CRT with something greater, Critical *Grace* Theory." The Apostle Paul's words offer a principle which to consider in response.

> We have divine power to demolish strongholds. We demolish arguments and every pretension that sets itself up against the knowledge of God, and we take captive every thought to make it obedient to Christ. (2 Corinthians 10:5-6).[50]

Does this qualify CRT as a pretension to be addressed by the church?

Rasool Berry does not think so, but questions the leaders of the church as to their own version of separatism. Berry asks,

> When it comes to theories of justice, postmodern theory, psychology or the Declaration of Independence we can use conceptual integration but when it comes to CRT, or the Black Lives Matter movement, the typical reaction by some Christians is to reject them wholesale and denounce anything of anyone associated with them?[51]

In so doing, is the church rejecting people whose identities are so bound together with their beliefs?

Grace sees the person behind the beliefs, even if the person being viewed cannot distinguish between the two. There is a cost to offering grace, especially to those who are not ready to accept it. But if the church expects to impact culture, and not the other way around, it must speak to and be able to parse the historic orthodox Christian positions on contemporary cultural issues such as CRT and race.

THE COST OF GRACE

Christian philosopher J. P. Moreland

> argues that common grace enables us to learn from all people. Common grace is the doctrine that God allows everyone including those who don't believe in him to understand truths about reality. As a result of common grace, we can learn from philosophers, scholars and activists regardless of their personal beliefs.[52]

There is no coincidence that even with the abuse of the Bible's teachings and the despicable practice of associating God's will with owning of human beings that grace was at work. Christians believe God is always at work. MLK believed this, otherwise he would have given up the fight for civil rights. Some of the most stalwart Christian churches were founded during times of tremendous persecution. Even so, one would be hard-pressed to find passages in the New Testament that illustrate that grace does not exist in the midst of persecution.

Historically, Americans, in general, have played a role in spreading the message that God's grace has been a part of the nation's history. By means of the efforts of many in Christian churches and abolitionists, challenges arose in the past to those who understood that the ownership of human beings was contrary to the gospel message. Two popular verses used at the time that provided clarity and hope were 2 Cor 5:17: "Therefore if anyone is in Christ, *this person is* a new creation; the old things passed away; behold, new things have come" (NASB), and John 8:36: "So if the Son sets you free, you really will be free" (NASB).

Although history is not clear on this point, but speculation exists as to whether MLK associated the words of an old Negro Spiritual, *Free at last, free at last, thank God Almighty, we are free at last*, based on verses found in the biblical books of Genesis, John, and both 1 and 2 Corinthians. Grace has always been paired with a sacrificial spirit in its expressions. Thus, "Greater love has no one than this, that a person will lay down his life for his friends."[53]

Although MLK paid the ultimate price because of his message and methods, the meaning associated with his life was a grace-centered message.[54] Despite the rejection of King by his detractors, through his personal sacrifice, God continues to shed His grace upon America. There are many biblical stories that demonstrate common grace. One of these stories involved Joseph, the second youngest son of Israel (Jacob). Another is the story of Job.

Joseph, after being sold into slavery by his brothers and whereupon being reunited in Egypt, proclaimed, "What you meant as evil, God meant for good."[55] Grace sees even the terrible negative circumstances of life and acknowledges the words of Isaiah 55:8, 'For My thoughts are not your thoughts, nor are your ways My ways,' declares the LORD" (NASB). Common grace provided for food during famine because of the wisdom of Joseph in preparing for bad times when times were good.

Job was tested, by losing his entire fortune and family, yet refused to curse God. His faith in God's grace and will led to a blessed ending to Job's years. Job 42:10 (NASB) records, "And the Lord restored the fortunes of Job when he had prayed for his friends, and the Lord increased all job had twofold."

Humans often feel the depths of despair in desperate situations in life. Nevertheless, grace expressed means that humans are not stuck there.

Seeking one's own pounds of flesh as payback eats away at the soul. The principle to take from here is that a *grace-centered life* views all aspects of one's life very differently than a life centered on human flesh, regardless the color. Seeing life through grace is not necessarily going to absolve anyone from difficulties in their lives. But it will enable them not to be absorbed by these difficulties and provide hope that in the end blessings await.

Personal Sacrifice and Grace

No one can truly understand the theological nature of grace in shedding of human blood as part of a grander plan of grace, as in the case of the death of Jesus Christ. But couldn't this be the meaning behind the lyric, "God shed His grace on thee"? There are many examples in history of how changes for the better resulted from personal sacrifices. There should not be taken from these sections that Black Americans, whose ancestors were enslaved, should just wake up one day and decide to forgive the past. Certainly, that would be ideal, and some may claim this is exactly where they are in life. But is also almost certainly and insultingly trite.

Even so, what is being asked is for grace to be applied to those in the present who have had no connection to slavery whose families came here for better lives, long after slavery and even Jim Crow ended. This is a request of personal sacrifice—the kind that requires letting go of resentment and a desire for revenge. The truth is there is no reason to indict an entire population based on skin color and hold them hostage to the sins of their forebears. America has already made this mistake and it was wrong. Even so, whatever side one takes, common grace messaging from the Book of Romans, at least reminds believers that

> The . . . Spirit . . . helps our weakness . . . the Spirit Himself intercedes for *us* . . . and He who searches the hearts knows what the mind of the Spirit is. . . . And we know that God causes all things to work together for good to those who love God, to those who are called according to *His* purpose . . . What then shall we say to these things? If God *is* for us, who *is* against us?[56]

The church should be the place of grace. Is this not why the church was the ignition point for cultural change under MLK.

There can be no doubt that grace has a memory, but this grace is of the head, and not the heart. Unfortunately, the battle today over race is a battle contrasting emotions and intellect. Finding grace in all things can be difficult. Still, grace is not punitive, especially where innocents are concerned. Consequently, holding people accountable for things they did not do is one thing. This is guilt by association. Taking responsibility for something and being guilty for those things is very different.

A legal parallel illustrates this point. In terms of law, it is unconstitutional to hold accountable a family member of a person accused of the crime of treason if other family members had nothing to do with the treason. This has been used to affirm no "corruption of blood," or guilt by association defenses (Article 3, Section 3).

The broader principle of guilt by association is a principle that is respected in America. Therefore, even with one of the highest crimes that could be committed against the United States, collective guilt is not only unconstitutional, it is immoral as well. What parent wants their own children accountable for extended family relatives' legal or moral failures? Under this principle, American parents find it reprehensible that their children are assumed guilty by association because of skin color. In other words, a white person should not be labeled as racist, even if there were racists in one's family history.

GRACE KNOWS NO RACE

Instead of expecting others to apologize for the wrongs of history, grace offers forgiveness for the past. In other words, *common grace* sees other people through the lens of forgiveness that may not be deserved,[57] and with good reason. The meaning

> of the word *grace*, as used in the New Testament, is not unlike its meaning as employed in common speech,—but for one important exception, namely, in the Bible the word often represents that which is limitless, since it represents realities which are infinite and eternal.[58]

The word "*favor* is the nearest Biblical synonym for the word *grace*."[59] According to Lewis Sperry Chafer, "Grace is favor, and favor is grace."[60] Likewise, "Grace means pure unrecompensed kindness and favor. What is done is done graciously. From this exact meaning there can be no departure; otherwise grace ceases to be grace."[61]

There is no white grace and there is no black grace. There is only grace and it has no attachment to race. Given this truth, the good news is humans are capable to view past wrongs without seeing skin color. Even in the midst of political polarization and cultural marginalization, grace could lead the way and fill human hearts with kindness and favor. The fact that it is undeserved means that grace is that much more meaningful. Since all people are helpless in changing their past, "grace finds its greatest triumph and glory in the sphere of human helplessness."[62] These are excellent words for today. Scripture adds other truths to consider.

The Apostle Paul provides some sound instruction to the church at Colossae. In Col 3:12–13, Paul writes,

> So, as those who have been chosen of God, holy and beloved, put on a heart of compassion, kindness, humility, gentleness and patience; bearing with one another, and forgiving each other, whoever has a complaint against anyone; just as the Lord forgave you, so also should you. (NASB)

A special emphasis

> is given as well to Christian kindness: Let all bitterness, and wrath, and anger, and clamor, and evil speaking, be put away from you, with all malice; and be ye kind one to another, tenderhearted, forgiving one another, even as God for Christ's sake hath forgiven you. (Ephesians 4:31-32)[63]

The Book of Matthew describes a conversation about forgiveness between Jesus and Peter, one of Jesus's disciples. The passage reads, "Then Peter came to Jesus and asked, Lord, how many times shall I forgive my brother who sins against me? Up to seven times? Jesus answered, I tell you, not just seven times, but seventy-seven times!" (Matthew 18:21–22, NASB).

Now, what has been written in the previous sections of this chapter can easily be dismissed by those who do not claim to be Christians. Others might disregard any pleas as a form of *white-splaining*. But for those who do claim the Christian faith as their own, a challenge is offered. Could it be that it is time to live within the common grace provided, in such a way that external characteristics that separate BIPOC and white are valid and important, but not more important as inner traits? Is this not what MLK had intended when he addressed the importance of character over color?

Authentic Grace

Authentic grace can change hearts and minds. The possession of this type of grace comes in knowing the *One in Whom* the depths of authentic grace exist. Looking to oneself or within one's color group is not the answer. Authenticity to oneself in the area of race places *Critical Race* over *Common Grace*. This leads to five areas of concern that illustrate the incompatibility of CRT with Christianity.

First, when race supersedes grace, the focus is on the external. This amounts to a point of soulful empowerment through external physical identification.

CRT supporters claim that race is not biological, yet they maintain that black is beautiful and, to some people, their biology is superior physically, compared to other races.[64] To recognize racial distinctions while offering criticism of others who recognize the same is to place oneself above another.

Authentic common grace pertains to inward character and should project truth in soulful, growing relationships with others. This type of grace overlooks the external appearance and accepts all people because its focus is on the deeper needs of humans. Authentic grace forgives. Authentic grace levels people as equals and accepts them as they are, and where they are in life. Even when behaviors and actions do not comport with certain cultural stereotypes, authentic grace offers forgiveness. When feasible, restoration of relationships is the goal. In other words, "If possible, so far as it depends on you, be at peace with all people."[65]

Grace levels humans as persons with common natures, whereas race is a social construct devised by humans. Grace is stalwart toward recognition and acceptance of differences as blessings found within the kaleidoscope of humanity. Race sees two kaleidoscopes. One contains various colors and the other is monochrome.

Second, assumptions that things must exist in the present because they existed in the past is a fallacy. Western civilization has elicited some of the best and the worst of humanity. Grace enables humans to understand the worst and then move to make conditions better between people. Race wants to punish the present for the past and leaves an unforgiving spirit intact. Grace offers forgiveness unconditionally.

Third, the Christian church in America must examine CRT but guard against buying into it wholesale. CRT advocates already occupy the pews and many of mainline denomination's pulpits and this is problematic. A good example of this is *woke-ism* and a bending of theology to fit the culture. A church that suddenly realizes its cultural awareness in support of a theory that does little to unite people focuses on white sins—while pushing grace into the background—is missing a key element of the Gospel message.

Fourth, a theology of liberation, or social justice, based on externals, is short on forgiveness and misses a critical piece of sound practical theology by leaving out grace. Most Americans are gracious and understand it is fine for colleges and universities to proclaim they are black or Hispanic serving institutions. But churches should not be places of exclusive races.

Last, American Christians are faced with choices. People are often made to choose between "the two extremes of wholeheartedly embracing CRT or rejecting all it has to say about race and justice. But is such a dichotomy necessary or even the right way to think about the issue?"[66] The Apostle Paul, in his letter to the Church at Galatia, declared, "There is neither Jew nor Greek, there is neither slave nor free, there is neither male nor female; for you are all one in Christ Jesus."[67] Likewise, "So if the Son makes you free, then you are unquestionably free."[68] In referencing those who claim the Christian faith, John 8:35–36 states, "A slave is not a permanent member of the family, but a son belongs to it forever. So if the Son sets you free, you will be free indeed" (NASB). The irony is that there is now equality under the law. The racism of the past is long gone. It is long gone by God's grace and forgiveness, and it is long gone in society, as a whole.

However, there is new racism in town willing to engage in punitive measures levied upon those who dare to disagree. R. R. Reno illustrates this clearly:

> The hysteria of the present moment is destructive. BLM activists and their fellow travelers police speech and topple statues, and although they are not yet burning books, they cancel careers, censor publications, and terrorize those they deem agents of white privilege.[69]

Where there is a hang-up today with CRT, is the message that "Christians can acknowledge the true observations that CRT makes without buying into the narrative or belief structure that goes along with it?"[70] CRT is as authentic to the theorists as grace is to the theologians.

GRACE AND GRADES

The term "*White privilege* refers to the myriad of social advantages, benefits, and courtesies that come with being a member of the dominant race."[71] Those who research white privilege in academe claim that

> white people benefit from a system of favors, exchanges, and courtesies from which outsiders of color are frequently excluded, including hiring one's neighbor's kids for summer jobs, a teacher's agreement to give a favored student an extra-credit assignment that will enable him or her to raise a grade of B+ to A-, or the kind of quiet networking that lands a borderline candidate a coveted position.[72]

But privilege has no color assigned to it, apart from those with power who do the assigning.

MLK would have a serious disagreement with Delgado and Stefancic over their use of the grade analogy to illustrate white privilege. King tells the story about his experience with grace, in his classic sermon "Man's Sin and God's Grace."[73]

While in graduate school, he explains a professor's actions: "There we were sitting there, sorrowful, feeling that we were going to have to take philosophical theology over again." And he said, "Well, you've been a loyal class, and I think, at bottom, maybe I should do something about this. And you will notice on your books that I have added ten points; to every examination I've added ten points." I got my little blue book and I noticed up there at the top, "75." Then under there I noticed the word "grace" and then it had "10" under there, right across from "grace." And then there was a line there, and it said "85" under there. "And that happened for every examination, there was this additional ten points, so that all of us were able to get by and pass the examination and get through the course. That was grace."[74] Could it be that a secular version of grace is really equity in disguise? If it is, then applying it subjectively, to one group over another, would disqualify it from any biblical connection, "for God is not one to show partiality."[75] The professor was not selective in his application of grace to just one group. The professor demonstrated equality because adding the ten points to each score still meant there was individuality in the scores of passage.

GRACE AND EQUITY

Equity, as Americans know it, can only be achieved by entities of authority stepping in to provide outcomes over access or possessions over possibilities. At first glance, the concept of equity seems to have something in common with grace. Certainly, all people are equal in value in God's economy, but not all people are equitable in the systems of humans. This is the dilemma faced by Americans today. The outcomes of humans both on a temporal and eternal scale are not equitable. Some live longer than others. People have more resources than others, and so on. Left to government, it would use its own discretion and remove goods and give them equitably to the less fortunate. However, there is no grace is mandatory equity.

Grace is not an outcome that is deserved because others are sinners of the past or present and must be responsible to give up something. Grace is unmerited favor and the Bible makes clear that all in the same boat, in that respect. "For all have sinned and fall short of the glory of God" (Roman 3:23, NASB). MLK was correct when he spoke of the content of character over color. The government cannot provide either.

A Christian

> does not love humanity. He loves God in Christ, and in so doing he is incorporated into the divine love that brings sun and rain upon the just and the unjust. . . . Our loves does not aim at the world—a vainglorious ambition that has shipwrecked many whose philanthropy withers into a hectoring moralism. The love that bears all things, believes all things, hopes all things, and endures all things seeks union with the Son of God.[76]

Externals seem to dissolve when there is authentic grace and godly blessing acting together in believers' lives. This would also be true of unbelievers working within common grace toward others. Grace should enjoin all Americans to pursue the greater good.

MLK knew the truth of Acts 2, and so do many spirit-filled graceful living people today.

> All the believers were together and had all things in common; and they would sell their property and possessions and share them with all, to the extent that anyone had need. Day by day continuing with one mind in the temple, and breaking bread from house to house, they were taking their meals together with gladness and sincerity of heart, praising God and having favor with all the people. And the Lord was adding to their number day by day those who were being saved.[77]

The spread of CRT and the teaching that designates people's value based on skin color do little to advance grace in practical terms. Churches that teach from their pulpits that all is well in American society cheapen grace. The onus on the faith communities that have an understanding of grace is pronounced. Conversely, those that preach a social gospel play directly into the hands of continued separation of people along racial lines. This is the place where the race-based radicals of today wish they could drag MLK.

In the extreme, the advocates of CRT are willing and able to ensnare those in need of grace. But they will do so by empowerment and action, rather than by humility. Delgado and Stefancic explain how this empowerment might play out:

> The peaceful transition [of power] . . . may not take place—the white establishment may resist an orderly progression toward power sharing. . . . As happened in South Africa, the change may be convulsive and cataclysmic. If so, critical theorists and activists will need to provide criminal defense for resistance movements and activists to articulate theories and strategies for that resistance.[78]

When a heart is captured, a disciple acts in favor of its teacher. Educators know this only too well. Such is the reality of CRT and the ground it is gaining in America's schools. How long before students come to believe another version of ensnarement that *Color is character.*

A REJECTION OF CRT

One of the reasons many people reject CRT is because many of its tenets are not based on truth. However, in this rejection, one must take care not to communicate a rejection of the person holding such a view. That is not grace-focused. CRT remains a theory based on assumptions—and these assumptions dismiss objective truth as opinion, thereby limiting dialogue or disagreement.

If no discourse or critique is allowed in the public square, there is only one chance for CRT to take hold and remain within American society. That is, it must be accomplished by federal, state, and local governmental forces. The irony in such an accomplishment is that the very institutions deemed as racist would be those called upon the establish antiracism. Critics refer to this as another form of racism.

Another reason most people reject CRT is the activism that spins out from its stances on religion, family, relationships and sex, and God. In the words of the late Francis Schaeffer, "Truth always carries with it confrontation. Truth demands confrontation; loving confrontation nevertheless. If our reflex action is always accommodation regardless of the centrality of the truth involved, there is something wrong."[79] If CRT is truth, it must be allowed open debate with critics, especially people of color who do not believe CRT is true.

Rasool Berry explains another reason why CRT is rejected by people. There is

> a sophisticated sleight-of-hand maneuver inherent in Critical Theory's philosophy. In order to undermine traditional theories, Critical Theorists often reject all narratives that seek to explain the world, with the notable exception of itself, because clearly critical theory is a narrative that seeks to explain the world. The CRT narrative is that the problem with the world are [*sic*] powerful people who create narratives that they say we must all believe in. The way we experience human liberation is to reject their narratives. Some have readily recognized this inherent inconsistency.[80]

In a message for the church, Berry says Christian believers

> should be aware . . . sin often blinds us and makes us susceptible to using culture and power for self-justification. Culture often blinds us to what the Bible is saying. Power allows us to insist our blinded version of reality MUST BE TRUE.

If believers are blind to their sin, how much more are non-believers also blind?[81]

The solemn reality, which should always be part of America's national psyche, is that individuals and groups are more likely to offer grace to others within their group, primarily because they have experienced grace in their own lives. The questions are then, where is *grace* and why should it be granted to groups in opposition to one another? The easy answer is that grace is best realized where it is needed the most. Essentially, and obviously, humans are in need of it most.

In closing out this chapter, there are three critical reminders to expressions of grace to consider. First, there must be the ability to forgive, whether the recipient accepts the forgiveness or not. Second, Americans must be exhorted not to hold past actions against others in the present, especially when they had nothing to do with the actions of the past. Christians, especially, have no right to ask for grace if they are unwilling to offer it first. Third, letting go of generational hurts means ending the label-making. The practice of these three elements offers a graceful start toward unity, which is so desperately needed in American society. The time has come to draw people together through realizing *common grace*. Only then can Americans of all colors begin to chip away at the ongoing cycle of *critical race*.

NOTES

1. "Booker T. Washington." *Goodreads Quotable Quotes*. Retrieved October 4, 2021, from https://www.goodreads.com/quotes/9580325-a-lie-doesn-t-become-truth-wrong-doesn-t-become-right-and.
2. Kirsten Powers. *Saving Grace: Speak Your Truth, Stay Centered, and Learn to Coexist with People Who Drive You Nuts*. New York City: Convergent Books, 2021, p. 1.
3. Staff. "What are the lyrics to America the Beautiful?" *Classical Music*. February 11, 2021. Retrieved September 8, 2021, from https://www.classical-music.com/features/articles/america-the-beautiful-lyrics/.
4. Josh Hayes. "Does God have a special relationship with America?" *Relevant Magazine*. March 24, 2017. Retrieved October 17, 2021, from https://www.relevant-magazine.com/culture/does-god-have-a-special-relationship-with-america/.
5. Scott Hancock. "The limits of Black forgiveness." *Journal of the Civil War Era*. June 18, 2020. Retrieved November 1, 2021, from https://www.journalofthecivilwarera.org/2020/06/the-limits-of-black-forgiveness/.
6. Ta-Nehisi Coates. "Why are Black people so forgiving?" *The Atlantic*. October 6, 2010. Retrieved November 1, 2021, from https://www.theatlantic.com/national/archive/2010/10/why-are-black-people-so-forgiving/64129/.
7. Jonathan Butcher and Mike Gonzalez. "Critical race theory, the new intolerance, and its grip on America." *The Heritage Foundation*. December 7, 2020. Retrieved November 5, 2021, from https://www.heritage.org/sites/default/files/2020-12/BG3567.pdf.
8. B. L. Wilson. "I'm your black friend but I won't educate you about racism. That's on you." *The Washington Post*. June 8, 2020. Retrieved November 5, 2021, from https://www.washingtonpost.com/outlook/2020/06/08/black-friends-educate-racism/.
9. Tyler O'Neil. "McAuliffe in 2019: Diversity, inclusion are as important as math and English in schools." *Fox News*. October 25, 2021. Retrieved October 26,

2021, from https://www.foxnews.com/politics/mcauliffe-diversity-inclusion-are-as-important-as-math-and-english-in-schools.

10. Edward F. DeRoche and Mary M. Williams. *Character Education: A School Guide for Administrators*. Lanham, MD: Scarecrow Press, Inc., 2001, p. 1.

11. Drew Desilver. "King's I have a Dream speech, by the numbers." *Pew Research Center*. August 28, 2013. Retrieved November 6, 2021, from https://www.pewresearch.org/fact-tank/2013/08/28/kings-i-have-a-dream-speech-by-the-numbers/.

12. Staff. "MLK's content of character quote inspires debate." *CBS News*. January 20, 2013. Retrieved November 6, 2021, from https://www.cbsnews.com/news/mlks-content-of-character-quote-inspires-debate/.

13. Kevin Ryan and Karen Bohlin. *Building Character in Schools: Practical Ways to Bring Moral Instruction to Life*. San Francisco, CA: Jossey-Bass Publishers, 1999, p. 9.

14. Ibid., p. 6.

15. Ibid.

16. Ibid.

17. Ibid.

18. Ibid., pp. 6–7.

19. 1 Corinthians 13:4, *New American Standard Bible*.

20. Martin Luther King Jr. "Man's sin and God's grace." *The Martin Luther King, Jr. Research and Education Institute*. January 1, 1954. Retrieved November 6, 2021, from https://kinginstitute.stanford.edu/king-papers/documents/mans-sin-and-gods-grace.

21. 1 Corinthians 13:13, *New American Standard Bible*.

22. Fabiola Cineas. "Don't ask what Martin Luther King Jr. would do today and then ignore his real message. *Vox*. January 18, 2021. Retrieved September 29, 2021, from https://www.vox.com/2021/1/18/22233296/martin-luther-king-jr-whitewashed-legacy-and-message.

23. Ibid.

24. Javonte Anderson. "Martin Luther King Jr.'s words of unity and truth transcend how they are often twisted." *USA Today*. January 18, 2021. Retrieved September 28, 2021, from https://www.usatoday.com/story/news/2021/01/18/king-holiday-martin-luther-king-jr-words-unity/4153503001/.

25. Jeanne Theoharis. "10 historians on what people still don't know about Martin Luther King Jr." *Time*. January 10, 2021. Retrieved September 28, 2021, from https://time.com/5197679/10-historians-martin-luther-king-jr/.

26. Wenyuan Wu. "The exhaustion of antiracism: Who has permission to quote MLK?" *National Association of Scholars*. October 18, 2021. Retrieved October 19, 2021, from https://www.mindingthecampus.org/2021/10/18/the-exhaustion-of-anti-racism-who-has-permission-to-quote-mlk/.

27. Ibid.

28. Ijeoma Oluo. *So You Want to Talk About Race*. New York: Seal Press, 2019, p. 203.

29. Ed Stetzer. "When will Christians learn from the unending engagement cycle of evangelicalism and race?" *USA Today*. September 28, 2021. Retrieved September 29, 2021, from https://www.usatoday.com/story/opinion/2021/09/28/bible-evangelicals-duty-fight-racism/5847173001/. Cf. Bob Smietana. "Christian author Josh McDowell steps away from ministry after comments about Black, minority families." *Religion News Service*. September 19, 2021. Retrieved September 20, 2021, from https://religionnews.com/2021/09/19/christian-author-josh-mcdowell-denounces-crt-says-black-and-minority-families-dont-value-hard-work-and-education/.

30. Brittany Wong. "White people, stop quoting MLK to police how black people protest." *The Huffington Post*. June 15, 2020. Retrieved October 16, 2021, from https://www.huffpost.com/entry/stop-quoting-mlk-black-people-protest_n_5ed554bac5b6d58c403814dc.

31. James Pasley. "The life and assassination of Malcolm X, the controversial civil rights activist who death remains a mystery." *Business Insider*. February 19, 2020. Retrieved November 8, 2021, from https://www.businessinsider.com/how-malcolm-x-lived-died-assassinated-death-reinvestigated-2020-2.

32. Ecclesiastes 3:1, *New American Standard Bible*.

33. Ecclesiastes 3:17, *New International Version*.

34. Staff. "Black Lives Matter activists aim to reclaim MLK as radical." *Fox News*. January 16, 2017. Retrieved October 17, 2021, from https://www.foxnews.com/us/black-lives-matter-activists-aim-to-reclaim-mlk-as-radical.

35. Ibid.

36. Lee Brown. "Black lives matter speaker declares war on filthy, disgusting animal cops." *New York Post*. August 19, 2020. Retrieved November 6, 2021, from https://nypost.com/2020/08/19/blm-speaker-declares-war-on-filthy-disgusting-animal-cops/.

37. The Doha Declaration. "Martin Luther King, Jr.'s six principles of nonviolence handout." *United Nations Office on Drugs and Crime*. 2021. Retrieved October 17, 2021, from https://www.unodc.org/documents/e4j/Secondary/Terrorism_Violent_Extremism_Six_Principles_of_Non-Violence.pdf). Cf. The King Institute. "Six principles of nonviolence." *Stanford University*. 2021. Retrieved October 17, 2021, from https://kinginstitute.stanford.edu/sites/mlk/files/lesson-activities/six_principles_of_nonviolence.pdf.

38. Wong. "White people, stop quoting MLK to police how black people protest." *The Huffington Post*.

39. Hanif Abdurraqib. "By the end of his life, Martin Luther King realized the validity of violence." *Timeline*. June 15, 2017. Retrieved October 17, 2021, from https://timeline.com/by-the-end-of-his-life-martin-luther-king-realized-the-validity-of-violence-4de177a8c87b.

40. Wong. "White people, stop quoting MLK to police how black people protest." *The Huffington Post*.

41. Oluo, *So You Want to Talk about Race*, pp. 203–204.

42. Carol M. Swain and Christopher J. Schorr. *Black Eye for America: How Critical Race Theory Is Burning Down the House*. Rockville, MD: Be the People Books, 2021, p. 37.

43. "Common Grace." *Theopedia*. 2021. Retrieved October 17, 2021, from https://www.theopedia.com/common-grace.

44. Louis Berkhof. *Systematic Theology*, 4th edition. Grand Rapids, MI: Eerdmans Publishers, 1979, p. 434.

45. Staff. "Echoes of faith: Church roots run deep among HBCUs." *Diverse Issues in Higher Education*. July 30, 2012. Retrieved September 30, 2021, from https://www.diverseeducation.com/demographics/african-american/article/15091579/echoes-of-faith-church-roots-run-deep-among-hbcus.

46. Swain and Schorr. *Black Eye for America*, p. 39.

47. R. R. Reno. "Antiracist hysteria." *First Things*. December 2020. Retrieved April 23, 2021, from https://www.firstthings.com/article/2020/12/antiracist-hysteria.

48. Rasool Berry. "Critical [g]race theory: The promise and perils of CRT." *Medium*. August 20, 2020. Retrieved August 8, 2021, from https://rasoolberry.medium.com/critical-g-race-theory-the-promise-perils-of-crt-c5de933d55a1.

49. Ibid.

50. Rasool Berry. "Critical [g]race theory: The promise and perils of CRT." *Medium*. August 20, 2020. Retrieved August 8, 2021, from https://rasoolberry.medium.com/critical-g-race-theory-the-promise-perils-of-crt-c5de933d55a1.

51. Ibid.

52. Ibid.

53. John 15:13, *New American Standard Bible*.

54. Jonathan Darman. "The persistence of grace: Martin Luther King Jr. *Yahoo News*. January 15, 1929—April 4, 1968." April 2, 2018. Retrieved November 6, 2021, from https://www.yahoo.com/news/persistence-grace-martin-luther-king-jr-jan-15-1929-april-4-1968-100804394.html.

55. Genesis 50:30, *New American Standard Bible*.

56. Romans 8:26–31, *New American Standard Bible*.

57. Mark M. Leach, Aisha Baker, and Virgil Zeigler-Hill. "The influence of Black racial identity on the forgiveness of Whites." *Journal of Black Psychology* 37, no. 2 (2011): 185–209. Retrieved November 1, 2021, from https://journals.sagepub.com/doi/pdf/10.1177/0095798410380201.

58. Lewis Sperry Chafer. *Grace: The Glorious Theme*. Grand Rapids, MI: Zondervan Publishing House, 1950 (1922), p. 3.

59. Ibid., pp. 3–4.

60. Ibid., p. 4.

61. Ibid.

62. Ibid.

63. Ibid., p. 329.

64. Matthew Hutson. "Whites see Blacks as superhuman." *Slate*. November 14, 2014. Retrieved October 26, 2021, from https://slate.com/technology/2014/11/whites-see-blacks-as-superhuman-strength-speed-pain-tolerance-and-the-magical-negro.html.

65. Romans 12:18, *New American Standard Bible*.

66. Berry. "Critical [g]race theory: The promise and perils of CRT." *Medium*.

67. Galatians 3:28, *New American Standard Bible*.

68. John 8:36, *Amplified Bible.*
69. R. R. Reno. "Antiracist hysteria." *First Things.*
70. Neal Hardin. "Is critical race theory biblical?" *The Religion & Politics Blog.* June 26, 2021. Retrieved July 1, 2021, from https://www.nealhardin.com/is-critical-race-theory-biblical/.
71. Delgado and Stefancic. *Critical Race Theory,* p. 87.
72. Ibid, p. 88.
73. King Jr. "Man's sin and God's grace."
74. Ibid.
75. Acts 10:34, *New American Standard Bible.*
76. R. R. Reno. "Antiracist hysteria." *First Things.*
77. Acts 2:44–47, *New American Standard Bible.*
78. Delgado and Stefancic. *Critical Race Theory,* p. 146.
79. Francis Schaeffer. *The Great Evangelical Disaster.* Wheaton, IL: Crossway Books, 1983, p. 64.
80. Berry. "Critical [g]race theory: The promise and perils of CRT." *Medium.*
81. Ibid.

Chapter 4

Analysis of Critical Race Theory

> CRT does not attribute racism to white people . . . Simply put, critical race theory states that U.S. social institutions . . . are laced with racism . . . that lead to differential outcomes by race . . . scholars have long noted that racism can exist without racists. . . . Many Americans are not able to separate their individual identity . . . from the social institutions . . . they interpret calling social institutions racist as calling them racist personally . . . There are also people who may recognize America's racist past but have bought into the false narrative that the U.S. is now an equitable democracy. They are simply unwilling to remove the blind spot obscuring the fact that America is still not great for everyone.[1]

> There is an alarming trend sweeping our nation's institutions. School children as young as five are being inculcated into antiracist activism. Administrators across the country are pushing that idea that merit is racist. Office workers are being pressured into DEI seminars where white people are forced to admit their irredeemable corruption. Journalists are losing their jobs because they uttered the wrong word.[2]

As King Solomon once claimed, "Futility of futilities, all is futility" (Ecclesiastes 1:2, NASB). Certainly, Solomon did not have CRT in mind when he wrote these words. However, the underlying assumptions that had birthed CRT are not really new ideas for humanity. Judging people based on externals has been part of humanity throughout all of recorded history. If polls are any indication, these types of judgment are not likely to end any time soon.[3]

CRITICAL RACE THEORY IS NOT A NEW IDEA

In biblical times, *people groups* were diminished and enslaved by Romans, and others, within the empire. The Jews have a lengthy history of experiencing this type of discrimination and mistreatment. Even the Jewish carpenter Jesus Christ was ridiculed because of where he lived in Nazareth. One of his early critics asked, "Can any good thing be from Nazareth?"[4]

Academics like to think their ideas are unique and have merit. Yet, as Solomon also penned, "What has been, it is what will be, and what has been done . . . it is what will be done. So there is nothing new under the sun."[5] People of all nations, all backgrounds, and all skin colors—and also by genders and sexes—have at one time or another been judged as inferior, because of some cultural ideology or expression of economic power.[6]

CRT originated from "postmodernist thought, which tends to be skeptical of the idea of universal values, objective knowledge, individual merit, Enlightenment rationalism, and liberalism—tenets that conservatives tend to hold dear."[7] CRT as a theory is contrary to the foundation of Western civilization. Yet, CRT advocates do not hesitate to use Western logical fallacies to explain subjective perspectives.

There is both irrationality and deception in play if a group claims not to believe in the very thing it uses as evidence to diminish another group. The bad news for CRT is that if there are no universals, such as life, objective knowledge, and merit, then there can be no values outside the subjective. Therefore, the fact that there is an objective statement as to there being *no objective values*, this subjective denial of such values becomes an objective statement.

Applying this to CRT means that any attribution assigned to a race cannot be taken as objective. Such contradictions amount to nullification of the major premises of CRT. As a result, America cannot be objectively declared as systemically racist, since objectives do not exist. By this, then, all whites are neither oppressors nor privileged racists, and whiteness is not evidence in support of systemic racism. Still, the narrative is presented accusing America as a racist nation from the beginning.

If CRT was illustrated as an anthropomorphism, then the theory, itself, comprises the head and the brain. BLM is the eyes and nose. DEI are the torso and arms, while white privilege and antiracism are the legs. What is missing from the figure is the mouth. That is for a reason since there is not a singular, consistent voice that comes from such a figure.

CRT and Voices

Stanley Kurtz of the *National Review* demonstrates there is a new type of race scholar that has emerged in American academe. This new type of scholar is fearful of critique. Ibram X. Kendi, Robin DiAngelo, and other woke professors, each of which claims to be part of the academy, refuse to debate anyone. The same is true for Hannah-Jones, founder of *The 1619 Project*, which has added to the conversation the phrase "cry-bully."[8] Apparently, grievances that make their ways into book form, or curriculum for schools, no longer have to be vetted, if a person is a member of a self-proclaimed grievance group or is a useful vessel for one.

On college campuses, far too often professors are left unchallenged and what emerges from this critical process usually finds its way into K-16 classrooms across America. Informal discussions with a sample of college students confirm the students' fears of challenging their instructors. The new phenomenon now has some professors fearful of being challenged from within their own disciplines, especially as untenured faculty.

Kurtz adds that some of the professors fear being challenged specifically on matters to do with race, so they acquiesce to the whim of the latest fad. In fact, writes Kurtz, "White guilt and the consequent double standard are tailor-made to produce the campus cry-baby persona."[9] The effects upon education are prominent and growing.

CRT AND ITS FOCUS ON AMERICAN EDUCATION

Thomas Sowell calls CRT brainwashing and warns of its effects. He asserts, "The educational consequences of ideological indoctrination efforts are likely to be far more serious than the political consequences. The ideologies of young people in schools or in colleges are not set in concrete."[10]

Efforts to convince students they are either oppressors or oppressed are a form of indoctrination that Sowell warns about. The contemporary shift to student brainwashing began with CRT, once it left academe. The theory was removed from the realm of the theoretical and conscientiously repackaged and instituted as truth. Sowell states,

> Whether blatant or subtle, brainwashing has become a major, time-consuming activity in American education at all levels. Some zealots have not hesitated to use the traditional brain-washing technique of emotional trauma in the classroom to soften up children for their message.[11]

To Sowell's point, schools today have incorporated trauma-informed instructions, social-emotional learning, and training in deconstructing whiteness. Misplaced empathy and student shame are as prominent as the CRT-related doctrinal tenets of white supremacy, original sin, and implicit bias, each of which is infused to induce trauma.

Strategies were attempted in earlier decades to produce similar results with students. Readers may remember the values clarification, affective education emphases, and the more recent comprehensive push for multicultural education. What CRT and these older education paradigms have in common are that they were specifically "designed to remold the emotions and values of students."[12]

Matt McManus elaborates on the strategy employed.

> Specifically, postmodern skepticism was adopted as a philosophical backdoor to justifying socialism along largely emotive lines. To paraphrase a memorable quote . . . postmodern Leftists came to say feelings were all that mattered and their feelings demanded socialism.[13]

While the reason was being

> culturally reduced to little more than an instrument for the achievement of our subjective desires, there were few reasons left to regard other human beings as possessing some intrinsic worth which we must not violate. . . . This is because when reason is purely instrumental, morality itself became purely a matter of subjective opinion.[14]

Unfortunately, this is where the nation finds itself in K-16 public education. Fluidity is valued over objective truth.

Educating for Activism

Neuroscientists inform education and posit that students learn best when their affect—the emotional center of their brains—is involved in learning. This does not just pertain to students' interests. The effects involve more than intellectual curiosity.[15] Rather, the more a student feels or emotes over a lesson topic, the greater the chance that such a student will become active in feeling associated with an issue related to the topic. Thus, what is happening in schools today is conscious training of activists to remake what they have been told is a system that needs a complete overhaul. Students are buying into the notion of overhaul.

The majority of the efforts to raise up activists rests on what Sowell refers to as "a seething hostility to the West."[16] Del Stover of the *American School Board Journal* understood that schools are the point of germination of social change. Back in 1990, he wrote, "Public schools are societies' best hope of beating racism."[17] Little did Stover realize that the empowerment of those considered disenfranchised at the time of his writing would now be the disenfranchisers—the very people which have pinned seemingly inescapable labels upon the heads of millions of America's children.

Stover was correct in that schools are where the battles lie for the hearts and minds of the current and next generations. He consistently argues that anyone could be a racist and demonstration of this racism is through the exercise of "prejudice or discrimination against someone else because of race."[18] Conversely, today's antiracists argue that it is impossible to be a racist without having power over others. The shift in power realized today is beginning to favor people of color over whites, and schools have become places where some teachers evangelize toward identification in social groups. Therefore, as these groups grow, they are empowered. This empowerment leads to enhanced battles against racism.

Teachers and students are being indoctrinated by leftist, Marxist ideology and actively being recruited as revolutionaries to remake America into a socialist nation. *Overthrow* and *dismantle* are two verbs often used in CRT "how-to" speeches. Parents used to believe that if they ignored some of which they viewed as fads in schools, especially things that came down from intellectuals at the higher education level, which somehow each new *ism* would eventually dissipate. CRT appears to be sticking around for a while.

Parents are now waking up to *the woke*. Thanks in no small part to the COVID-19 pandemic, they had front row seats to what their children were learning in schools. Thus, parents could not ignore what began overtaking American culture and society, by coming directly into their living rooms. To assist parents in staying abreast of the problem, William A. Jacobson has founded the website *Legal Insurrection*. As stated on the website, the goal is to be "a resource for parents and students who no longer can assume they will be left alone . . . the entire ideology of CRT and anti-racist training is that silence is violence."[19]

Legal Insurrection adds,

> The impact [of CRT] on education has been enormous, and destructive. What started on college campuses has moved to primary and secondary education, and into the broader culture. Government agencies and private corporations now are some of the worst offenders of the obsessive focus on race.[20]

CRT is a divisive set of tenets and parents felt something was drastically wrong.

Also taking advantage of this moment in history is the LGBTQ+ movement. Examinations of current sex education standards and curriculum in some states reveal that CRT includes gender theory as part of the education. BLM has made no secret of this inclusion in school curricula. Some of the leaders of the BLM organization are themselves members of the LGBTQ+ amalgamation. Readers are encouraged to research the topics of QueerCrit,

GenderCrit, and others to understand the vast array of critical theory applications.

The reason BLM exists in the first place is to fight injustice and police brutality. It is based, however, on the notion that America is systemically racist and this racism is endemic in law enforcement and other institutions. In just a few short years, BLM has added other groups to their list of grievances. The group now includes attacks on the nuclear family, heterosexuality as the dominant reality, and whiteness in general. In short, Mark Levin writes, "The group Black Lives Matter . . . is a product of the fusion of Marxism and CRT."[21] Additional information can be found in my book *When the Secular Becomes Sacred.*[22]

CRT CORE PROBLEMS

CRT has

> redefined the concept of white supremacy and given it an entirely new meaning. Now being born into the white race automatically makes one a supremacist unless one is explicitly *anti-white*. Indeed, CRT is a total rejection of America's liberal tradition in terms of how we ought to treat each other as morally equal and autonomous individuals in possession of natural rights.[23]

Several of the core problems with CRT include that it puts

> social significance back into racial categories . . . inflames racism, tends to be purely theoretical, uses postmodern knowledge and political principles, is profoundly aggressive, asserts its relevance to all aspects of Social Justice, and—not least—begins from the assumption that racism is both ordinary and permanent, everywhere and always.[24]

This all sounds quite like a deterministic type of social Calvinism.

The concern about this type of social justice theology is real: *The chosen are the woke.* Conversely, once a person is branded a racist, that person would be considered hopelessly lost. Another problem is associating this type of racism with a god who is prejudged to be *the god of whiteness*—one who is willing to accept some people and not others.

Another problem with CRT is the interpreting of everything

> as racist and saying so almost constantly is unlikely to produce the desired results in white people (or for minorities). . . . Some studies have already shown that diversity courses, in which members of dominant groups are told that

racism is everywhere and that they themselves perpetuate it, have resulted in increased hostility towards marginalized groups.[25]

This is precisely the strategy employed for a group concerned with indoctrinating children. Is the desired result violence?

Once this mindset works it's way into all student learning and it is anyone's guess as to how many violent Portland-types may eventually emerge. If the nation is concerned about the rise of domestic terrorism, yet shuns a deep examination of racial indoctrination in schools, then is it really concerned?

CRT GENERATES HOSTILITIES

Generally, when people become angry and hostilities escalate, there are usually unbecoming behaviors that result. These can occur by words and deeds. When people are told repeatedly they are unchangeable and minimized, sparks usually fly. The reason is that an emotion such as "anger signals your body to prepare for a fight."[26] Most Americans were taught from an early age that name-calling and ad hominem attacks on individuals or groups are wrong. The advent of social media and its use by socialists and neo-Marxist revolutionary-minded progressives leave little to desire, in terms of honoring a traditional American ethos.

As a result of this shift in American society, the shaming, cancellation, and ruination of people, who are on opposite sides, have become increasingly nastier. Objections to tactics can lead to bullying, labeling, mob-type actions, and even to physical hostilities. Once an individual or a group approaches its zenith of opposition, the accused seem to come ready "for a fight all the time."[27] Examples of this phenomenon are best viewed on social media sites, such as Twitter.

The result of these conflagrations is often punitive to those targeted by BLM, including LGBTQ+ factions. It is not uncommon for professional people to experience doxing, physical threats and protests at their residences, death threats, and calls for their firing from employers.

Those dealing with the threats are increasingly overlooked by media and district attorneys, especially in large cities. This surge of threats does not occur in a vacuum. This does bring to mind as to what type of activism is being taught in America's high schools as part of civics classes. By the looks of what is transpiring in American society, coupled with personal comments from professors and teachers, the future of academic freedom and expression of opposing viewpoints on school campuses seem quite insecure.

Calls for unity and words from politicians that seem to imply a desire to work together on racial reconciliation and social justice are not enough. Even

BLM knows that talk is cheap. In terms of the psychology of relationships, it is not helpful for a president or any elected official of the United States to ask for unity[28] and then "to tell people who do not believe that they are racist—who may even actually despise racism—that there is nothing they can do to stop themselves from being racist—and then ask them to help you."[29]

The unfortunate reality is that when the main focal point is skin color, coupled with rejections of people which claim to be color blind, one result is a "refusal to attach social significance to race." In order to circumvent that, "critical race theory threatens to undo the social taboo against evaluating people by their race."[30] However, this does not pertain to whites. The implications for students in America's K-12 schools are most glaring.

THE 1619 PROJECT: LOSING SIGHT OF HISTORY

The United States is heading rapidly toward losing its status as the dominant intellectual world power in mathematics and science. Some would argue it already has. The federal government appears more concerned about focusing on social and racial equity outcomes, other than outcomes in academics. This concern plays itself out and is clearly illustrated in *The New York Times 1619 Project*.

In the words of Swain and Schorr, "The tragedy of CRT's spread throughout the American body politic is that Americans are now losing sight of their country's true history and of the remarkable racial progress it has made."[31] The lack of instruction in US history opens the door to first-generation ideas that create narratives, from which falsehoods are propagated. This establishes doubts about the nation and its people. History then becomes subjective and fluid, and students without prior knowledge are ripe for a feelings-based schema.

Thus, accurate history is an essential element of a quality education. The lens through which a person evaluates historical events does not have to be completely magnanimous, or one-sided, but it has to be accurate. In this season of skepticism over American history, to say that *The 1619 Project* does not *teach* CRT is deceptive and incorrect.

Peter Wood, the president of the *National Association of Scholars*, wrote quite a dismantling critique of *The New York Times 1619 Project*. His book *1620: A Critical Response to the 1619 Project* exposes *The 1619 Project* developer and journalist Nikole Hannah-Jones for her "journalistic malfeasance"[32] that masquerades as the history of the founding of America.[33]

What *The 1619 Project* amounts to is a non-scholastic endeavor that takes liberties through narratives to claim the real history of America's founding is ushered in directly on the backs of slaves and the institution of slavery. Even after the *New York Times* debunked the project's journalistic integrity and scores of history professors objected in writing to the project as credible history, public schools across America adopted the project into their curriculum pipeline for instruction.[34] The truth is that *The 1619 Project* has been highly criticized as *fake history*.[35] Now it is revised and expanded, yet to new project release seeks to "normalize and ideologically divisive story about this country's founding and history by pushing questionable stories on public school students."[36] Christine Rosen, of Commentary, writes that the purpose of the new 1619 Project "isn't to expand our understanding of our nations rich, complicated, and yes, flawed past. It is to enforce ideological conformity in the present. That's not a project; it's a recipe for a more divided, self-censoring citizenry."[37]

CRT inspired *The 1619 Project*, which *is a* distortion of American history "by treating aberrations from founding principles as founding principles themselves. Such efforts are, moreover, riddled with factual errors."[38] Observe four glaring errors in the following section.

Sample Errors in *The New York Times 1619 Project*

Example #1: *The colonists' main reason for fighting in the American Revolution was to protect and preserve the peculiar institution of slavery.* Fact checker Leslie M. Harris concluded the claim to be erroneous, and not just a mere opinion. Harris writes, "I vigorously disputed the claim. Although slavery was certainly an issue in the American Revolution, the protection of slavery was not one of the main reasons the 13 Colonies went to war."[39]

Example #2: *There are multiple errors attributing falsehoods to Abraham Lincoln's sentiments about slavery and equality.* Nikole Hannah-Jones writes, "Like many white Americans . . . [Lincoln] opposed slavery as a cruel system at odds with American ideals, but he also opposed black equality."[40] In the words of Sean Wilentz of *The Atlantic*, "To state flatly, as Hannah-Jones's essay does, that Lincoln opposed black equality, is to deny the very basis of his opposition to slavery."[41]

Example #3: *The project credits slavery for the prosperity of the United States, especially in the South.* The fact is slavery was responsible for slowed economic growth in the South.[42] This is usually used as one of the points of justification for reparations for black families with ties to slavery, which amounts to requests for trillions of dollars to be handed over to people who were never enslaved.[43]

Example #4: *The first Africans brought to America were slaves.* Historians are aware that "the first Africans brought to American in 1619 were not slaves but rather indentured servants. After fulfilling their contracts, some of these previously indentured servants—all blacks themselves—contracted black and white indentured servants of their own."[44]

These errors briefly presented do not lessen the history of the impact of slavery in the South and the horrific nature of the system that supported the practice. However, these facts do point out that *The 1619 Project* has faulty history and bases certain premises on these faults.[45]

What is of great concern is that the students who will be taught this narrative will be learning erroneous history and shaping a part of their understanding of America's founding on falsehoods and errors. As a small deviation from a straight line illustrates, the farther the deviation, the more errant the line. Thus, in the lineage of *The 1619 Project*, there is a great error.

As evidence that race is more important to some than history itself, woke "historian Nell Irvin Painter, knowing full well what *The 1619 Project* was trafficking in falsehoods, nonetheless refused to sign a letter of scholarly protest" against the project.[46] The historian did not sign the letter of protest, so as to avoid taking sides and escalating the disagreement into a racial divide. Wood, in response to Painter's refusal, responded that it was "condescending to black journalists."[47]

THE CRT PERSPECTIVE

Critical race theorists

> have built on everyday experiences with perspective viewpoint, and the power of stories and persuasion to come to a deeper understanding of how Americans see race. They have written parables, autobiography, and counterstories and have investigated the factual background and personalities . . . Legal storytellers, such as Derrick Bell and Patricia Williams, draw on a long history with roots going back to the slave narratives . . . Although some writers criticize CRT for excessive negativity and failure to develop a positive program, legal storytelling and narrative analysis are clear-cut advances that the movement can claim.[48]

Since critical theories are not science, they unfold in academe as *truths* in the *social sciences*, humanities, women and gender studies, and legal studies classes. Subjective truths, and even assumptions, can result in radically progressive ideas. For example, if one assumes to know the value of "x," and that "x" is a specific number, then it is sensible to assume that this person is also aware of the "constructed truth" of x + 1. If so, then x + 2 must also be true and so on. But with progressive and subjective assumptions, the theoretical becomes quite amorphous, as the reader will see.

CRT and Subjectivity

What if one challenges the basic premise about the assumption of the value of x? For example, what if a person assumed that the value of "x" was "−1," "−2," and so on? In many schools in the United States, the subjective truth for mathematics is becoming more acceptable. In other words, 1 + 1 does not always have to equal 2. In terms of CRT, it is one's perspective that dictates the correct response. Mathematics, as it is taught, has been designated as a subject developed by whites. Its whiteness in *thought constructs* is rejected by advocates of CRT and antiracists.

CRT begins with assumptions and these assumptions are accepted as true. CRT disallows any alternative assumptions to its predetermined truths. Here is another example. If "x" (white people are all racists), then x + 1 equates racists plus something else. Is it more racists, or another quantity? In order for any CRT idea to work, it must be first based on an assumption. In this case, it is based on a subjective value for x. What if the assumption for −x is *that a group of white people are not racists*? Would then the equation (−x −x = −2x) equal less racists? CRT would disallow such an equation because it is not based on the presumed perspective that theorists apply to the value of x. The point is whomever calls the shots for the variables exercises control over the outcome.

CRT comes up short on logic and common sense, and yet, the contention is that CRT is strictly theoretical. If CRT is true, then researchers adding more grievance concepts to CRT is, for them, also true. What then does it come down to, in terms of the assumed value of *x*, by adding to the variable *white privilege*, *intersectionality*, *Queer-feminism*, *supremacy*, *implicit bias*, *culturally responsive teaching*, and so on. In short, since CRT is assumed as true, and not simply theoretical, then adding other CRT concepts are also considered as true. All of this is reminiscent of a *Post Hoc Ergo Propter Hoc* [after this, therefore because of this] fallacy.

Questioning the CRT Perspective

Two critical questions must be considered during any analysis of CRT. These include the following: (1) Does there exist a certain level of envy of whites as an implicit driver behind the push for CRT? (2) Why some people of color, who reject CRT, are themselves rejected as truly people of color?

In today's America, blacks marry non-blacks.

> In 2015, 17% of all U.S. newlyweds had a spouse of a different race or ethnicity, marking more than a fivefold increase since 1967, when 3% of newlyweds were intermarried . . . one-in-ten married people in 2015—not just those who *recently* married—had a spouse of a different race or ethnicity. This translates into 11 million people who were intermarried. . . . Asian and Hispanic newlyweds are by far the most likely to intermarry in the U.S. About three-in-ten Asian newlyweds (29%) did so in 2015, and the share was 27% among recently married Hispanics. For these groups, intermarriage is even more prevalent among the U.S. born: 39% of U.S.-born Hispanic newlyweds and almost half (46%) of U.S.-born Asian newlyweds have a spouse of a different race or ethnicity.[49]

Interracial Marriage

People are marrying outside their races in greater numbers in America. But why is this? If CRT is correct, then this should not be happening. America's racism, according to black activists, would not allow for this. Yet, here it is. In fact, "one-in-ten married people in 2015—not just those who *recently* married—had a spouse of a different race or ethnicity. This translates into 11 million people who were intermarried."[50]

Are these people interracially marrying because of racism to avoid a racist label, or are they marrying for other reasons? Could they be envious of whiteness or the skin color of another race? The nation—and most people in particular—marry for love and have racism as one of the farthest things from their minds. A theory behind one of the factors of interracial marriage is the availability of males of color in the age brackets desired for marriage.[51] Apparently, for millions of people, availability of a partner is much more important than skin color.

Another idea is that people marry outside their race for economics. CRT activists are not certain what to make of all the intermarriage and how to consider their children of these marriages. For example, is Barack Obama a racist because his mother and grandparents were white? Or can someone simply claim that away by identifying as another race? Are Obama's children racists, because they are 25 percent white? These questions are seemingly ridiculous to be asking. However, the nation's schools have many mixed-race children and desire to know where they fit. CRT has no answer for them, except to allow students to identify as they will. Students should be able to ask these questions and they should not be labeled as racists for the asking.

White Adjacency

In a CRT-idealistic world, categorizing whiteness[52] by degree or adjacency is sensible. However, such ideas in practice come across as punitive and potentially psychologically damaging. If the American system is oppressive and was built out of the interests of whites, then why are black and interracial couples moving into so-called white neighborhoods? Is there an envy because of the possessions whites have? Why would people consider moving into such places if they truly believed in the tenets of CRT? One might ask some of the founders of BLM, why they bought homes in exclusive, mostly white neighborhoods? Is there some envy involved and some desire for the same American privilege assigned to whites? Others might question why blacks place their children in expensive private schools. Isn't the private American education enterprise just another institution of white supremacy? Some Christian blacks even attend churches with mostly white members. The deeper one delves into the foundation of CRT, the more ridiculous CRT appears when challenged by real-world experiences.

Proponents of CRT do not want to answer these questions and they certainly avoid debating the issues. The answers may result in disproof of the narrative constructed out of premises of the theory—those very premises that seem to have taken a page from a nineteenth-century racial and cultural demagoguery.[53] There should be little question as to why the CRT advocates do not want to debate the merits of their theory. The legs of the theory are too weak to stand on.

Economics and CRT

Some blacks seek and attain similar jobs and incomes as their white counterparts. The jobs are sought based on merit. Black athletes and artists use their talents and skills in a competition to get ahead in athletics, arts, music, and other professions. The number of black millionaires is growing in America, and there are just under ten black billionaires in the United States.[54] America is still capitalist enough for all to have the opportunity to become wealthy. The truth is, either the supposed systemic racism that is claimed to be embedded in America's capitalist society is either stalled or it doesn't exist as people have been told.

There are more minorities on network and cable television, in both programming and advertising. In fact, there are more interracial relationships in media advertising than ever before, and some would argue disproportionately so.[55] In 2021, about 70 percent of ads portraying interracial couples feature white men with black women.[56]

The reality is that CRT advocates wish the world was as they see it, which is one reason why they are working so feverishly to change the framework of history to their liking. They are stuck in narratives they created, while quick to use incidents of racism to prove a point. Maybe those claiming America is racist should give up their professorial positions, write their books on racism for no royalties, and give up their nice homes and cars. Where are the exemplars shunning the material wealth generated by claims of America's institutional racism?

Ibram X. Kendi is a prime example. But there are others. Kendi was recently paid $20,000 to hold a 45-minute virtual discussion and 15-minute question-and-answer session at the University of Michigan. His topic mainly covered sections of his 2017 book *Stamped from the Beginning*. Kendi did not offer any reasons why he would claim to be oppressed and somehow achieve wealth and notoriety in the midst of such oppression. Kendi benefited from the very privilege he would assign to whites,[57] while condemning the system as oppressive. The irony is the very thing so many CRT advocates promulgate and lobby against is what they have become. Are these not neo-Marxist provocateurs showing off a new capitalist class?

American students are waking up and they are beginning to see the hypocrisy involved in the racial-political identity movement. Yet, they remain reluctant to speak out. How long before these potential students seeking admission to higher education institutions see themselves as victims and construct grievances of their own to take advantage of the opportunities for material wealth that capitalism offers?[58]

ANALYSIS OF THE CRT NARRATIVE

As a classic example of an examination of a narrative, C. S. Lewis, a devout atheist in his early days, began to check the exclusive claims of Jesus. When Lewis converted to Christianity he stated,

> I did not then see what is now the most shining and obvious thing; the Divine humility which will accept a convert even on such terms. The Prodigal Son at least walked home on his own feet. But who can duly adore that Love which will open the high gates to a prodigal who is brought in kicking, struggling, resentful, and darting his eyes in every direction for a chance of escape?[59]

Lewis was compelled in 1931 to believe by the evidence he examined over a period of time. He weighed the exclusive claims made by Jesus. As the story is told, Lewis becomes one of the most ardent apologists of the twentieth century and impacted the world until his death in 1963.

Lewis went on to write many books in defense of the biblical Jesus and Christianity. So, how does this apply to CRT and its exclusive claims by its leaders on racial identity issues? It applies because of the vetting and questioning that Lewis undertook before he believed. This is the caveat emptor. Before believing what is told, each should be encouraged to think critically.

As if with something to hide, this type of vetting is not allowed by unbelievers of CRT. Any such questioning challenges indoctrination and is met by accusations of fragility and racism.

Standpoint Theory

In flipping the script, some people claim that whites are fragile about their whiteness, and this is why they get defensive when they are called "racists." Robin DiAngelo has made a small fortune informing fellow whites of their fragility. Whites are told by DiAngelo, and others, that they carry unconscious and implicit biases against people of color and that their skin color gives them a privilege in a nation that is systemically racist, from the beginning. These claims are made spuriously and are exclusively applied to whites.

CRT promotes the idea that America is thoroughly and endemically corrupt. As a result, critical race theorists focus on developing a narrative that revises history and fits their assumptions. This is a type of *eisegesis*, which is cherry picking to justify assumptions, which are often criticized as non-contextual.

For example, revisionist historians apply labels such as *colonizer* and genocidal *conqueror* to historical figures like Christopher Columbus, but somehow leave out Francisco Pizarro, Mansa Musa (who had 12,000 slaves of his own and remains the richest person in history), Hernan Cortez, Genghis Khan, and Saladin. The assumption is drawn based on what Columbus must have been like because he was a European Caucasian Christian.

Historians reexamine

> America's historical record, replacing comforting majoritarian interpretations of events with ones that square more accurately with minorities' experiences. . . . Revisionist historians often strive to unearth little-known chapters of racial struggle, sometimes in ways that reinforce current reform efforts. . . . Revisionism is often materialist in thrust, holding that to understand the zigs and zags of black, Latino, and Asian fortunes, one must look to things like profit, labor, supply . . . and the interest of other whites.[60]

Authors such as DiAngelo and Kendi then write from this revisionist perspective and make exclusive claims to then generalize them to a majority of people. This is not scholarship. It is revisionist activism. In the activist's mind, having a specific perspective, and filtering ideas about life through this perspective is just the subjective perspective that comes standard with many liberal scholars. But, other viewpoints that lay claim to the same opportunity to filter history from a different perspective are generally not provided. This is referred to as "a form of *standpoint theory*—the belief that knowledge comes from the lived experience of different identity groups, who are differently positioned in society and thus see different aspects of it."[61]

Two Assumptions. Standpoint theory

> operates on two assumptions. One is that people occupying the same social positions, that is, identities—race, gender, sex, sexuality, ability status, and so on—will have the same experiences of dominance and oppression and will . . . interpret them in the same ways. . . . The other is that one's relative position within a social power dynamic dictates what one can and cannot know. . . . Standpoint theory can be understood by analogy to a kind of color blindness, in which the more privileged a person is, the fewer colors she can see.[62]

Essentialism. Standpoint theory "often finds itself criticized for *essentialism,*"[63] which basically reduces those in a group to near-identical levels of thought and feelings about their experiences. The idea that captures standpoint theory well—and can describe any group—according to Standpoint theorist Sandra Harding is the notion that all people within a group feel a certain way about something.[64]

One of the more influential black feminists, Kristie Dotson, has written extensively on standpoint theory. She arrives at the point of intersection between Standpoint Theory and CRT[65] and "argues that it is almost impossible for dominant groups to see outside of their own system of knowledge."[66] Her message is clear. It is almost impossible for whites to see outside of their white-constructed system of thought.

According to the theorists like Dotson,

> the systems of knowledge—*schemata*—have been specifically set up to work for dominant groups and exclude others . . . the knowledge produced by dominant groups—including science and reason—is also merely the product of their cultural traditions and is not superior to the knowledge produced by other cultural traditions.[67]

The media idealists and groups like BLM have taken the nation along for the ride with *separation perspective*. Even in this push for the separation of people into groups, why is there such a great push to show interracial relationships and disproportional support of minority groups in the media. This needs to be answered, especially since theories and subsequent policies abound which may codify concepts like *interest convergence*, *white adjacency*, and *white privilege.*

ANALYSIS OF ANTIRACISM

At first take, someone *antiracist* would seem like a person to be admired. However, in order to understand the term, one must delve more deeply into the meaning behind the term. As with all terms that are birthed from within the social sciences, there is often more to the story.

As author of *How to Be an Antiracist* Kendi provides definitions to the terms such as "racism," "racial inequity," "racist policies," and "institutional," "structural," and "systemic racism." As a point of foundation, Kendi posits: "racial inequity is when two or more racial groups are not standing on approximately equal footing."[68] Equity means being given opportunities that others either do not have, possibly do not deserve, or are not allowed, in order to level the playing field. Favoring equity is an antiracist action.

The push for equity is having a serious effect on children. Parents and teachers have begun documenting these effects. For example, a teacher in Virginia's Loudoun County Public Schools stated that she "witnessed the *heartbreaking* effects of critical race theory on children firsthand and described its implementation as extremely *damaging* to students, where I have witnessed students of color excluding their White peers."[69]

The teacher Monica Gill "asserted that teachers and students are being taught that if you claim to be color blind you are engaging in microaggressions and a form of racism."[70] Gill referred to the teachings of CRT as "the antithesis of the teachings of Martin Luther King Jr., who famously advocated for judgment to be based on character and contribution, rather than physical characteristics." [71]

Kendi believes that because members of certain races do not own and occupy homes at the same percentage rates as whites, this proves unequal economic outcomes. Kendi cherry-picks numbers and wishes that the decades of the "forties, seventies, or . . . nineties"[72] could have demonstrated more racial equity. He is not alone in this desire. However, wishful thinking in the present does not change the past.

Kendi continues by defining a *racist policy* as "any measure that produces or sustains racial inequity between racial groups."[73] Conversely,

> an antiracist policy is any measure that produces or sustains racial equity between racial groups. . . . There is no such thing as a nonracist or race-neutral policy. Every policy in every institution in every community in every nation is producing or sustaining racial inequity or equity between racial groups.[74]

Observe the effort put into demarcating and thereby marginalizing groups. In the end, a group is either racist or antiracist, and there is no one in-between.

Racist policies have been described using other terms, according to Kendi. Three of these terms are also CRT terms and include "institutional racism, structural racism, and systemic racism. . . . Racism itself is institutional, structural, and systemic."[75] Kendi uses the term "equity" over equality and the two mean totally different things.

In higher education, equity means something different than equality. Many universities and colleges are no longer requiring rigorous academic preparation for admission to some of America's elite institutions of higher learning. Critical race theorists bring race into the discussion of college admissions. The assumption is that "real inequities exist in American education, and they are reflected in every measure."[76] In California, toward the pursuit of admission and matriculation into higher education academics, the regents agreed that the metrics for previously evaluating students on the SAT and the ACT were "racist metrics."[77]

The University of California system, once the premier system of higher education, announced early in 2021 a shift to equity-based admissions. After the announcement, "the system received the highest number of undergraduate applications in its history for the fall 2021 admission, which included surges among African American and Chicano/Latino students. California Community college transfer applications grew by an impressive margin."[78] This is the result of reducing the rigors of admission, moving into an equity mode of admissions, and dismissing assessments—all of which are intended as tactics to begin to undo a systemic racism in higher education admission.

Equity is to guarantee outcomes as self-esteem is to *everyone receives a trophy*. The children of the 1970s and 1980s self-esteem movement are now professors in our colleges.

Equity is certainly not a new educational concept. It is just a smoother-sounding term for Affirmative Action again favoring people by skin color.

What may eventually occur as a result of the shift to equity in higher education admissions is found in at least one of four outcomes. The following summary statements are critiques of Kendi's original statements included in *How to Be an Antiracist.*

(1) Higher graduation rates in public schools will pump in more college students, and the standards will have to be reduced to allow more lower-achieving high school students admission. Meanwhile, some qualified students which have academic merit are not admitted, all in the name of equity. Such actions are associated with Affirmative Action programs in the recent past.
(2) The reputation of people being admitted to college will result in a cadre of unqualified students. However, because they are the right color/gender, they would be given eventual employment as a continuation of equity-based outcomes with higher education networking.
(3) If colleges only drop admission requirements and do not adjust the academic rigors to suit incoming students graduating from high school with limited reading and math proficiencies, then students will fail at the college level. Those that favor equity had better plan to deal with the

massive achievement gaps that result from equity-based outcomes. Will colleges become large institutions of remediation out of necessity? If BIPOC occupy these college classes in greater numbers, will the classes be deemed as racist?

(4) Colleges will have to reconstitute their programs, when complaints about having any standards equate to holdovers of White supremacy, and racist *whiteness* expectations. How will colleges handle the accusations and lawsuits that will come their way when graduation is not a reality for some students? The Catch-22 is that if they do not graduate, then equity was truly all about access and opportunity, and not a guarantee of an outcome.

A specific action of antiracism, according to Kendi, is "the practice of actively countering racism. It moves past passive practices when someone says they are not racist but do not take action in the face of racist actions—and often requires conscious efforts."[79] The question is, are these conscious efforts of admissions adjustments enough to demonstrate antiracism and appease critics?

According to John Marshall, chief equity officer for Jefferson County Public Schools in Louisville, Kentucky,[80] being an antiracist is "very binary . . . if you're not antiracist, what are you?"[81] Antiracism also implies that a person who is an antiracist is compelled to call it out as it occurs.

EQUITY OVER EQUALITY

CRTs believe racism to be a mere social construct and exists whether it is seen or not. Kendi tries to modify racism in his latest book, which is "a memoirish argument that Americans of all races must confront their roles in a racist system" and become antiracists.[82] But what exactly is antiracism is not clearly defined outside of examples?

For example, Kendi writes,

> An antiracist idea is any idea that suggests the racial groups are equals in all their apparent differences—that there is nothing right or wrong with any racial group. Antiracist ideas argue that racist policies are the cause of racial inequities.[83]

However, Kendi misses the mark here, because he does not address the basic nature of humanity.

Antiracists like to proclaim that whites by nature are racists. Some researchers have stated (1) racism is beyond one race, (2) that race is merely a construct, and (3) blacks may be genetically superior and possibly more diverse when compared to whites.[84] Kendi asks, "So what is a racist idea?"[85] His response to his own query is "a racist idea is any idea that suggests one racial group is inferior or superior to another racial group in any way."[86] Based on this, would not this then implicate Kendi, antiracism, and CRT as racist?

A recent, but controversial, Cornell University study concluded that some blacks may be superior to whites genetically, have less deleterious genetic variations in the DNA, and are more diverse as a group.[87] Is Kendi ready to call out this study as racist? If merit, intelligence, or physical accomplishments are the criteria for superiority, then does this not invalidate the equity policies in place around the nation?

Would it not be antiracist to fight against any notion that blacks are superior to whites, as it would be to battle the idea that whites hold any superiority over blacks? During this modern era of CRT, with its antiracist indoctrination, consider the impact upon students in schools who learn that one race may be superior to other races? Does pondering this broad-reaching definition of racism—the likes of which smack of 1930s and 1940s Nazi Germany—frighten anyone? This is exactly at the heart of MLK's call for character over color.

The truth is that policies are not the real reason for any inequities between races. Any culture that promotes superiority or inferiority is subjective. A government that recognizes inferiority and superiority of people and groups reinforces these subjective values and empowers the select group. Since public schools are government schools, whatever the government endorses quickly shows up in the education of America's children.

INDOCTRINATION SPREADS

The US military has gone woke and is being required to be trained in concepts related to CRT. For example, the US Air Force Academy, where "the decades old theory has gotten significantly more attention in recent months that schools and military institutions have begun introducing core tenets in the classroom."[88] What is now taking place in military education and training is also taking place in K-12 schools. As with the entire educational system in the United States, there is a serious power imbalance that does not allow debate of any sort. According to Colonel Mark Anarumo,

> the president of Norwich University and formerly the director and permanent professor for the Center for Character and Leadership Development at the Air Force Academy . . . there is a natural power dynamic in higher education, or really in any education, where if the professors are steering you towards a certain way to think, and you buck that, your grade suffers.[89]

CRT proponents understand that real teaching does not go by the controversial term Critical Race Theory, per se. This is why, when asked, district school superintendents can reply *our district will not be teaching CRT.*[90] Parents, especially, should be extra careful. This is not actually a victory.

By removing the acronym CRT, the real concerns for parents then become (1) another CRT (Culturally Responsive Teaching), (2) antiracism curriculum in history and social sciences, (3) gender and sex curriculum that supplants the nuclear family, (4) neo-segregationism, where whites are told by woke racists that they do not belong because they are white, and (5) race-based BLM, neo-Marxism that separates into groups by skin color.[91]

Mark Twain has been associated with the phrase "History may not repeat itself, but it often rhymes." This quote has been used over the years to point out to readers when analysts believe historical events and presidential decisions appear troublesome to the memories of antagonists, or when these events mimic the past.[92] As someone who had spent several summer breaks in the former Soviet Union, the trending is clear. America is headed down a path that has failed whenever groups of people are pitted against each other.

Anti-Semitism

In a frightening historical parallel, past and present anti-Semitic writers have stated warnings about Jews. Some antiracist writers

> cannot help but call to mind those who warn that America is caught in a spiderweb of *systemic racism.* They speak of *white privilege* in a language not unlike that in which Drumont, Bailly, Maurras, and other spoke of *Jewish power. . . . White Fragility*, like *La France juive*, ... Substitute whiteness for the Jewish race, and portions of Robin DiAngelo's book read like turn-of-the-century Anti-Semitic tracts, which combined ersatz race science with wild speculation. On DiAngelo's account, racism *is hard to see and recognize.* Like the Jewish syndicate, it is hidden and all the more powerful for being invisible. . . . In his foreword to White Fragility, Michael Eric Dyson adapts anti-Semitic tropes to the antiracist agenda. . . . Dyson notes that whites may wish to see themselves as Americans, not as *whites.* But this is an illusion. Whiteness is inescapable. And it is most useful when its existence is denied. That's its twisted genius. . . . For Drumont and others, *Jewishness* mattered above all. For Dyson, DiAngelo, Ta-Nehesi Coates, Ibram X. Kendi, and others, *whiteness* is of transcendent significance. It is the all-explaining source of inequality, injustice, oppression, and suffering.[93]

Black-White Binary

Bigotry can be a source to justify a racially binary system. Discrimination can be its practice. The black-white binary

> effectively dictates that nonblack minority groups must compare their treatment to that of African Americans to redress their grievances. The paradigm holds that one group, blacks, constitutes the prototypical minority group. *Race* means quintessentially, African American. Other groups, such as Asians, American Indians, and Latinos/as are minorities only insofar as their experience and treatment can be analogized to those of blacks.[94]

Binary thinking, by definition, necessarily focuses on just two groups,

> usually whites and one other, can thus conceal the checkerboard of racial progress and retrenchment and hide the way dominant society often casts minority groups against one another to the detriment of all. . . . In addition to pitting one minority group against another, binary thinking can induce a minority group to identify with whites in exaggerated fashion at the expense of other groups.[95]

Swain and Schorr clarify,

> According to CRT, science, reason, and objectivity are *white ways of knowing* whereas black ways of knowing involve storytelling based on *lived experiences*. . . . CRT's claims are not merely absurd and dangerous, they are racist. . . . CRT demeans people of color by denying them ownership of and control over their own lives.[96]

The binary concept, according to Swain and Schorr, is reinforced in concepts deleterious to unity, "such as colorblindness, assimilation, and merit are dismissed as cynical means by which whites maintain their power and privilege in American society."[97] Ladson-Billings agrees and posits,

> Colorblindness, a legal corollary to equality of opportunity and the idealized goal of the Black Civil Rights Movement of the 1950s and 1960s, is currently used by Whites to justify the status quo by asserting that policies intended to improve the educational options of people of color because of a legacy of racism are discriminatory toward White people.[98]

A reason that CRT is damaging to students is that classrooms are not only comprised of black and white students. School rooms have long left the binary demarcations behind. This fact means that students who come from or share mixed-race families feel out-of-place, within the racial focus of CRT. In fact, these students are often labeled as "White-adjacent,"[99] if they are partly white. Asians and black students are also saddled with this label because of their economic and social success, if they have had adjacency to whites.

Again, it bears repeating, white adjacency is a major issue that stereotypes blacks in mixed marriages, as not really black. Is this a reason marketers spend so much time on commercials and advertising that show multiracial families?[100]

CRT AND TEACHER TRAINING

Teachers coming out of current teacher education programs are not likely to resemble the previous generations of teachers. If they have spent the majority of their K-12 years in public education as students, they are more likely to have emerged *lit with the fire of activism.*

At the time of this writing, at least twelve states have banned CRT from being included, taught, or referred to in classrooms throughout their states. That does not mean these states are forbidden to teach how to be activists against whiteness, or "about slavery, segregation, race-and gender-based pay gaps, or other aspects of U.S. history."[101] But it does limit the extent and depth of the instruction pertaining to race and the consensus is that more teachers need training in the teaching of civics.[102] The question is how does this play out for teacher training, with more time spent on CRT training and less time on content mastery?

Terms such as "intersectionality, whiteness, and systemic racism have become buzzwords. *Woke* and *anti-woke* are not just descriptors but group identities, and serve as the fault upon which the culture war rages."[103] Make no mistake about it. Teachers in training will still be subjected to CRT, even if their state legislators forbid its teaching in their states' schools.

The truth is,

> CRT has been making big inroads into the wider culture these last few years. If you've heard the terms intersectionality, whiteness, microaggressions, white privilege, systemic racism, etc., then you have been exposed to ideas that have been shaped by or come directly from Critical Race Theory.[104]

CRT has grown beyond education.

The largest teachers' union in the United States basically undercut its own secret. The union

> has moved to undermine the left-wing talking point that critical race theory is not taught to children—by voting (to) promote it and arguing it is reasonable and appropriate to use CRT in social studies classes. The *National Education Association* has approved a plan to publicize critical race theory and dedicate a team of staffers to assist union members looking to fight back against anti-CRT

> rhetoric. Additionally, the resolution calls for the union to join with Black Lives Matter at school and the Zinn Education Project to call for a rally on . . . George Floyd's birthday . . . as a national day of action to teach lessons about structural racism and oppression.[105]

CRT has become a political pawn, and some might argue it has become a weapon for political victory, especially for Republicans, who are being accused of lying about the existence of CRT and that it is being taught in schools.[106] Teachers are the deliverers of instruction and their methods affect students and their learning. Teachers are in the best positions to know whether CRT is taught in schools, or not. Countering the liberal narrative that CRT either does not exist or that it is not in school is quite simple by evidence.

Educators Daniel Buck and David Kinnett highlight prevarications surrounding CRT. They declare,

> When asked about whether or not CRT was taught in schools, Secretary of Education Miguel Cardona said simply that it was not taught. Likewise after Glenn Youngkin's victory in Georgia, Joy Reid spent a segment asserting that critical race theory is not actually taught in any public school. We're both educators. These assertions are patently false. . . . Indianapolis Public Schools advised their principals to tell parents that CRT is not taught in their schools while offering professional development for their teachers that explicitly outlines the tenets of CRT, recommends strategies for incorporating it, and suggests further reading — including Ibram X. Kendi.[107]

W. James Antle III says CRT is

> a fusion of Marxism and racial essentialism that neatly separates groups of people into victims and oppressors based on characteristics they cannot control [and] is hardly the intellectual framework for counteracting racism, not only because of how easily it bleeds into something uncomfortably resembling prejudice. As flawed as its exaggeration of America's past is when the facts are already quite bad enough, it is also not an honest depiction of the present.[108]

ACTIVISM AMONG US

As a result of the pressures now being brought upon public school board members over CRT, some teachers have decided that taking matters into their own hands is the best thing to do. Regardless of whether parental pressure changes the board policy about teaching CRT, some teachers have vowed to teach its concepts anyway.

Other teachers are less visibly supportive about their support for CRT, but like the fact that parents have little idea about its tenets. In states like Florida, Iowa, Virginia, and others, elementary and secondary teachers sneak the tenets into their lessons in a variety of ways.

College activist professors are more brazen about their teaching of CRT,[109] and they are keen on professional development to hone their skills and incorporate CRT into their courses.[110]

Some districts are either naïve or they are purposefully ignorant in their assertions, they do not have CRT taught at their schools. For example, the Hernando Public Schools in Florida claim that CRT "has never been taught in Hernando schools and won't ever be."[111] Officials in the Hernando schools are not alone in their claims. Other districts officials in Florida have made the same claim. Then they follow up the claim by "noting that the theory is largely a college-level topic."[112]

The ignorance over CRT in Florida either means the state is out-of-touch or that CRT has gone the route of other states. This includes incorporating CRT as social-emotional learning (SEL), through training in diversity, equity, inclusion, implicit bias theory, and under a host of other titles. Nomenclature aside, districts truly must dig more deeply into what is taught to their students. SEL is viewed by many as a gateway ideology and set of practices to groom students for social justice, equity, and other CRT ideas. Any idea that begins with the premise of white supremacy and asserts that racism is in all systems and institutions—including housing and employment—is a CRT idea.

CRT has grown far beyond its point of inception as a theory of legal analysis. According to Richard Delgado, Jean Stefancic, and Angela Harris,

> Although CRT began as a movement in the law, it has rapidly spread beyond that discipline. Today, many in the field of education consider themselves critical race theorists who use CRT's ideas to understand issues of school discipline and hierarchy, tracking, controversies over curriculum and history, and IQ and achievement testing. Political scientists ponder voting strategies coined by critical race theorists. . . . It not only tries to understand our social situation, but to change it; it sets out not only to ascertain how society organizes itself along racial lines and hierarchies, but to transform it for the better.[113]

This tells the reader all one needs to know about CRT.

Karen Niemi, the president and CEO of CASEL,

recently announced that CASEL has revised its definition of and framework for social-emotional learning to highlight the value of SEL as a weapon for social justice. She emphasizes student identities and marginalization, equity, just communities, and the collective rather than the individual. . . . Social-emotional learning must actively contribute to anti-racism.[114]

Known far-left media establishments like

The New York Times, *Washington Post*, *MSNBC*, and elsewhere have begun spinning a new mythology that presents critical race theory as a benign academic concept, casts its detractors as right-wing extremists driven by racial resentment, and portrays legislation against critical race theory as an attempt to ban teaching about the history of slavery and racism. All three charges are false.[115]

CRT PLAYS OUT IN REAL TIME

Rufo sums up what has played out in Portland with devastating effects on schools and communities. He writes,

I have spent months investigating the structure of political education in three Portland-area school districts: Tigard-Tualatin School District, Beaverton School District, and Portland Public Schools. . . . We can best understand the political education program in Portland schools by dividing it into three parts: theory, praxis (or practice), and power. The schools have self-consciously adopted the *pedagogy of the oppressed* as their theoretical orientation, activated it through a curriculum of critical race theory, and enforced it through the appointment of de facto political officers within individual schools, generally under the cover of *equity and social-justice* programming. In short, they have begun to replace education with activism.[116]

Does anyone still wonder why cities like Portland are in serious trouble and under siege?

The good news, according to optimist Kotkin, is that

CRT's racialist agenda may not become a permanent fixture. The vast majority of Americans—including millennials and minorities—do not, for example, favor defunding the police. Most American voters—by wide margins—reject the notion of teaching Critical Race Theory in schools, even though the effort is adopted by the billionaire class as well as the corporate HR departments, most Democratic politicians . . . and the powerful teachers' union.[117]

This is usually the way of fads and cultural upheavals that involve younger generations. The passage of time will be the ultimate judge.

One of the reasons CRT might fizzle is because it does little to help those that are in need.

> Whether they realize it or not, CRT and its backers appear to be undermining whatever it takes to address poverty and distress, whether in the south Chicago ghetto, Appalachia or the British Midlands . . . the percentage of Americans who consider relations between Black and white communities as *poor* has almost doubled, to nearly 60%.[118]

What began as a serious slide under Obama[119] was exacerbated under Trump[120] and has now reached another level under Biden.[121] A biased media are always on the spot to take sides and to make matters worse. There can be no mistaking the fact that

> policies of *reverse discrimination* seem likely to stir resentment. People don't like to be forced to beg for forgiveness and make recompense for the sins of their fathers, especially when they have no reason to believe their fathers, most of whom immigrated well after the Civil War, have done nothing wrong.[122]

When authoritarianism arises and leaders begin to wrest power from the people of a nation, one of the first things to be discarded is a nation's history.

Back in the 1990s, Black Harvard sociology professor Orlando Patterson, a Democrat, assessed that the United States

> is now the least racist white-majority society in the world; has a better record of legal protection of minorities than any other society, white or black; offers more opportunities to a greater number of black persons than any other society, including all of those of Africa![123]

Specifically, in 1997, conservative analysts Stephan and Abigail Thernstrom argued that "the foundation of progress for many Blacks is no longer fragile. Progress is real and solid." Patterson agreed that "being Afro-American is no longer a significant obstacle to participation in the public life of the nation."

Is America still making progress? The focus on deconstruction of whiteness in America, the revision of its history—and the marginalization of groups by law—smacks of a period in history which many thought long gone. The CRT expansion and race-based advocacy groups have birthed a new form of racism. Their actions have laser-focused on race to the extreme. The signs indicate that these actions amount to a hyper-racism of the twenty-first century, and the pendulum of progress has resulted in a newer diminution of millions of people, based on the color of their skin.

It is worth noting that beyond shaming and labeling, there is no plan for either CRT or antiracism for improving American society. Modification is not in the CRT lexicon. The aim, however, is to gain as much power as possible and then make certain to deconstruct America, so that white Americans feel what contemporary blacks felt for decades. The power shift has already begun. Once Americans took the blame for the ill-treatment that their nation committed centuries ago, the political left in America had them right where they wanted.

Whether it's by the Taliban or BLM statue paranoia,

> it does little good to demolish the historical bonds Americans possess. All of our greatest heroes—whether it's America's Founding Fathers, Lincoln, Churchill, Roosevelt or Martin Luther King—each was flawed as a human as are we all. Without awareness of our history, its differing tangents and permutations, as classicist Michael Grant once noted, will be *blindfolded in our efforts to grapple with our future.*[124]

Today's revolutionaries aim to overthrow oppressors and their racist institutions. CRT has turned a corner. In terms of educators stuck in a *system of oppression*, they are either revolutionaries or they are oppressors.[125] For example, if events continue to unfold as they have in Oregon, Rufo observes that in America,

> Educators and parents in Portland are playing with fire. They have filled the heads of the young with dark visions of America and then told them to find fulfillment through Revolution. . . . For all the talk about liberation and critical consciousness, they are indoctrinating these children in a profoundly pessimistic worldview, in which racism and oppression pervade every institution, with no way out but revolution.[126]

All across the nation in public schools and now even in some private schools, students are being taught about the oppression that exists in America and that the only way to remedy this oppression is to dismantle, defund, and overthrow the system that allows it. The Kendian approach of discrimination in order to end discrimination is not lost on the students. Sitting in classes with teachers which actively indoctrinate recruits, by stirring up angst against the country they call home is distressing for some. Fortunately, some public school students have not succumbed to the pressures placed on them by modern BLM proponents.

Once students go off to college, the pressure is even greater to conform to the academic, social, and personal expectations of higher education. Add to these expectations, the cost of non-complying with *the woke crowd*, and the costs may turn out to be enormous.

Many students are repeatedly told by their teachers that their nation is racist from the beginning and that whites are privileged. This not only impacts academics but also causes issues psychologically and emotionally. The bottom line is that focusing daily on racism can have deleterious consequences on children of all races, particularly for cognitive and emotional development.[127]

Whatever is indoctrinated is eventually cultivated. That which is cultivated is then activated and serves as a precedent to expanded action. Indoctrination occurs in schools, and when students are enamored by what they hear, or idolize the messenger, they may eventually feel encouraged to take action. At the risk of tainting true civic education, only in some distorted, dystopian neo-Marxist universe can actions like those described actually become credited to a student as community service.

NOTES

1. Rashawn Ray and Alexandra Gibbons. "Why are states banning critical race theory?" *Brookings Institution*. August 2021. Retrieved November 3, 2021, from https://www.brookings.edu/blog/fixgov/2021/07/02/why-are-states-banning-critical-race-theory/.

2. Angel Eduardo. "Stop telling critical race theory's critics we don't know what it is." *Newsweek*. June 16, 2021. Retrieved July 2, 2021, from https://www.newsweek.com/stop-telling-critical-race-theorys-critics-we-dont-know-what-it-opinion-1600535.

3. Staff. "On views of race and inequality, Blacks and Whites are worlds apart." *Pew Research Center*. June 27, 2018. Retrieved October 5, 2021, from https://www.pewresearch.org/social-trends/2016/06/27/on-views-of-race-and-inequality-blacks-and-whites-are-worlds-apart/.

4. John 1:46, *New American Standard Bible*.

5. Ecclesiastes 1:9, *New American Standard Bible*.

6. Jeff Grabmeier. "When Europeans were slaves: Research suggests white slavery was much more common than previously believed." *Ohio State News*. March 7, 2004. Retrieved August 23, 2021, from https://news.osu.edu/when-europeans-were-slaves--research-suggests-white-slavery-was-much-more-common-than-previously-believed/.

7. Stephen Sawchuk. "What is critical race theory, and why is it under attack." *EdWeek*. May 18, 2021, p. 4. Retrieved May 20, 2021, from https://www.edweek.org/leadership/what-is-critical-race-theory-and-why-is-it-under-attack/2021/05.

8. Stanley Kurtz. "A book for our Times: Peter Wood's 1620 skewers 1619 project." *National Review*. November 16, 2020. Retrieved September 12, 2021, from https://www.nationalreview.com/corner/a-book-for-our-times-peter-woods-1620-skewers-1619-project/.

9. Ibid.
10. Thomas Sowell. *Inside American Education.* New York: The Free Press, 1993, p. 17.
11. Ibid.
12. Ibid., p. 33.
13. Matt McManus. "The Frankfurt School and postmodern philosophy." *Quillette.* January 3, 2019. Retrieved August 20, 2021, from https://quillette.com/2019/01/03/the-frankfurt-school-and-postmodern-philosophy/.
14. Ibid.
15. Ernest J. Zarra III. *Teacher-Student Relationships: Crossing into the Emotional, Physical, and Sexual Realms.* 2013. Lanham, MD: Rowman & Littlefield Publishers. See Chapter 3. Cf. *The Entitled Generation: Helping Teachers Teach and Reach the Minds and Hearts of Generation Z.* Lanham, MD: Rowman & Littlefield Publishers, 2017. See Chapters 1, 4.
16. Thomas Sowell. *Inside American Education.* New York: The Free Press, 1993, p. 71.
17. Del Stover. "The New Racism." *American School Board Journal.* June 1990, p. 14.
18. Karen B. McLean Donaldson. *Combating racism in United States Schools.* Westport, CT: Praeger Publishers, 1996, p. 13.
19. William A. Jacobson. "Critical race training in education." *Legal Insurrection.* February 2, 2021. Retrieved September 11, 2021, from https://legalinsurrection.com/2021/02/legal-insurrection-launches-critical-race-training-in-higher-education-website/.
20. Ibid.
21. Mark R. Levin. *American Marxism.* New York: Simon & Schuster, Inc., 2021, p. 118.
22. Ernest J. Zarra III. *When the Secular Becomes Sacred: Religious Secular Humanism and Its Effects Upon America' Public Learning Institutions.* Lanham, MD: Rowman & Littlefield Publishers, 2021.
23. Carol M. Swain and Christopher J. Schorr. *Black Eye for America: How Critical Race Theory Is Burning Down the House.* Rockville, MD: Be the People Books, 2021, p. 32.
24. Helen Pluckrose and James Lindsay. *Cynical Theories: How Activist Scholarship Made Everything about Race, Gender, and Identity and Why This Harms Everybody.* Durham, NC: Pitchstone Publishing, 2020, p. 133.
25. Ibid., p. 134.
26. William H. Blahd Jr., Adam Husney, Kathleen Romito, et al. "Anger, hostility, and violent behavior." *University of Michigan Heath System.* February 26, 2020. Retrieved September 8, 2021, from https://www.uofmhealth.org/health-library/anger.
27. Ibid.
28. Heather Mac Donald. "The divisive double standard in Joe Biden's unity speech." *Newsweek.* November 13, 2020. Retrieved October 6, 2021, from https://www.newsweek.com/divisive-double-standard-joe-bidens-unity-speech-opinion-1547002. Cf. Kat Stafford and Aaron Morrison. "Biden repudiates white supremacy,

calls for racial justice." *US News and World Report.* January 20, 2021. Retrieved January 22, 2021, from https://www.usnews.com/news/world/articles/2021-01-20/biden-repudiates-white-supremacy-calls-for-racial-justice.

29. Pluckrose and Lindsay. *Cynical Theories*, p. 134.

30. Ibid.

31. Swain and Schorr. *Black Eye for America*, p. 34.

32. Peter W. Wood. *1620: A Critical Response to the 1619 Project.* New York: Encounter Books.

33. Kurtz. "A book for our Times," *National Review.*

34. Ibid.

35. James Freeman. "American history and the New York Times." October 7, 2020. *The New York Times.* Retrieved September 12, 2021, from https://www.wsj.com/articles/american-history-and-the-new-york-times-11602093219.

36. Christine Rosen. "The falsification project." *Commentary.* November 11, 2021. Retrieved November 12, 2021, from https://www.commentary.org/christine-rosen/the-falsification-project/.

37. Ibid.

38. Swain and Schorr, *Black Eye for America*, p. 33.

39. Leslie M. Harris. "I helped fact-check the 1619 Project. The Times ignored me." *Politico.* March 6, 2021. Retrieved September 30, 2021, from https://www.politico.com/news/magazine/2020/03/06/1619-project-new-york-times-mistake-122248.

40. Sean Wilentz. "A matter of facts." *The Atlantic.* January 22, 2020. Retrieved September 29, 2021, from https://www.theatlantic.com/ideas/archive/2020/01/1619-project-new-york-times-wilentz/605152/.

41. Ibid.

42. Ben Johnson. "Karl Marx: Intellectual father of the 1619 Project?" *Intellectual Takeout.* September 5, 2019. Retrieved September 30, 2021, from https://www.intellectualtakeout.org/article/karl-marx-intellectual-father-1619-project/.

43. Swain and Schorr. *Black Eye for America,* pp. 33–34.

44. Ibid., p. 33.

45. Harris. "I helped fact-check the 1619 Project." *Politico.*

46. Kurtz. "A book for our times." *National Review.*

47. Ibid.

48. Delgado and Stefancic. *Critical Race Theory*, pp. 44–45.

49. Gretchen Livingston and Anna Brown. "Intermarriage in the U.S. 50 years after Loving v. Virginia." *Pew Research Center.* May 18, 2017. Retrieved October 4, 2021, from https://www.pewresearch.org/social-trends/2017/05/18/intermarriage-in-the-u-s-50-years-after-loving-v-virginia/.

50. Ibid.

51. Nicole Cardos. "Why one sociologist says it's time for black women to date white men." *WTTW News.* April 17, 2019. Retrieved October 18, 2021, from https://news.wttw.com/2019/04/17/sociologist-cheryl-judice-interracial-relationships.

52. Christopher F. Rufo. "The child soldiers of Portland." *City Journal.* Spring 2021. Retrieved May 22, 2021, from https://www.city-journal.org/critical-race-theory-portland-public-schools?mc_cid=9ddf5edee7&mc_eid=dd2cd80aa4.

53. Sorin Voicu. "Editorial: Critical race theory is racist." *The Neshoba Democrat*. October 18, 2021. Retrieved October 19, 2021, from https://neshobademocrat.com/stories/editorialcritical-race-theory-is-racist,51088. Cf. Anthony Zurcher. "Critical race theory: The concept dividing the US." *BBC News US and Canada*. July 22, 2021. Retrieved October 18, 2021, from https://www.bbc.com/news/world-us-canada-57908808.

54. Staff. "Millionaire statistics." *Balancing Everything*. September 17, 2021. Retrieved October 18, 2021, from https://balancingeverything.com/millionaire-statistics/.

55. Carly Mallenbaum. "Black representation grows on TV—but diversity behind the scenes lags, UCLA report finds." *USA Today*. October 22, 2020. Retrieved September 5, 2021, from https://www.usatoday.com/story/entertainment/tv/2020/10/22/black-representation-tv-grows-but-diversity-off-screen-lags-study/3720579001/.

56. Deborah Block. "Americans see more interracial relationships in advertising." *Voice of America*. March 7, 2021. Retrieved August 30, 2021, from https://www.voanews.com/usa/race-america/americans-see-more-interracial-relationships-advertising.

57. Jessica Chasmar. "U. Michigan paid critical race theory advocate $20,000 for a one-hour virtual discussion; Report." *Fox News*. October 17, 2021. Retrieved October 18, 2021, from https://www.foxnews.com/us/university-michigan-ibram-x-kendi-20000-virtual-discussion.

58. Scott Jaschik. "Do applicants lie about their race?" *Inside Higher Ed*. October 25, 2021. Retrieved November 9, 2021, from https://www.insidehighered.com/admissions/article/2021/10/25/survey-asks-if-applicants-are-truthful-about-race.

59. Lyle W. Dorsett. *The Essential C. S. Lewis*. New York: Scribner, 2017, p. 50.

60. Delgado and Stefancic. *Critical Race Theory*, p. 24.

61. Pluckrose and Lindsay. *Cynical Theories*, p. 75. Cf. Gurminder K. Bhambra, Dalia Gebrial, and Kerem Nisancioglu, eds. *Decolonising the University*. London, UK: Pluto Press, pp. 2–3.

62. Pluckrose and Lindsay. *Cynical Theories*, pp. 194–195.

63. Ibid., p. 195.

64. Sandra Harding. *Whose Science, Whose Knowledge?* Ithaca, NY: Cornell University Press, 1991.

65. James Bohman. "Critical theory." *Stanford Encyclopedia of Philosophy*, 2005, p. 22. Retrieved May 28, 2021, from https://plato.stanford.edu/entries/critical-theory/#6.

66. Pluckrose and Lindsay. *Cynical Theories*, p. 196.

67. Ibid., p. 196.

68. Ibram X. Kendi. *How to Be an Antiracist*. New York: One World, Random House, 2019, p. 18.

69. Nikolas Lanum. "Virginia teacher says it's been heartbreaking to watch effects of critical race theory on kids." *Fox News*. August 12, 2021. Retrieved August 13, 2021, from https://www.foxnews.com/media/critical-race-theory-loudoun-virginia-teacher-heartbreaking-effects.

70. Ibid.

71. Ibid.
72. Kendi. *How to Be an Antiracist*, p. 18.
73. Ibid.
74. Ibid.
75. Ibid.
76. Danielle Wallace. "University of California agrees to nix SAT, ACT in admissions decisions in settlement with minority students." *Fox News*. May 16, 2021. Retrieved May 17, 2021, from https://www.foxnews.com/us/university-of-california-sat-act-admissions-settlement-minority-students
77. Ibid.
78. Ibid.
79. Olivia Krauth. "Schools keep taking about critical race theory and DEI. What do those terms really mean?" *USA Today*. July 22, 2021. Retrieved August 8, 2021, from https://www.usatoday.com/story/news/education/2021/07/22/critical-race-theory-defined/8045511002/.
80. Staff. "Education Week names JCPS diversity chief John Marshall 'leader to learn from.'" *Jefferson County Public Schools*. 2018. Retrieved August 9, 2021, from https://www.jefferson.kyschools.us/departments/communications/monday-memo/diversity-chief-john-marshall-named-Leader-to-learn-from.
81. Krauth. "Schools keep taking about critical race theory and DEI." *USA Today*.
82. Ben Smith. "He redefined racist. Now he's trying to build a newsroom." *The New York Times*. March 22, 2021. Retrieved March 22, 2021, from https://www.nytimes.com/2021/03/21/business/media/boston-globe-ibram-kendi.html.
83. Kendi. *How to Be an Antiracist*, p. 20.
84. Staff. "White genetically weaker than Blacks, study finds." *Fox News*. February 22, 2008. Retrieved October 8, 2021, from https://www.foxnews.com/story/whites-genetically-weaker-than-blacks-study-finds.
85. Kendi, *How to Be an antiracist*, p. 20.
86. Ibid
87. Kirk E. Lohmueller, Amit R. Indap, Steffen Schmidt, et al. "Proportionally more deleterious genetic variation in European than African populations." *Nature* 451 (February 21, 2008): 994–997. Retrieved October 8, 2021, from https://www.nature.com/articles/nature06611.
88. Mike Brest. "Air Force Academy requires training linked to critical race theory and Black Lives Matter." *Washington Examiner*. August 18, 2021. Retrieved August 19, 2021, from https://www.washingtonexaminer.com/news/air-force-academy-requires-training-linked-critical-race-theory-black-lives-matter.
89. Ibid.
90. Staff. "Kern High School District will not teach critical race theory." *California News Times*. June 28, 2021. Retrieved July 7, 2021, from https://californianewstimes.com/kern-high-school-district-will-not-teach-critical-race-theory/417701/.
91. Tyler Kingkade, Brandy Zadrozny, and Ben Collins. "Is critical race theory taking over your school board? A national organization could be why." *NBC News*. June 15, 2021. Retrieved June 15, 2021, from https://www.nbcnews.com/

news/us-news/critical-race-theory-invades-school-boards-help-conservative-groups-n1270794.

92. Brian Adams. "History doesn't repeat, but it often rhymes." *Huffington Post*. January 18, 2017. Retrieved September 14, 2021, from https://www.huffpost.com/entry/history-doesnt-repeat-but-it-often-rhymes_b_61087610e4b0999d2084fb15.

93. R. R. Reno. "Antiracist hysteria." *First Things*. December 2020. Retrieved April 23, 2021, from https://www.firstthings.com/article/2020/12/antiracist-hysteria.

94. Delgado and Stefancic. *Critical Race Theory*, pp. 75–76.

95. Ibid., pp. 79–81.

96. Swain and Schorr. *Black Eye for America*, p. 18. Cf. James Lindsay. "Ways of knowing." *New Discourses*. April 21, 2020. Retrieved September 29, 2021, from https://newdiscourses.com/tftw-ways-of-knowing/.

97. Swain and Schorr. *Black Eye for America*, p. 18. Cf. James Lindsay. "Ways of knowing." *New Discourses*.

98. Gloria Ladson-Billings. *Critical Race Theory in Education*. New York: Teachers College, Columbia University, 2021, p. 196.

99. Lanum. "Virginia teacher says it's been heartbreaking to watch effects of critical race theory on kids." *Fox News*.

100. Deborah Block. "Relationships in advertising." *Voice of America*. March 7, 2021. Retrieved August 29, 2021, from https://www.voanews.com/usa/race-america/americans-see-more-interracial-relationships-advertising.

101. Julia H. Kaufman and Alice Huguet. "How state critical race theory bans could trickle down to the classroom." *The RAND Corporation Blog*. August 31, 2021. Retrieved September 12, 2021, from https://www.rand.org/blog/2021/08/how-state-critical-race-theory-bans-could-trickle-down.html.

102. Ibid.

103. Eduardo. "Stop telling critical race theory's critics we don't know what it is." *Newsweek*.

104. Neal Hardin. "Is critical race theory biblical?" *The Religion & Politics Blog*. June 26, 2021. Retrieved July 1, 2021, from https://www.nealhardin.com/is-critical-race-theory-biblical/.

105. Michael Ruiz. "Largest teachers union says critical race theory is reasonable and appropriate for kids." *Fox News Education*. July 4, 2021. Retrieved August 15, 2021, from https://www.foxnews.com/us/largest-teachers-union-critical-race-theory-reasonable-and-appropriate.

106. Daniel Buck and Anthony Kinnett, "We're educators. Critical race theory is, in fact, in the schools." *National Review*. November 6, 2021. Retrieved November 8, 2021, from https://www.nationalreview.com/2021/11/were-educators-critical-race-theory-is-in-fact-in-the-schools/.

107. Ibid.

108. W. James Antle. "The democrats' deception on critical race theory." *The Week*. November 5, 2021. Retrieved November 6, 2021, from https://theweek.com/critical-race-theory/1006859/the-dishonest-discourse-of-critical-race-theory.

109. Jon Brown. "Iowa professor explains how she circumvents state ban on teaching CRT." *Fox News*. September 20, 2021. Retrieved September 22, 2021, from

https://www.foxnews.com/politics/blm-propose-day-of-civil-disobedience-to-teach-critical-race-theory-in-iowa-despite-state-ban.

110. Patricia Tolson. "Despite bans on CRT, educators are teaching other educators how to back-door it into the classroom." *The Epoch Times*. September 22, 2021. Retrieved September 24, 2021, from https://www.theepochtimes.com/despite-bans-on-crt-educators-are-teaching-other-educators-how-to-back-door-it-into-the-classroom_4008873.html.

111. Jake Sheridan. "Critical race theory sparks debate in Hernando schools." *Tampa Bay Times*. August 26, 2021. Retrieved September 12, 2021, from https://www.tampabay.com/news/education/2021/08/26/critical-race-theory-sparks-debate-in-hernando-schools/.

112. Ibid.

113. Richard Delgado, Jean Stefancic, and Angela Harris. *Critical Race Theory: An Introduction*. New York: New York University Press, 2006. See Chapter 1. Retrieved August 23, 2021, from https://jordaninstituteforfamilies.org/wp-content/uploads/2020/04/Delgado_and_Stefancic_on_Critical_Race_Theory.pdf. Cf. Ben Shapiro. "The movement against critical race theory is deeply necessary." *Inside Scoop Politics*. June 23, 2021. Retrieved June 24, 2021, from https://insidescooppolitics.com/archives/3657.

114. Tony Monzo. "Social-emotional learning—A gateway to CRT." *Cape May County Herald*. September 22, 2021. Retrieved September 23, 2021, from https://www.capemaycountyherald.com/opinion/article_d9540a74-1b13-11ec-b38b-4baac4f36e76.html.

115. Christopher F. Rufo. "Battle over critical race theory." *Wall Street Journal*. June 27, 2021. Retrieved June 28, 2021, from https://www.wsj.com/articles/battle-over-critical-race-theory-11624810791.

116. Christopher F. Rufo. "The child soldiers of Portland." *City Journal*. Spring 2021. Retrieved May 22, 2021, from https://www.city-journal.org/critical-race-theory-portland-public-schools?mc_cid=9ddf5edee7&mc_eid=dd2cd80aa4.

117. Kotkin and Heyman. "Critical race theory ignores anti-Semitism." *UnHerd*.

118. Ibid.

119. Jennifer Agiesta. "Most say race relations worsened under Obama, poll finds." *CNN*. October 6, 2016. Retrieved June 16, 2021, from https://www.cnn.com/2016/10/05/politics/obama-race-relations-poll/index.html.

120. Domenico Montanaro. "Americans say President Trump has worsened race relations since George Floyd's death." *NPR*. June 5, 2020. Retrieved July 9, 2021, from https://www.npr.org/2020/06/05/871083543/americans-say-president-trump-has-worsened-race-relations-since-george-floyds-de.

121. Megan Brenan. "Ratings of Black-White relations at new low." *Gallup*. July 21, 2021. Retrieved July 23, 2021, from https://news.gallup.com/poll/352457/ratings-black-white-relations-new-low.aspx.

122. Kotkin and Heyman. "Critical race theory ignores anti-Semitism." *UnHerd*.

123. Walter E. Williams. "Walter Williams: Blind to real problems." *Daily Citizen-News*. June 21, 2018. Retrieved October 28, 2021, from https://www.dailycitizen.news/opinion/columns/walter-williams-blind-to-real-problems/article_fa2ba9d3

-2a71-5cee-958a-295c3467ad2b.html. Cf. Orlando Patterson. *The Ordeal of integration: Progress and resentment in America's racial crisis.* New York: Civitas, 1997, p. 17.

124. Kotkin and Heyman. "Critical race theory ignores anti-Semitism." *UnHerd.*

125. Christopher F. Rufo. "The child soldiers of Portland." *City Journal.*

126. Ibid.

127. Maria Trent, Danielle G. Dooley, and Jacqueline Douge. "The impact of racism on child and adolescent health." *Pediatrics* 144, no. 2 (August 1, 2019): 1–16. Retrieved August 19, 2021, from https://pediatrics.aappublications.org/content/pediatrics/144/2/e20191765.full.pdf. Cf. J. T. Young. "Critical race theory and the threat to Democrats." *The Hill.* July 23, 2021. Retrieved September 12, 2021, from https://thehill.com/opinion/campaign/564588-crts-threat-to-democrats. Cf. also, Jessica Lynn. "Republicans weaponized critical race theory for kindergarteners." *Medium.* July 20, 2021. Retrieved September 12, 2021, from https://medium.com/the-rant/republicans-weaponize-critical-race-theory-for-kindergarteners-3a10c16f2128.

Chapter 5

Critical Flaws of Critical Race Theory

> The precise relationship of CRT to the most extreme expressions of woke anti-racism and the Black Lives Matter movement has yet to be made clear. How do we get from a niche academic discipline to calls to defund the police, lamentations over the existence of America itself and expressions of loathing towards white people?[1]

> Racial inequality, baked into the fabric of American society, can only be undone by a brand of anti-racism rooted in Kendi's view that, when he sees racial disparities, he sees racism. As nature abhors a vacuum, Kendi abhors any analysis of racial inequality that "racism" cannot explain. . . . This reflexive mono-causality gives us a basic logical fallacy in Kendi's work: the fallacy of affirming the consequent.[2]

Some of the flaws of CRT are critiqued in previous chapters, within the context of various premises and positions posed by proponents of the theory. Several other flaws of CRT, such as its illogical foundation, internal inconsistencies in application of the theory, hypocrisy, and inadequacy of the theory are addressed in this chapter.[3]

As a point of beginning this chapter, it must be pointed out that the logic of the CRT, itself, and the actions that spin out from it are definitely open to criticism. If CRT is found to be logical, it should be able to support analogous applications to other examples and contexts. Likewise, the additional elements added to the theory should not internally contradict themselves, nor should the actions taken circumvent the postulates of the theory. On that note, below are five flaws of CRT to consider as this chapter begins.

FLAW 1: CRITICAL RACE THEORY IS ILLOGICAL

Consider the Democratic Party. Since its inception in the South, it had been the political party that favored enslavement of blacks. Past leaders of the party legislated Jim Crow laws, and many voted against the Civil Rights and Voting Rights Acts of the 1960s. They supported segregationists and birthed the Ku Klux Klan, and most of the impoverished and high-crime areas to this day are the inner cities run for decades by Democratic political machines.

Sociologically and economically, based on the criteria for dismantling and deconstructing society, would it not be sensible for critical *political* theorists and advocates to call for the destruction of these horrific inner-city political machines? Since race and poverty are inexorably connected to inner cities, that would be the sensible thing to do.

Racist Policing?

If *critical political theory* is true, then the same criteria applied to one political party must also be applied to the other, given that racism is an issue that arises in both. But this is not what we are seeing in America today. It is the Republican Party which is branded as racist, which goes against over 100 years of American history. More specifically, it is the color of the skin of those claiming to be Republican that are really the racists.

Another point to consider is the theoretical notion that is applied to law enforcement in America today. Again, Americans are told that institutions are corrupt, and this includes the system of policing and law enforcement. Proponents of CRT, including BLM advocates, claim that sporadic incidents involving black men and police are evidence of institutional racism. However, large numbers of inner-city police forces are racial and ethnic minorities.

The facts are that in the South some of the first types of policing occurred. The

> policing in the South was known as slave patrol, which began in the colonies of Carolina in 1704. The patrol was usually made up of three to six men riding horseback and carrying whips, ropes, and even guns. The group's main duties included chasing and hunting escaped slaves, releasing terror on slave communities to prevent riots, and to keep plantation owners in check. . . . The slave patrols lasted until the Civil War and eventually gave way to the Ku Klux Klan.[4]

The politicians of the Democrat-run cities of today's America are left in power, while the police are being forced from their jobs in those same cities. The proponents of racial demagoguery use incidents between police as validation to vilify institutions as racist, when they have stated that racism is not incidental. An interesting question is, how many of today's modern Democrats have ancestors that were slave patrol enforcers and slave owners in the South during slavery?

Certainly, it is morally wrong for one group to assign inescapable blame to another group, just by being members of the latter or bearing a job title. In reality, today's entrenched inner-city Democrat politicians bear no resemblance to the KKK, and the diversity of law enforcement officers of all colors that serve and protect the people of those cities, is a far cry from the demographic of nineteenth century slave patrols.

Illogical Inconsistencies

What we find today is that any argument that points out the fallacies or suppositions that result in labeling institutions as racist is disallowed. What this reveals is an insecurity of a theory and that amounts to a major critical flaw. Take, for example, the following which illustrates a critical flaw of CRT thinking. Observe the objective assumptions in the premises and the absurdity in each conclusion.

Example 1	Example 2
All whites are racists from birth.	It is true that whites are racists.
Whites are responsible for creating systemic racism.	Denying this truth is racist.
Therefore, all whites and their systems are racist.	White denials prove they are racists.

Another example of the inconsistency of logic pertains to personal application. Calls for ending law enforcement in cities, while hiring private law enforcement from within the supposed same racist institution created to control blacks, both enslaved and free,[5] are illogical. If an institution is racist, are not those within it still racists when they work privately as well?[6]

If law enforcement is systemically corrupt, how is the corruption negated because law enforcement is hired by elites whether people of color or not? Are so-called white neighborhoods that have been labeled as racist enclaves somehow less racist because people of color live there? The practices do not always justify the premises.

Another way to describe the illogical nature of the claims associated with CRT is to examine the thinking of the antiracist Ibram X. Kendi. According to Jonathan Church, Kendi falls into *affirming the consequent* fallacy in his reasoning. The fallacy considers:

(1) If P, then Q.
(2) Q.
Therefore,
(3) P.

> Racism (P) certainly can lead to racial inequality (Q). But it does not follow that, if racial inequality (Q), then racism (P). The contrapositive (if not Q, then not P), yes, but not Q, then P. Of course, we should acknowledge that, for Kendi, it is not about "racism" but about policy. . . . Thus, when Kendi says policy is racist when inequality results, he is saying policy is indistinguishable from racism or, more plainly, that policy is racism. Kendi affirms the consequent. Why is this a problem? Because other factors may be at work.[7]

Removing theology from the equation and using two common psychological constructs yield interesting conclusions for CRT. Assume that (1) mankind are born with a good nature[8] or (2) mankind are born with a blank slate.[9] Inserting a third construct is theological, which places all humans with a sinful nature. How then does any three of these explain the view that only whites are born racists and possess implicit bias, and that racism is hardwired into their white melanin?

What psychological theory is relied on to answer this question? Even returning theology to the query implicates all humans with the same nature. Either way, there is no logical way for CRT to justify one race as different by nature. Since systems are created by these same people, what is the basis for assuming racism throughout?

If the obvious conclusion is true, then racists are not born. Racism must be a socio-political, human-racial construct, like many other things claimed by social scientists. We can look to other nations of the world for easy proof that racism is not left to one race. Therefore, racism must be in human nature.

Questioning the society that developed this construct and fixing it would be the logical thing to do. Logically, if racism is a social construct then it is logical that people of any race can then be racists. Lest one dismisses this statement as whiteness defending itself from within its frailty, consider that racism does not just occur between blacks and whites.[10]

Ijeoma Oluo promotes the view that

> you are racist because you were born and bred in a racist, white supremacist society. White Supremacy is . . . insidious by design. The racism required to uphold White Supremacy is woven into every area of our lives. There is no way you can inherit white privilege from birth, learn white supremacist history in schools, consume racist and white supremacist movies and films, work in a

racist and white supremacist workforce, and vote for racist and white supremacist governments and not be racist.[11]

One has to wonder if this same logic holds true for the people in mostly black African nations, or whether Oluo thinks such statements are attributed to other groups aside from whites in America. What does she do with the Nation of Islam, Anti-Israel groups, New Black Panthers, Black Nationalists such as the NFAC, and others? In Oluo, there is the presumption of racism everywhere in America, both seen and unseen. This borders on hysteria and is somewhat irrational.

The Motte and Bailey Doctrine

In 2005, "philosopher Nicholas Shackel wrote about the Motte and Bailey Doctrine, which some refer to a fallacy argument."[12] The name of the doctrine comes from a castle-defense system developed in the 10th century in northern Europe. One part was a courtyard area, called a *bailey*, where people would trade, eat, and work. On a nearby hill was a fortified tower called a *motte*. The motte was an unproductive place to hang out, but it was safe. So, during attacks, residents would flee the bailey for the motte, where they could ward off enemies.

In short, when it comes to logic, the doctrine can be interpreted in the following manner. The bailey is the desired but hard-to-defend controversial opinion. The motte is the less desired yet defensible opinion that nearly everyone agrees with, and which the arguer retreats to if unable to defend the bailey.

Stephen Johnson writes, The *Motte and Bailey Doctrine* "describes a rhetorical move in which an arguer advances an indefensible opinion, but when challenged, retreats and falls back to a similar yet easier-to-defend opinion. Motte-and-baileys have become a weapon of choice in political and culture-war arguments."[13] What is interesting is that despite its transparent theoretical weakness in practice, proponents of CRT use this doctrine to try to stem criticism against their beliefs. The motte-and-bailey is actually both a deflection and a surrender. Here are three hypothetical examples of the Motte and Bailey Doctrine.

Example 1

A: America and Whites are systemically, institutionally, and intrinsically racist from the beginning. (*The Indefensible Position*)

B: Show me the evidence where racism exists in institutions, in people, and is system-wide. (*The Challenge*)

A: The reality is that racism is rampant and that you are part of that. (*The Retreat*)

Example 2

A: Homeopathic medicine can cure cancer. (*The Indefensible Position*)
B: There's no evidence showing homeopathy is effective. (*The Challenge*)
A: Actually there are many ways for people to be healthy besides taking doctor-prescribed drugs. (*The Retreat*)

Example 3

A: Medical experts agree that vaccines for children protect them and others from contracting and spreading COVID. (*The Indefensible Position*)
B: Where are the studies of children 12 and under showing the need for children to be vaccinated? (*The Challenge*)
A: Most would agree vaccines save lives and are beneficial for people. (*The Retreat*)

Certainly, one of the reasons critical race theorists do not want to debate scholars of departments outside social science is because of the inability to defend indefensible and illogical positions. Consider briefly another area where CRT is illogical.

Mathematics as a discipline has been accused of originating out of a white supremacist culture of the Western world. The accusation is that mathematics and its penchant for right and wrong answers is a form of white oppression because it controls logic and mathematical thinking toward only one correct answer for even the simplest of equations. Any "teaching that math is racist will taint the field for everyone, including those who need it most."[14]

Traditional white math logic says 1 + 1 = 2. But math using non-white logic says something quite different. Examine the directions and consider the following solutions to the stated problem.

Directions: Translate the following word problem into two similar mathematical equations.
Problem: A man walks into a store and steals an item.
Solution 1: One man robs one store and walks out with one item. Therefore, 1 + 1 = 1.
Solution 2: One chicken plus one rooster equals 1 egg. Therefore, 1 + 1 = 1.

According to proponents of CRT, this type of reasoning is not only accurate, but it should be allowed and accepted as a counter to the white supremacy mathematics that is forced upon all public school students. There is a concerted effort across America to dismantle racism in mathematics instruction. For example, *The California Mathematics Project* aims to do just that.

The themes built into the pages of the eighty-eight-page manual of instructional practice exercises comprise "a pathway to equitable math instruction: Dismantling racism in mathematics instruction."[15] The pathway encompasses two major themes, which include, (1) culturally relevant curricula and the (2) promotion of antiracist mathematics instruction. There are "exercises for educators to reflect on their own biases to transform their instructional practices."[16]

After several hours of informal conversations with civil engineers, teachers online and in person, and several scientists and architects, there were given many comments to this author—two of which are paraphrased in the following: "I would hate to have that type of logic applied to bridge building" and (2) "Could you imagine the house which could be built from that type of reasoning?"

FLAW 2: CRT IS INCONSISTENT

Although not white, Asians are no longer considered as people of color. No one is certain exactly whose idea it was to not view Asians as oppressed minorities,[17] but critical theorist ideology appears to be the source. A large school district in Washington State, the North Thurston Public Schools, "lumped Asians in with whites and measured their academic achievement against students of color . . . Asians are now white."[18]

Asians are now generally placed in the same "privileged" class as whites because they generally achieve high in academic and economic pursuits. Could this be one reason why Asians are discriminated against and why colleges and universities are restricting their admissions, while favoring other students, particularly those of non-Asian descent?

Higher education institutions and many secondary schools are restructuring courses and curricula to fit lower-achieving student demographics, thus discriminating against higher-achieving students. This begs the question, *in what ways are lower standards of rigor equitable for all students—and what about those students who achieve at high levels with more rigorous standards?* This type of educational dumbing down is directly related to CRT but also about ideas regarding equity for all students. However, this is a word game. What is meant by all students really only pertains to those identified as oppressed. It is not only illogical to conclude that the lowering standards challenge students, but it is equally insulting. Only in the minds of CRTs can equity for a select group be good for all.

An irony of CRT is that it criticizes American Caucasian culture, yet BIPOC have access to all sectors in American society. CRT maintains that

American society is associated with whiteness and white supremacy and therefore needs to be challenged on every front and dismantled. Yet, many BIPOC choose to participate in the society at all levels successfully.[19]

The question should be asked that, if America is such an unchanged, racist nation, then why are so many people of color participating successfully in such a racist system. For example, why would a former leader of BLM suddenly have enough wealth to purchase millions of dollars[20] of real estate[21] and do so in exclusive white enclaves?[22]

As stated in an earlier question, the real question is, why would she even want to live surrounded by wealthy racists, in the first place? Furthermore, most Americans making the claim that America is a racist nation would be hard-pressed to form an intelligent answer as to why hundreds of thousands to millions of people of color flock to America's borders seeking entry.

Shame-Blame Hypocrisy

For critical race proponents to bully whites into shame and require them to disown their very culture—yet participate in the *shamed* white culture themselves—is more than a flaw. Such a practice is hypocritical. Cries of systemic racism fall on deaf ears when *the oppressed* participate widely in the system they claim is systemically oppressive. Seeking to revolutionize what is deemed as white supremacist capitalism, while personally and professionally benefiting from it, is a demonstration that material gains often win out over the theoretical and that capitalism really does trump socialism.

The reality in shaming whites for desiring the best for their children, in terms of education and jobs—all while accessing the very system for other races and their families—demonstrates that the system is not so racist after all. What is sad is that such accusations are particularly harmful to children of all races and the schools are where the neo-Marxists intend to shape the future.

CRT has a lot for which to answer, including the material wealth and power its spokespersons have amassed. This is inconsistent with its narrative. Current race leaders appear to be about money and power, with ideas sprinkled with a new neo-Marxist ideology, the likes of which are based on racial classification, rather than social class structures.[23] But are the ideologues using race as an issue just to gain monetary wealth and notoriety?

FLAW 3: CORRECTING PAST ERRORS BY COMMITTING PRESENT ERRORS

The commission of actions in the present, which were deemed wrong in the past, is as immoral as it is illogical. Active racial discrimination, so that whites come to understand what it is like to be discriminated against is a page taken from the writings of Ibram X. Kendi. No one should be surprised by the activist rhetoric of antiracists. Kendi writes, "The only remedy to racist discrimination is antiracist discrimination. The only remedy to past discrimination is present discrimination. The only remedy to present discrimination is future discrimination."[24] In Kendi, we see the clear motive of CRT and antiracism activism. The motive is best understood as a distortion of a biblical principle which now reads, "Do unto others as they have done unto you."

CRT and its practices are dis-unifying, fracturing racial relationships, and disrespectful of Martin Luther King's hard-fought legacy. Character over color was the mantra then.[25] Today, melanin over merit is the practice. It is discriminatory and racist to state that one has to be of the right skin color to advance, while all others are increasingly instructed not to apply. In 2022, President Biden illustrated this by selecting a nominee to the U.S Supreme Court strictly by melanin and gender. How can a practice labeled so wrong for over 200 years now be adopted as a morally just practice? Such a practice is neither corrective nor considers the content of one's character. The practice actually amounts to an emboldening of vindictive hearts. Again, there is the appearance of economic gain that is the main driver of CRT.

FLAW 4: CRITICAL RACE THEORY IS SEPARATIST AND LEADS TO RACIAL SEGREGATION

CRT is becoming more and more aggressive and expansive in American society. It has infected the minds of millions of people in America and continues to grow by elevating divisiveness and racial separation. America's K-16 public learning institutions were always meant to be places of unity around American principles. If it was wrong for America to separate by race in the past—and it was—then it is still wrong to separate today. Common sense and human decency dictate that any theory that encourages this type of practice must be rejected.[26]

People can be *enlightened* by truth and love, academic challenge, and their better angels. People can also claim to know the truth and become *woke* to something qualitatively lesser and quantitatively more racially divisive. The shiny object that dangles before people is an angel of light. Behind the glow is vengeance and discrimination disguised as equity and fairness. America's students are attracted to the glow, as they receive heavy doses of indoctrination at the schools they attend?[27] The fruit of the tree of vengeance is sweet only upon the first bite.

There are examples of racial segregation that are showing up in communities across the nation. This is not by accident segregation, incidents are becoming more and more prevalent. Blacks are being placed into separate classrooms, as if those are racial safe spaces, while whites are segregated away from them. But people are speaking up![28]

Recently, a civil rights complaint was filed by Kila Posey, with the United States Department of Education (USDOE). Posey, who is black, claimed that the racial segregation of students into black and white classes violated "Title VI of the Civil Rights Act of 1964." Posey claims that the principal of the school placed all black students in separate classes at the Mary Lin Elementary School in Atlanta, Georgia. The principal, Sharyn Briscoe, is also black.[29]

Posey is the vice president of operations for the district's parent-teacher association. After contacting the principal of the school to inquire about her daughter being placed with a teacher of the parent's choice, she was told that could not happen. The principal stated that the requested teacher was not a teacher of one of the black students' classrooms.[30] Thus, separatist segregation is back, as if the nation had not learned from its past. MLK's character mantra has been effectively canceled, and *Brown v. Board* is being patently overstepped.

When educators become activists, their *wokeness* often blinds their sensibilities, much like converts to a new religion. They tend to lose sight of the larger picture. The notion that black students would learn better in environments where everyone looked like them, placing students in classrooms to avoid white supremacy, or even be free of microaggressions by others is tethered to CRT. Posey realized this, and she is pleased that her complaint is being investigated by the USDOE.[31]

CRT is predicated on falsehoods about people, while marginalizing these same people in the process. Students today are told to see skin color first and to feel guilty if they are the wrong color. Again, to repeat: *If it was wrong for America to separate by race in the past—and it was—then it is still wrong to separate today.* Such separatist ideologies must not be tolerated.[32] Common sense dictates that any theory that encourages this type of discussion or practice must be discarded.

FLAW 5: CRT IS INADEQUATE FOR TEACHER TRAINING

Critical Theory is full of tensions and concerns. One of these tensions rests in the claim that it has been tested as a "viable alternative for social and political philosophy today."[33] This alternative has found its way into most university educational philosophies. With the emergence of

> new forms of critical theory . . . related to racism, sexism, and colonialization, reflective social agents have transformed . . . democratic ideals and practices in

> the interest of emancipation. In entrenching new social facts, agents transform the ideals themselves as well as their institutional form.[34]

In this sense, teachers are being trained to guide students in such transformations.[35]

Those training to be teachers in America's public schools are forced to take courses on the permanence of racism and whiteness, as these relate to (1) classroom understanding for students of color, (2) personal trauma, (3) students' families, and (4) teachers who are white.

Teachers who are students in graduate schools seeking advanced degrees are confronted with the assumption that racism exists in their schools, and their assignments are presented to them without allowance of criticism or critique. In fact, any such efforts to criticize or question the underlying assumptions upon which CRT is built is ample evidence of a person's whiteness or adjacency to whiteness. This is definitely a hallmark of a theory that cannot be trusted. If the foundation of CRT can be disproven, then any school teaching the elements stemming from an erroneous theory become guilty of teaching pure indoctrination.

One teacher earning a graduate degree shared his lesson requirements for a class leading to his advanced degree. His identity is kept anonymous, but his story appeared in a recent issue of *The American Conservative*. The teacher wrote:

> I'm a high school teacher . . . and currently taking the last class required for my master's degree in education. . . . The class covers some of the science behind how people (and specifically children) learn. The latest modules, however, deal with CRT and its tenets, such as the permanence of racism, the failure of liberalism, the myth of colorblindness, and others. It has been difficult to complete the assignments because I disagree with nearly all of them. I find myself staring at the screen in gridlock because the work presupposes all of these beliefs. How can I answer from a perspective I feel is inherently wrong? . . . . These ideologues must insist that reality conform to the tenets of the ideology.[36]

An example of one of the activity assignments required by the graduate course in question is found in Module Four: Critical Race Theory: A Tool for Analyzing Equity/Inequity in Schools. The activity is a checklist of CRT Tenets 1–2, taking a deeper dive into the permanence of racism and whiteness as property. The leading statement that sets the tone for the modified Likert Scale activity reads, "As discussed in this module, racism does not need to be intentional to be considered racism—a racist policy or practice has a disproportionately negative effect on racial minorities' access to or quality of goods and services."[37]

Readers should carefully observe the biases, assumptions, and preconceptions that are found in the graduate student's following assignment for CRT Tenets 1–2. Each statement in question is listed here and was expected to have been answered by one of three responses: "Affirmative, Negative, or Unsure."[38]

CRT Tenets 1–2: (Responses: *Affirmative, Negative, or Unsure*)

- Underrepresentation of people of color in curriculum and examples that teachers use during instruction; focus on the *white* canon of authors, scientists, artists, etc.; cultural irrelevancy of curriculum to students of color
- Family and community depicted as a *problem* or hurdle to students of color in achieving excellence; *subtractive schooling* where community culture is marginalized/judges as negative, and norms associated with *school culture* are celebrated
- Overrepresentation of students of color in special education and lower tracked classes
- Underrepresentation of students of color in AP, GT, and honors classes
- Higher drop-out rates and discipline referral rate for students of color
- Less or inappropriate/outdated materials and resources for students of color who attend more segregated schools, more dilapidated buildings for students of color that attend more segregated schools
- Less per pupil spending in schools or districts with higher numbers of students of color
- Less experienced teachers in classrooms with higher numbers of students of color

There are many examples like these that are being used in teacher training courses in higher education, as well as in district-level professional development. Some of the college classes where topics and assignments like these are found include psychologies, trauma-informed instruction, culturally relevant teaching (another CRT), ethnic studies, instructional methods, and others.[39]

FLAW 6: CRT IMAGINES IT CAN END DISCRIMINATION BY DISCRIMINATING AGAINST OTHERS

The late U.S. Supreme Court justice Harry Blackmun wrote the following in 1978, "In order to get beyond racism, we must first take account of race. There is no other way. And in order to treat some persons equally, we must treat them differently." Attaining equality is not the focal point of advancement today.[40] People understand that equality is no longer a thing to be grasped, because of the recognition that people are equal under the law and equal before God.[41] The twenty-first-century concern is equity, which Blackmun implies in the last phrase.[42]

Treating people differently impacts education in several ways, not the least of which might occur in any ordinary public school classroom. What differences are there of greater and lesser importance? What if a student is better at math or can run faster, or whose hair is different. What should be made of these differences, because some students are inferior in certain academic content areas? But this inferiority may be due to a host of reasons. Is race one of them?

Asians do not always like to hear they are good at math, because everyone understands that all Asians are not good at math. According to Kendi, this *idea* is stereotypical and racist, and so too would be generalizations about racial groups. Yet, Kendi has right before his eyes what CRT and antiracism claim about all whites and does not call this out as racist.

Therefore, it must be asked if it is racist to make the claim that families in inner cities, whose children grow up without dads, are more likely to find themselves in trouble, join gangs, drop out of school, and have children out-of-wedlock. Are these a series of facts or are they racist tropes? Why are questions like these anathema to critical theory? According to Kendi's logic, they are anathema because of the all-purpose smear of racism.

The implication that a person is racist for stating children with intact nuclear families have greater opportunities afforded them is quite ridiculous. Kendi himself had this privilege. BLM, before they redesigned their website, had as one of its goals the dissolution of the nuclear family, which they deemed anti-LGBTQ+ and a hallmark of white supremacy. Kendi seemed in agreement, when he penned, "Racist ideas have defined our society since its beginning and can feel as natural and obvious as to be banal, but antiracist ideas remain difficult to comprehend, in part because they go against the flow of this country's history."[43]

Kendi defines "anti-Black racist ideas . . . as any idea suggesting that Black people, or any group of Black people, are inferior in any way to another racial group"[44] and then links this to the history of America. So, what does it say about an education system that does away with requirements, standardized tests, and admits based on skin color? Does this *not* at least imply that Blacks are inferior and need assistance?

Certainly, discrimination against higher-achieving students, in order to end lack of access to challenging classes and programs, is a flawed policy. To suggest any group lacks abilities is racism, at least—and just as much racist as reducing challenging classes for others because of a lack of achievement.

Kendi concludes,

> In other words, to call women as a group stupid is sexism. To call Black people as a group stupid is racism. To call Black women as a group stupid is gender racism. Such intersections have also led to articulations of class racism (demeaning the Black poor and Black elites) queer racism (demeaning Black lesbians, gays, bisexuals, transgender, and queer people) and ethnic racism (concocting a hierarchy of Black ethnic groups), to name a few.[45]

In order to be consistent, classifying all whites as racists, implicitly biased, and nationalists is demeaning an entire race and is racist per se, if we apply the same Kendian critical standards.

The CRT Manifesto

In 2020, several hundred Princeton University faculty members "signed an anti-racist manifesto that described the school as founded upon the pillars of its oppressive past, requiring an overhaul of faculty, curriculum, and admissions procedures to fumigate the campus of an all-permeating racism."[46]

Along with a list of demands, the manifesto established a faculty committee to oversee faculty and keep an eye on those who might need to be disciplined, because of "racist behaviors, incidents, research, and publication on the part of the faculty."[47] This is frightening. But it gets worse, as the declaration shifted its indictment to implicate the United States as being anti-black.

The faculty letter to the university administration begins as follows:

> Anti-Blackness is foundational to America. It plays a role in where we live and where we are welcome. It influences the level of healthcare we receive. It determines the degree of risk we are assumed to pose in contexts from retail to lending and beyond. It informs the expectations and tactics of law-enforcement. Anti-Black racism has hamstrung our political process. It is rampant in even our most "progressive" communities. And it plays a powerful role at institutions like Princeton, despite declared values of diversity and inclusion.[48]

Manifestos lead to watchful faculty eyes, seeking to remove disagreeable professors from campus or require them to mute themselves from microaggressions. However, there is something even more sinister occurring on college campuses.

Antiracist Snitch Teams at Learning Institutions

Snitch teams are designed to catch and remove professors who write something, say something in class, or otherwise cause negative attention to themselves. Outing professors who do not fall into compliance is reminiscent of fascist and socialist revolutionaries bent on purifying their ranks for their *cause*. These discriminatory antiracist teams have spread their ideologies to infect a host of colleges, universities, and K-12 schools across the nation. They strike fear into the heart of education as they follow an antiracist maxim of *see something* and *do something*.[49]

Teacher education departments in many states are now required to train teachers in CRT and antiracism, as part of their credentialing for their states. Some states have thankfully restricted this training and have banned the ideas from K-16 classrooms throughout their state learning institutions.[50]

Antiracist activists have invaded learning institutions such as Bryn Mawr College, New York City's elite Dalton School, Northwestern University, Princeton University, and hundreds of others across America. John McWhorter reminds readers, "American universities have long been more committed to antiracism than almost any other institutions."[51] This should come as no surprise to anyone who is following the course of actions taken on college campuses today. The squeakiest of wheels still gets its share of lubricant.

When it comes to advocates of CRT, there must be activists to advance the message and the cause. Otherwise, critical race theorists serve little purpose. Unless there are activists, CRT is reduced to a theory without legs. Theories without legs are like cars without wheels. There is a lot of noise when they start up, but no movement. Colleges are hotbeds of activism.

At Bryn Mawr, *woke* ideals are largely unquestioned. Dalton has made inroads to establish a substantially non-white student body, and at Northwestern the debate still rages as to what percentage of black students should matriculate, in order to be considered representative of remedy of past discrimination.[52]

At Amherst University, the admissions department has changed its admissions policy. The college website states that the college is ending its long-standing practice of legacy admission preference. Paired with a new expanded financial aid program for lower- and middle-income families, *the College is sending a clear signal to prospective students that its education is within reach*. Parents who have donated large amounts of money will no longer be able to count on their children attending Amherst, as they did. Equity policies now will make available the college for those who, before, had little hope of attending.[53]

McWhorter offers reasons why institutions should not yield to CRT and antiracism. First, declares an adamant McWhorter,

> They must resist destructive demands, even by self-proclaimed representatives of people of color, and even in a society where racism is real. To give in to anti-intellectual, under-considered, disproportionate, or hostile demands is condescending to the signatories (of the university letter to the Princeton administration) and the protesters. It implies that they can do no better, and that authorities must suspend their sense of logic, civility, and progress as some kind of penance for slavery, Jim Crow, redlining, and the deaths of people such as Floyd. That *penance* would hurt only the community in the end, through lower educational quality.[54]

Next, McWhorter claims that the "writers of manifestos might classify resistance as racist, denialist backlash. But the civil, firm dismissal of irrational demands is, rather, a kind of civic valor."[55] It is one thing for a group of scholars to begin with an assumption and develop a theoretical framework around this assumption. What is meant as theory usually does not remain as such. Ivory towers leak into mainstream America over time.

Scholars publish their work and present it as tenable. What begins as an ivory tower assumption, over time, is more broadly shared outside of academe. Elites with microphones, and with the support of media technopolies and sycophants, parrot the notions that are posited by academics. The bullhorns of media then magnify the theoretical into the general marketplace of ideas. The insertion of politics into the spread of the messaging yields a joint narrative of the triad of alignment of academe, social and economic elites, and the media.

A most obvious example of this alignment is the rapid reemergence of racial and identity politics. There is nothing new under the sun, said Solomon, thousands of years earlier. Groups like BLM and proponents of CRT are illustrative of contemporary activism meant to wrest power from the dominant culture—all abetted by the triad. They make no effort to hide this fact.[56]

Truth Test for Discrimination

Anyone with concerns about their children's schools and who want to challenge the existence of CRT should apply a truth test. Truth tests are best applied when younger school-age children are present with their parents and, if possible, supporting teachers. Parents should be requested to bring their children to school board meetings when CRT is being discussed. Concerned stakeholders should make public statements with their children by their sides.

The truth test is presented in asking board members, administrators, and classroom teachers to state directly to the children that if children are born white in America, they are racists—and that their parents are also racists, by being born white, as well.

If the adults who make decisions that affect children and their families are unwilling to be honest about their positions on CRT or refuse to answer how they feel about whiteness, then they should be challenged with the follow up: *Why it is all right for their children's teachers to teach what leaders are unwilling to affirm, and do so with impunity and without parents' knowledge or permission?*

Few things could be more damaging than telling children that both they and their parents are racists. Furthermore, how inverted is a system that claims to care about children when they tell them (1) that their value is in their skin color, (2) that in their skin color there is a cemented racism, an evil, and (3) that they possess the innate ability to oppress children of color?[57] The effect of labeling is not lost on schoolchildren, as one six-year-old illustrates. After arriving home from school one day, a Loudoun County student asked her mother "if she was born evil because she's white,"[58] which was prompted as a result of statements made during her class's history lesson.

CRT SHORTCOMINGS

James Lindsay has written a piece analyzing CRT and explains why its use is terrible for dealing with issues of racism in America.[59] In this article, Lindsay addresses eight reasons and demonstrates their shortcomings. A summary of this list of reasons is included in the following, along with extended remarks and/or examples.

(1) *CRT presents as fact that racism is present, whether consciously aware, or not, in every aspect of life in America.* The assumption is that the presence of racism affects every relationship and every interaction that occurs in society at all levels. Hence, it is ubiquitous and omnipresent. Not surprisingly, such an assumption also similarly hurts those who are only accused of racism.

(2) *The only times that Blacks are given opportunities to achieve in America comes when Whites have something to gain from granting these opportunities.* In other words, there is a self-serving that takes place and it makes Whites feel good when Blacks succeed as a result of opportunities provide for them by Whites. For example, when Whites are interested in something Blacks are interested in, there is a *convergence of interests*

that plays into benefitting Whites by granting Blacks opportunities in these areas of interest. Moreover, Whites offer these opportunities when they can claim higher moral ground, elevate their status by their deeds, or benefit economically and/or socially. In other words, there are no such things as pure hearts, or humble motives in the actions stemming from convergence of interests.

(3) *Critical Race Theory disallows freedoms within so-called societies.* Such restrictions are illiberal, small-minded, and even bigoted.[60]

Free societies are anathema to critical race theorists because such societies are free to maintain what theorists' view as inequities and manipulations, in culling freedom for all. Some theorists argue they are against free societies and favor racial politics. This would lead to the bolstering of race, resulting in the limitation of freedom for others. This is a primary reason why CRT is a stark and contrasted opposite to freedom. Essentially, critical race theorists support a new version of restricted practice which some whites were rightfully accused of throughout the twentieth century.

(4) *In order for Critical Race Theory to flourish, it must delineate people into groups.* CRT cannot be sustained where individual rights are enabled and upheld. As a result, critical race theory cannot support the individual. That is too risky and more closely aligned with the U.S. Constitution, for the sake of comfort. CRT views people by groups, and one of these groups is by race. There are other critical theories that are applied, similarly, such as to gender, sex, age, queerness, and socio-economic class status.

Individuals cannot be granted exclusive freedom within CRT. If people are free to believe, accept, and practice what they will, they might decide within their group against CRT. Therefore, social groups are empowered as units to reduce the risk of dissent. This is why CRT advocates can claim "all whites" are oppressors and all blacks are the oppressed. Even as this is the case, CRT *folks* use individual examples as their reasons to apply group-think and group-action. The term *folks* is used as part of the racial narrative, to achieve *simpatico* within a specific group based on skin color.

(5) *Critical Race Theory is predicated on the idea that academe in America is based on whiteness and a White way of thinking.* Therefore, content areas such as science, mathematics, logic and reasoning, history, economics and capitalism are all based in White supremacy. Race theorists counter these areas with narratives and story-telling, such as is found in the *New York Times 1619 Project*. Theorists claim, for example, that everyday science and mathematics, exude the power of whiteness and reinforce the reality that whoever controls the narrative in these and other

disciplines holds the power over others. Since the claim is that Whites are solely responsible for these disciplines in western society, they hold the power over the narrative. Critical Race Theory aims to dismantle this and other perceived White narratives.

(6) *Critical Race Theory makes clear that it cannot abide competition.* Criticism, or alternate theories are not acceptable. Disputes or rejections are racist. It sets itself up as the objective truth about White America, while at the same time supporting the façade that theirs is the only narrative, and that no one truth exists. For example, if a person or group makes the claim of being colorblind, or that there are other ways to view America, besides through a critical lens based on race, such claims are racist even to suggest. The thinking is circular. All Whites are racists. Claims of not being racists are racist in-and-of-themselves, as are any alternatives or challenges to CRT. In short, the assumed racism is validated by any and all other claims of disagreement. Ironically, even the claim of racism directed toward others can equally be determined as racist.

(7) *Disagreement with any of the premises or conclusions of Critical Race Theory is intolerable.* People who offer alternatives, or find fault in the premises or assumptions are only doing so because of their racism and White supremacy ideology that is ingrained in them. This is also the case with BIPOC who are not accepted by the *kin folks*. Being Black only in their skin color is not enough. One must agree with and align with the deeper racial identity of racial wokeness. Therefore, even according to Kendi, Blacks can also be separatists and racists, especially if they have been affected by the dominant culture.

The phrase used for blacks that do not ascribe to CRT is *Blacks are part of us because of skin, but not of kin.* In other words, not ascribing to antiracism brings the label *skin folk, not kin folk.* Even the creator of the *New York Times 1619 Project* Nikole Hannah-Jones once posted to one of her social media pages that there are distinctions between people who are black by race and those who are black politically.[61]

(8) *Regardless of progress and logical flaws, there is no compromise that is found in Critical Race Theory.* The lines are drawn too deeply in American society. The theory is reinforced by its antiracist advocates by proclaiming dissatisfaction with any evidence from science, *mathematics*, or biology that goes against the tenets of the theory. There is no acceptable dissent.

Peter Wood highlights the fact that "the proponents of so-called *Antiracism* . . . assert that anyone who dissents from their view that America is a systemically racist nation perpetuates racism and deserves to be silenced.

Neo-racism's proponents explicitly advocate for censorship."[62] The built-in assumption that racism exists as stated cannot abide any other view. If it did, then the theory would come crashing down like a house of race cards.

CRT is taking a page from the Jim Crow era and presuming upon whites today, ideas that are both unreasonable and immoral. In CRT we have a form of inescapable moral slavery imputed to a race because of the immutability of skin color. There is also discrimination of a race because of perceived implicit bias and privilege. Both of these were deemed wrong and made illegal in the past. Holding others to past racist standards is unreasonable and immoral.

PEDAGOGY AS WEAPONRY

There are only two racial lenses through which to view the western world. One lens views a racist, white supremacy world, which includes oppressors with implicit and explicit biases, and deeds that are self-serving. The other lens is one of antiracism. This lens sees and roots out any vestiges of beliefs, actions, traditions, and behaviors in the United States, which are assumed to have their origins in racism. Since the assumption of antiracism is that all whites are racists from early on in life, if whites rise up to demand their removal from the racist class, the result is then prima facie evidence that they are already racists.[63]

CRT comes across as a pedagogical weapon in education. As such its purpose is to demoralize and demean white students by telling them that not only are their views illegitimate so also their very lives. This is most harmful and, according to Wood, "Critical Race Theory is a way of playing with the minds of vulnerable children who are in no position to assert their own critical independence."[64] As educators play with the minds of students, they use tactics and insert narratives that capture their attention and, in so doing, offer them alternative truths.

Several questions come to mind, in terms of the reforms advocated through CRT pedagogy. Five good starter questions include the following:

- What shall we make of a generation of students who are being indoctrinated to believe that melanin is their merit, and equity their pathway?
- How should American people adjust to the enablement of a new form of racism that results in the creation of superior identities and uncompromising arrogance?
- To what extent is a politically divided nation to respond to the demands that all people must actively recognize the recipients of equity for what and whom they claim to be, absent science, biology, and history of humankind?

- In what ways can a nation focused on CRT, and group separation by skin color, unite in academic and social purposes to ensure equity for all students?
- What are the emotional and psychological effects upon children who are taught that they are either oppressors, as whites, or that they are oppressed and consciously overlooked by established institutions and systems?

CRT AS A NEW RELIGION?

First, in order to be an exclusive member of this new religion, one has to be born into it by having the correct melanin. Next a person has to have an epiphany and become woke to the truth as a convert. Last, as a disciple of this religion, it is incumbent upon all followers to become active in sharing it and defending it against all unbelievers.

According to John McWhorter, and others, CRT has become a religion of its own, complete with doctrinal tenets, beliefs that lead to and call for conversion. Woke-ism is an aim of antiracism, and the practice of identity across every aspect of American culture, from gender and sex to politics.[65] Others see CRT as more than one religion blended, and even as two separate religions. Regardless of the perspective, consensus is the result of a growing number of scholars who claim that CRT is a cult and it has crept and slinked its way into schools at every level.

Carol Swain and Christopher Schorr address the impact of CRT on Christian church doctrine.

> In terms of Christianity itself, the creeping influence of CRT on doctrine is unmistakable. In evangelical Christianity, this *Woke Church* holds that whites carry a special inherited sin as descendants of slave owners and beneficiaries of systemic racism. . . . CRT preaches a different gospel. It should not be leading and guiding the work of the church.[66]

There was a time in the United States when blacks were considered marked because of a sin committed by the biblical character Ham, one of the sons of Noah.[67] The result of that sin was twisted into the erroneous idea of an assigned physical marking of dark skin. In an interesting turnabout and reversal, *woke religious doctrine* implies that the true original sin is actually whiteness.[68]

Asra Nomani, an immigrant from India, former journalist for the *Wall Street Journal*, and current vice president for *Parents Defending Education*, relates why CRT is most problematic. According to Nomani, it is "so repulsive . . . because it perpetuates . . . separation of people based on identity . . . What I reject in Muslim supremacy is what I reject in this leftist supremacy."[69] Economist Glenn Loury adds, "CRT wipes out agency by downgrading western concepts and *impedes the acquisition of traits that are valued in the marketplace and are essential for human development*."[70]

When asked about the pursuit of diversity and equity on college campuses, regarding skin color in admissions, Loury reasoned,

> You can't do affirmative action, maintain black dignity, and maintain the standards at the same time. That's a trilemma . . . if you lower standards for black people to admit them to elite venues of intellectual performance and the standards are correlated with performance, you assure as a statistical necessity, on average, lower performance of the blacks whom you've admitted.[71]

Racial Activism as Religious Expression

Shunning the 1972 Amendments to the Civil Rights Act, thousands of teachers have already placed their names on a list of lawbreakers and made a "pledge to teach the truth despite new state bills against it."[72] The subjective truth that the potential lawbreaking teachers will continue to proclaim is the divisive rhetoric that America is founded

> on dispossession of Native Americans, slavery, structural racism and oppression; and structural racism is a defining characteristic of our society today. . . . We, the educators, refuse to lie to young people about the U.S. history and current events—regardless of the law.[73]

Examples of rebellious teacher attitudes are the actions found among the teachers unwilling to go along with any laws that limit or restrict their version of the truth. Liz Jarvis, ESL teacher at Cornerstone Prep in Memphis, Tennessee, said she would not abide by any bill and that any such bill "will not make it harder"[74] for her personal students or classroom because she would simply "ignore it."[75]

Should this same lawbreaking attitude prevail in those which are against any laws passed in states requiring the teaching of CRT through ethnic studies or culturally relevant teaching curriculum? Oppositional positions that lead to reactions by parents may just bring down the full force of the federal, state, and local governments upon parents and criminalize such dissent. It is just too early to tell what the devotees to the rebellion and supporters of the opposition will do. The trend today is to support BIPOC and overlook complainants from the oppressor group.

CRT NARRATIVES

Critical race theorists are keen on stories that elevate subjective narratives to the level of the objective. In so doing, the narratives become established truth, albeit flawed. Theorists reject objective and absolute knowledge and truth, and they support replacing what they reject with their own narratives of truth. Three aspects of such flawed narratives and their impacts are included below:

Aspect 1: Use of narratives as truth-telling. This restricts the development of critical thinking abilities. The irony here is that CRT emphasizes less criticism and more subjectivity by the tactic of story-telling.

Aspect 2: Theorists assert that the world is separated into two camps. The first camp is those that oppress. The second camp consists of those who *feel* oppressed. Oppressors, or those in power, versus the oppressed, the victims of the oppressed are the categories that set up *us-versus-them classifications*. How does a person come to understand he or she is oppressed, unless they are told? To what extent can a person trust what another person *feels* is true?

Aspect 3: Reliance on narratives implies a less rigorous set of methodologies to arrive at a deeper understanding. Such a reduction leads to stereotypes that blacks are not as interested in quantitative measures, or about authentic critical thinking, when compared to their white counterparts. Such stereotypes should not be reinforced by segregating searches for knowledge and history based on skin color and story-telling.

Theorists claim that those in racial minority groups in the United States have to think about racism all the time and that white privilege enables whites to avoid such stress. This is an assumption that is not supported by evidence. What is true is that those that are most concerned about being actively *anti-racist*, probably think about racism more than others think about it. These activists claim to find it everywhere they look.

Pluckrose and Lindsay state,

> we hear the language of critical race theory from activists in all walks of life, and one could be easily forgiven—if critical race theory didn't consider it racist to forgive this—for thinking that critical race theory sounds rather racist itself, in ascribing profound failures of morals and character to white people (as consequences of being white in a white-dominant society).[76]

These authors summarize the assertions of the CRT narrative.[77]

- We are told that racism is embedded in culture and that we cannot escape it.
- We hear that white people are inherently racist.
- We are told that racism is *prejudice plus power*, therefore, only white people can be racist.
- We are informed that only people of color can talk about racism, that White people need to just listen, and that they don't have the racial stamina to engage it.
- We hear that not seeing people in terms of their race (being color-blind) is, in fact, racist and an attempt to ignore the pervasive racism that dominates society and perpetuates white privilege.
- We can hear these mantras in many spheres of life, but they are particularly prevalent on college campuses.

As a result of focusing on racial diversity and a conscious effort to dismantle whiteness at the university levels, the result is

> many . . . leading academic and research institutions, including the national Academies of Science, the American Academy of Arts and Sciences, the National Science Foundation, and the National Institutes of Health, [that] scientific excellence is being supplanted by diversity as the determining factor for eligibility in regard to prizes and other distinctions.[78]

If America has any chance of competing with emerging powers in math and science, it must correct its flaws and focus points and redirect its policies and investments.

American educators

> must return to a process of recruitment and promotion based on merit, at all levels of education and research—a step that will require a policy U-turn at the federal, state, and local levels. . . . Instead of implementing divisive policies based on the premise of rooting out invisible forms of racism, or seeking to deconstruct the idea of merit in spurious ways, organizations should redirect their DEI budget toward more constructive goals.[79]

Before closing this chapter, a return to the insights of Pluckrose and Lindsay are in order. They affirm,

> What is, perhaps, most frustrating about [critical race] theory is that it tends to get literally every issue it's primarily concerned with backwards, largely due to its rejection of human nature, science, and liberalism. It allows social significance to racial categories, which inflames racism. It attempts to depict

> categories of sex, gender, and sexuality as mere social constructions, which undermines the fact that sexual expression varies naturally. . . . Theory is highly likely to spontaneously combust at some point, but it could cause a lot of human suffering and societal damage before it does.[80]

Finally, as with most cultural fads and educational theories, they are eventually discarded, replaced, or legislated into oblivion. This process does take some time. Americans are beginning to awaken from the nation's COVID-19 slumber. Let us pray a national awakening occurs sooner, rather than later. In this way, the effects of errant ideas can be minimized and the trajectories of the minds and hearts of children and grandchildren may be redirected.

NOTES

1. Samuel Kronen. "The trouble with critical race theory." *Areo*. September 11, 2020. Retrieved November 3, 2021, from https://areomagazine.com/2020/11/09/the-trouble-with-critical-race-theory/.
2. Jonathan Church. "Ibram Kendi's thesis could use a lot more rigor." *Merion West*. November 7, 2020. Retrieved November 3, 2021, from https://merionwest.com/2020/11/07/ibram-kendis-thesis-could-use-a-lot-more-rigor/.
3. Kevin Narizny. "The flawed foundations of critical race theory." *Lehigh University*. 2020. Retrieved November 3, 2021, from https://www.lehigh.edu/~ken207/.
4. Frank Olito. "Photos show how policing has evolved in the US since its beginnings in the 1600s. *Insider*. April 26, 2021. Retrieved November 3, 2021, from https://www.insider.com/history-of-police-in-the-us-photos-2020-6.
5. Jim Lepore. "The invention of the police." *The New Yorker*. July 20, 2020. Retrieved October 27, 2021, from https://www.newyorker.com/magazine/2020/07/20/the-invention-of-the-police.
6. Dorothy Moses Schulz. "We don't need cops—we have private security." *City Journal*. September 13, 2021. Retrieved October 21, 2021, from https://www.city-journal.org/police-defunding-advocates-spend-big-on-private-security.
7. Jonathan Church. "Ibram Kendi's thesis could use a lot more rigor." *Merion West*. November 7, 2020. Retrieved November 3, 2021, from https://merionwest.com/2020/11/07/ibram-kendis-thesis-could-use-a-lot-more-rigor/.
8. Abigail Tucker. "Are babies born good?" *Smithsonian Magazine*. January 2013. Retrieved November 3, 2021, from https://www.smithsonianmag.com/science-nature/are-babies-born-good-165443013/.
9. Nigel Barber. "The blank slate controversy: How much of our individuality is determined at conception?" *Psychology Today*. September 21, 2016. Retrieved November 3, 2021, from https://www.psychologytoday.com/us/blog/the-human-beast/201609/the-blank-slate-controversy.

10. Eusebius McKaiser. "In South Africa, police violence isn't black and white." *Foreign Policy.* October 21, 2020. Retrieved November 3, 2021, from https://foreignpolicy.com/2020/10/21/in-south-africa-police-violence-isnt-black-and-white/. Cf. Xianan Jin. "How COVID-19 exposed China's anti-Black racism." *Open Democracy.* March 2, 2021. Retrieved November 3, 2021, from https://www.opendemocracy.net/en/pandemic-border/how-covid-19-exposed-chinas-anti-black-racism/. Cf. also, Michelle Nichols. "U.S. and China spar over racism at United Nations." *Reuters.* March 19, 2021. Retrieved November 3, 2021, from https://www.reuters.com/article/us-usa-china-un/u-s-and-china-spar-over-racism-at-united-nations-idUSKBN2BB29E.

11. Ijeoma Oluo. *So You Want to Talk About Race.* New York: Seal Press, 2019, p. 12.

12. Nicholas Shackel. "The vacuity of Postmodernist Methodology." *Metaphilosophy* 36 (April 2005): 295–320. Retrieved October 2, 2021, from https://philpapers.org/archive/SHATVO-2.pdf.

13. Stephen Johnson. "The Motte & Bailey meme reveals what's wrong with political arguments in 2020." *Big Think.* September 4, 2020. Retrieved October 24, 2021, from https://bigthink.com/neuropsych/motte-bailey-meme/#rebelltitem2.

14. Kenin M. Spivak. "The folly of woke math." *National Review.* September 16, 2021. Retrieved September 24, 2021, from https://www.nationalreview.com/2021/09/the-folly-of-woke-math/.

15. Sonia Michele Cintron, Dani Wadlington, Andre ChenFeng, et al. "A pathway to equitable math instruction: Dismantling racism in mathematics instruction." *California Mathematics Project: Stride 1.* November 2, 2020. Retrieved October 27, 2021, from https://equitablemath.org/wp-content/uploads/sites/2/2020/11/1_STRIDE1.pdf.

16. Ibid.

17. Naseeb Bhangal and Oiyan Poon. "Are Asian Americans white? Or people of color?" *Yes Magazine.* January 15, 2020. Retrieved February 17, 2020, from https://www.yesmagazine.org/social-justice/2020/01/15/asian-americans-people-of-color.

18. Eugene Volokh and Robby Soave. "School district decides Asians aren't students of color." *The Volokh Conspiracy.* November 16, 2020. Retrieved October 27, 2021, from https://reason.com/volokh/2020/11/16/school-district-decides-asians-arent-students-of-color/.

19. Vicky Colas. "10 Inspirational BIPOC chefs and restauranteurs share the top things you need to succeed as a chef." *Entrepreneur.* March 11, 2021. Retrieved November 9, 2021, from https://www.entrepreneur.com/slideshow/360566. Cf. Staff. "Comcast supporting BIPOC business owners." *BusinessNH.* May 13, 2021. Retrieved November 9, 2021, from https://www.businessnhmagazine.com/article/comcast-supporting-bipoc-business-owners.

20. Isabel Vincent. "Marxist BLM leader buys $1.4 million home in ritzy enclave." *New York Post.* April 10, 2021. Retrieved May 21, 2021, from https://nypost.com/2021/04/10/marxist-blm-leader-buys-1-4-million-home-in-ritzy-la-enclave/.

21. Rick Rouan. "Fact check: Missing context in claim about Black Lives Matter co-founder's property purchases." *USA Today.* April 26, 2021. Retrieved May 27,

2021, from https://www.usatoday.com/story/news/factcheck/2021/04/19/fact-check-misleading-claim-blm-co-founders-real-estate/7241450002/.

22. David Rutz. "Black Lives Matter co-founder defends ritzy home purchases: I live my life in 'direct support to Black people.'" *Fox News*. April 16, 2021. Retrieved May 27, 2021, from https://www.foxnews.com/media/black-lives-matter-co-founder-responds-to-criticism-of-ritzy-home-purchase.

23. Staff. "Ben Domenech on Bill Barr speech: Critical race theory is public schools pushing religion." *The Federalist*. May 20, 2021. Retrieved May 21, 2021, from https://thefederalist.com/2021/05/20/ben-domenech-on-bill-barr-speech-critical-race-theory-is-public-schools-pushing-religion/.

24. Ibram X. Kendi. *How to be an Antiracist*. New York: One World, Random House, 2019.

25. Martin Luther King, Jr. "I have a Dream." *YouTube*. January 20, 2011 (August 28, 1963). Retrieved June 3, 2021, from https://www.youtube.com/watch?v=1eCYysxNimo.

26. Samantha Harris. "Critical race theory is dangerous. Here's how to fight it." *National Review*. March 13, 2021. Retrieved May 25, 2021, from https://www.nationalreview.com/2021/03/critical-race-theory-is-dangerous-heres-how-to-fight-it/.

27. John McWhorter. "Schools must resist destructive anti-racist demands." *The Atlantic*. January 29, 2021. Retrieved May 24, 2021, from https://www.theatlantic.com/ideas/archive/2021/01/when-antiracist-manifestos-become-antiracist-wrecking-balls/617841/.

28. Niara Savage. "It was just disbelief: Parent files complaint against Atlanta elementary school after learning the principal segregated students based on race." *Atlanta Blackstar*. August 10, 2021. Retrieved August 11, 2021, from https://atlantablackstar.com/2021/08/10/it-was-just-disbelief-parent-files-complaint-against-atlanta-elementary-school-after-learning-the-principal-segregated-students-based-on-race/, Cf. Tom Jones. "Video: Segregation investigation." *WSBTV*. August 8, 2021. Retrieved August 25, 2021, from https://www.wsbtv.com/news/local/parent-files-complaint-against-atlanta-elementary-school-alleges-its-segregating-classes/2PNTBQDPQRCM7CXJTESRXUTMJE/.

29. Savage. "It was just disbelief: Parent files complaint against Atlanta elementary school after learning the principal segregated students based on race." *Atlanta Blackstar*.

30. Ibid.

31. Ibid.

32. Harris. "Critical race theory is dangerous. Here's how to fight it." *National Review*.

33. James Bohman. "Critical theory." *Stanford Encyclopedia of Philosophy*. 2005. Retrieved May 28, 2021, from https://plato.stanford.edu/entries/critical-theory/#6.

34. Ibid.

35. Staff. "Explained: The truth about how critical race theory and how it shows up in your child's classroom." *Education Post*. May 5, 2021. Retrieved October 21. 2021, from https://educationpost.org/explained-the-truth-about-critical-race-theory-and-how-it-shows-up-in-your-childs-classroom/.

36. Rod Dreher. "The CRT Commissars in Public Education." *The American Conservative*. April 12, 2021. Retrieved April 23, 2021, from https://www.theamericanconservative.com/dreher/crt-commissars-public-education-critical-race-theory/.
37. Ibid.
38. Ibid.
39. Andrea N. Smith. "Critical race theory: Disruption in teacher education pedagogy." *Journal of Culture and Values in Education* 3, no. 20 (June 6, 2020): pp. 52–71. Retrieved October 21, 2021, from https://doi.org/10.46303/jcve.03.01.4. Cf. Robert Kim. "What critical race theory is and what it means for teachers?" *Learning for Justice*. August 23, 2021. Retrieved October 21, 2021, from https://www.learningforjustice.org/magazine/what-critical-race-theory-is-and-what-it-means-for-teachers?gclid=CjwKCAjwn8SLBhAyEiwAHNTJbcca1HhUhs-M9i87d7MpK8nmiw0gDOr1Eo7WDQzCi7fsQprxNcRtLxoCHfsQAvD_BwE.
40. Adam Harris. "The Supreme Court justice who forever changed affirmative action." *The Atlantic*. October 13, 2018. Retrieved October 21, 2021, from https://www.theatlantic.com/education/archive/2018/10/how-lewis-powell-changed-affirmative-action/572938/.
41. John Stossel. "Jordan Peterson: The full interview." *YouTube*. November 9, 2021. Retrieved November 10, 2021, from https://www.facebook.com/watch?v=2765775003722755.
42. Ibram X. Kendi. *How to be an Antiracist*. p. 19.
43. Ibid, p. 21.
44. Ibram X. Kendi. *Stamped from the Beginning: The Definitive History of Racist Ideas in America*. New York: Bold Type Books, p. 5.
45. Ibid, p. 6.
46. John McWhorter. "Schools must resist destructive anti-racist demands." *The Atlantic*. January 29, 2021. Retrieved May 21, 2021, from https://www.theatlantic.com/ideas/archive/2021/01/when-antiracist-manifestos-become-antiracist-wrecking-balls/617841/. Cf. Brett Tomlinson. "Faculty members propose an anti-racism agenda." *Princeton Alumni Weekly*. July 13, 2020. Retrieved October 12, 2021, from https://paw.princeton.edu/article/faculty-members-propose-anti-racism-agenda.
47. McWhorter. "Schools must resist destructive anti-racist demands." *The Atlantic*.
48. "Faculty letter to the Administration." *Princeton University*. July 4, 2020. Retrieved May 21, 2021, from https://docs.google.com/forms/d/e/1FAIpQLSfPmfeDKBi25_7rUTKkhZ3cyMICQicp05ReVaeBpEdYUCkyIA/viewform.
49. Ibram X. Kendi. *Be Antiracist: A Journal for Awareness, Reflection, and Action*. New York: One World Publishing, 2020.
50. Ellie Bufkin. "States push back against critical race theory in education." *Sinclair Broadcast Group*. May 6, 2021. Retrieved May 21, 2021, from https://foxbaltimore.com/news/nation-world/states-push-back-against-critical-race-theory-in-education.
51. McWhorter. Schools must resist destructive anti-racist demands." *The Atlantic*.
52. Ibid.

53. "Staff. "Amherst Ending legacy admissions preferences." *Amherst College.* 2021-2022. Retrieved October 21, 2021, from https://www.amherst.edu/. Cf. Scott Jaschik. "The benefit of legacy admissions." *Inside Higher Education.* April 22, 2019. Retrieved October 21, 2021, from https://www.insidehighered.com/admissions/article/2019/04/22/study-shows-significant-impact-legacy-status-admissions-and-applicants.

54. McWhorter. Schools must resist destructive anti-racist demands." *The Atlantic.*

55. Ibid.

56. Philip Montgomery. "Get up, stand up." *Wired.* November 2015. Retrieved November 9, 2021, from https://www.wired.com/2015/10/how-black-lives-matter-uses-social-media-to-fight-the-power/.

57. Emma Mayer. "CRT teaches my daughter her mother is evil: Father gives testimony before school board." *Newsweek.* July 8, 2021. Retrieved July 12, 2021, from https://www.newsweek.com/crt-teaches-my-daughter-her-mother-evil-father-gives-testimony-before-school-board-1607992.

58. Emma Colton. "Loudoun County mom says 6-year-old asked her if she was born evil because she's white." *Fox News.* October 31, 2021. Retrieved October 31, 2021, from https://www.foxnews.com/us/loudoun-county-mom-6-year-old-born-evil-because-white.

59. James Lindsay. "Eight big reasons critical race theory is terrible for dealing with racism." New Discourses. June 12, 2020. Retrieved August 16, 2021, from https://newdiscourses.com/2020/06/reasons-critical-race-theory-terrible-dealing-racism/.

60. Helen Pluckrose and James Lindsay. *Cynical Theories: How Activist Scholarship Made Everything about Race, Gender, and Identity and Why This Harms Everybody.* Durham, NC: Pitchstone Publishing, 2020, p. 115.

61. Sam Dorman. "NYT reporter, in now-deleted tweet, claims there's a difference between being politically black and racially black." *Fox News.* May 23, 2020. Retrieved November 3, 2021, from https://www.foxnews.com/media/nikole-hannah-jones-politically-racially-black.

62. Peter Wood. "Keeping the republic." *National Association of Scholars.* May 17, 2021. Retrieved May 19, 2021, from https://www.nas.org/blogs/article/keeping-the-republic.

63. Ibid.

64. Ibid.

65. John McWhorter. "Antiracism, our flawed new religion." *Daily Beast.* April 14, 2017. Retrieved September 30, 2021, from https://www.thedailybeast.com/antiracism-our-flawed-new-religion. Cf. Ernest J. Zarra, III. *When the secular becomes sacred: Religious secular humanism and its effects upon America's public learning institutions.* 2021. Lanham, Maryland: Rowman & Littlefield Publishers, pp. 22, 81–83.

66. Carol M. Swain and Christopher J. Schorr. *Black Eye for America: How Critical Race Theory Is Burning Down the House.* Rockville, MD: Be the People Books, 2021, p. 44.

67. Garrett Kell. "Damn the curse of Ham: How Genesis 9 got twisted into racist propaganda." *The Gospel Coalition.* January 9, 2021. Retrieved September 30, 2021, from https://www.thegospelcoalition.org/article/damn-curse-ham/.

68. Paris Amanda Spies-Gans. "James Madison." *Princeton & Slavery*. 2021. Retrieved September 9, 2021, from https://slavery.princeton.edu/stories/james-madison#anchor-author. Cf. Swain and Schorr. *Black Eye for America,* pp. 44–45.

69. Ryan Mills. "Parents find new allies in fight against racial indoctrination in schools." *National Review*. May 21, 2021. Retrieved June 15, 2021, from https://www.nationalreview.com/news/parents-in-fight-against-racial-indoctrination-in-schools/.

70. Glen C. Loury. "Why does racial inequality persist? Culture, causation, and responsibility." *Manhattan Institute*. May 7, 2019. Retrieved July 7, 2021, from https://www.manhattan-institute.org/why-does-racial-inequality-persist. Cf. Joel Kotkin and Edward Heyman. "Critical race theory ignores anti-Semitism." *UnHerd*. August 9, 2021. Retrieved August 10, 2021, from https://unherd.com/2021/08/critical-race-theory-rewrites-history/.

71. Bari Weiss. "Wrongthink on race with Glenn C. Loury." *Substack*. September 29, 2021. Retrieved September 30, 2021, from https://bariweiss.substack.com/p/wrongthink-on-race-with-glenn-c-loury.

72. Luke Rosiak. "Here are the thousands of teachers who say they're willing to violate law to keep pushing CRT." *Daily Wire*. June 23, 2021. Retrieved August 8, 2021, from https://www.dailywire.com/news/here-are-the-thousands-of-teachers-who-say-theyre-willing-to-violate-law-to-keep-pushing-crt. Cf. Kiara Alfonseca. "Teachers protest bills targeting critical race theory, race education." *ABC News*. August 26, 2021. Retrieved August 26, 2021, from https://abcnews.go.com/US/teachers-protest-bills-targeting-critical-race-theory-race/story?id=79642784.

73. Luke Rosiak. "Here are the thousands of teachers who say they're willing to violate law to keep pushing CRT." *Daily Wire*.

74. Ibid.

75. Ibid.

76. Pluckrose and Lindsay. *Cynical Theories*. p. 121.

77. Ibid.

78. Percy Deift, Svetlana Jitomirskaya, and Sergiu Klainerman. "As US schools prioritize diversity over merit, China is becoming the world's STEM leader." *Quillette*. August 19, 2021. Retrieved August 20, 2021, from https://quillette.com/2021/08/19/as-us-schools-prioritize-diversity-over-merit-china-is-becoming-the-worlds-stem-leader/.

79. Ibid.

80. Pluckrose and Lindsay. *Cynical Theories*, pp. 258–259.

Chapter 6

Communities Fighting Back

> If more judges view equity as the perverse discrimination it really is, then critical race theory will indeed have its day in court. And it will be exposed for the sham that it is.[1]
>
> —Professor William Jacobson,
> Cornell Law School

> Schools across the country are working to address systemic racism and inject an anti-racist mind-set into campus life. But where advocates see racial progress, opponents see an effort to shame White teachers and sometimes students for being part of an oppressive system.[2]

The main idea "behind CRT and antiracism is the acceptance of a worldview that encompasses specific notions about history, philosophy, sociology, and public policy."[3] Standing up against CRT brings some hateful rhetoric, as exemplified by Eric Hananoki. The group, *No Left Turn in Education* addresses this rhetoric. They write:

> Hananoki has become one of the leading groups' fearmongering about the teaching of critical race theory in schools. The group and its founder Elana Yaron Fishbein have frequently used toxic and bigoted rhetoric on social media and in right-wing media, including comparing the efforts of educators to that of Pol Pot, Vladimir Lenin, and Adolf Hitler; claiming that black bigotry toward whites is a very real problem.[4]

Since when is criticism hateful, and language considered as violence? Is America at the point in history where speech that is critical of another person, his or her viewpoints or policies, now considered violent? Unfortunately, the answer is affirmative. The political left in America has been doing this for years, and it is more acute during election cycles.[5] Be that as it may, now that a groundswell of parent groups are speaking out on behalf of their children, there is a heightened sense of awareness of the tactics used to shutter dissent. All one has to do is review the 2021 election result for governor of Virginia to see the impact parents can have when they unite.

The US Congressman Burgess Owens understands the struggle. He addresses the dismissal of parents by school board leaders and other elected officials, in a recent *New York Post* article. Owens, who is black, writes "Parents' passionate concerns and debate regarding the divisive practices of CRT, school safety and other education decisions that directly impact their children should be encouraged and supported, not attacked and disregarded."[6]

In terms of CRT, in general, Owens finds

> it divisive, racist, destructive, and anti-American. It violates equal protection under the law, fundamentally diminishes the accomplishments of the Civil Rights movement, and perpetuates policies of discrimination based on race. It seeks to portray our country not as a beacon of freedom and opportunity but as a nation of victimized groups based on sex, race, ethnicity, and national origin. And in our classrooms, it teaches our youngest learners to view American history through a lens of hatred and oppression.[7]

Whoever has the power in politics seems to inflate the actions of opponents by injecting hyperbole. This definitely describes parents from both ends of the political spectrum, as well as concerned educators who have expressed more than a little disdain for their local school boards, in recent days.[8] Many districts are finding parents taking actions to unseat board members[9] who are liberals and desire to move forward with CRT agenda. Also under scrutiny is the advance of the LGBTQ+ narratives about gender and sex.[10]

Former CNN news anchor Chris Cuomo recently expressed his support of what he referred to as peaceful protests by BLM. The CNN anchor, upon reporting on some of the violence during the protests in the streets of major US cities, questioned, "Who says protests are supposed to be polite and peaceful?"[11] The answer for Cuomo, and others, is the First Amendment. That being said, one wonders whether Cuomo would be supportive of the many angry parents expressing themselves to their local school boards, or whether that kind of protest is deemed as domestic terrorism.[12]

While drafting this chapter, the National School Boards Association (NSBA) apologized for the language used in a statement to the Executive Branch about boisterous parents as potential threats to school board members. After working in conjunction with the Biden administration on the letter, the NSBA retracted some of the accusations in the letter in just five days after it was published online. In addition to vitriolic verbiage, the letter called for the FBI to investigate activist parents. The letter was entered into the *Congressional Record*, and afterward the heavy-handed approach against parents backfired.

The NSBA claims that it now regrets its hyperbole and issued apologies for the language in the original letter. Even as several states, including South Carolina, Montana, New Hampshire, Missouri, Louisiana, Pennsylvania, and Ohio state school board associations voted to leave the NBSA over the heavy-handedness of the national organization,[13] no one at the national level has backtracked on their beliefs that parents are a rising danger at school board meetings.

The debate is raging over CRT and parents are noticing a radical shift in the direction of their children's education. In the middle of this, what could be more toxic than labeling children and adults of all of one race as racists? Elana Yaron Fishbein is deeply bothered by the shift in her child's schooling was particularly outraged by the material stemming from the *Cultural Proficiency Committee* that "imposed a lesson plan to indoctrinate the children into the woke culture, using reprehensible resources designed to inoculate Caucasian children with feelings of guilt for the color of their skin and the *sins* of their forefathers."[14] This hate is already showing up in classrooms. Fishbein goes on to say, "Whatever the school's intentions are, this proficiency program threatens to unleash hate upon white children."[15]

THE AMERICAN PEOPLE ARE SLOW TO ENGAGE

Peter Wood relates, radical activists

> now confront America with . . . radical critiques of who we are as a nation, accompanied by equally radical proposals to remake our basic institutions. These critiques are false. America is exceptional not least because of its long traditions of antislavery, abolition, and dedication to civic equality that transcends race.[16]

Americans are beginning to understand the urgency of the mission to get involved and the importance of the battle against race-based education. However, they are often a few steps behind in their responses. Playing catch-up is not easy. There is now, nationally, a growing level of reluctance by parents of all races and ethnicities, to release their children to the public, government schools for an average of seven hours per day. The numbers are clear.

> Parents oppose critical race theory in the public school curriculum by a massive 42-point margin, and a strong majority of black and Hispanic parents oppose critical race theory and support removing concepts such as white privilege and systemic racism from the curriculum . . . most parents, including minorities, oppose critical race theory.[17]

Children do not need to become activists.
Still, the mission of radical activists is

> to transform . . . all of American society. Their proposals to accomplish this are sweeping. They include a call to establish *equity* that requires a quasi-totalitarian imposition of job quotas and the suppression of all opposing speech. . . . They require a transformation of our schools from places that teach students to seek out truth to places that teach students to seek out power so as to revolutionize America.[18]

Parents in communities across the nation have begun expressing shock and dismay at what their children were being exposed to online and in person. In order for the radical transformation to occur, the children must be indoctrinated to the cause.

As Sawchuk points out in his *EdWeek* article titled, "What Is Critical Race Theory, and Why Is it under Attack," most Americans simply do not know much about CRT, while others are assigning to it outlandish assumptions reacting emotionally, based on what little they know. Sawchuk explains the core idea of CRT: "The core idea is that racism is a social construct, and that it is not merely the product of individual bias or prejudice, but something embedded in legal systems and policies."[19] Typical of many who would deflect from the ongoing battles in education, Sawchuk places CRT into a category that comes across as beyond the concerns of most parents. However, this is somewhat deceptive and not consistent with a proper understanding of the evolution of CRT and its presence in culture. For more information on this, and other inconsistencies, refer to chapter 4.

Racism, according to Sawchuk, is embedded in all American institutions, including families. If this is the case, then it is therefore logical to conclude that if people live in a socially constructed racist society, then they are members of that society as well. As a result, any person can then participate in the practice of racism and not be aware of this practice.

CRT proponents allude to this, by the statement, *people are not aware until they are woke to the fact that they are aware*. This is confirmed by Sawchuk's statement: "The theory says that racism is part of everyday life, so people—White or non-White—who don't intend to be racist can nevertheless make choices that fuel racism."[20] In other words, people just cannot help but be racists. And why is this the case? The answer is because they are racists. The battle for the minds and hearts of students is real and it is escalating.

PARENTS AND THE CRT BATTLE

As the reader by now has realized, CRT is embedded in public school policies and practices. It is found in curriculum frameworks and in state standards, including recent additions to some preschool programs.[21] CRT has also arrived at the point of educational delivery, which equates to what teachers present and require of students each day in classes. For example, in Herriman, Utah, students were required to fill out a privilege checklist, by way of a football field grid, in order to gauge their white privilege.

In another example, in the Clover Park School District in Lakewood, Washington, students were given the exercise to examine the diversity in their lives. This was done by the use of white and multicolor beads. The assignment included the caveat, *the white beads are not bad, and they are just beads*.

CRT has caused uproars at school board meetings and resulted in the federal government's attention.[22] As a result of content and activities such as these, CRT now has a major opponent in millions of parents.[23] The fear by some is that there will be great political fallout in the next election cycle because of the inroads made by social activists and politicians who support indoctrinating children.

CRT Makes Inroads

CRT has made serious inroads into K-12 public schools. Manhattan fellow Rufo shares:

> By high school, the basic education about *skin color* and *justice fighters* turns into advanced race theory and live-action street protesting. At Lincoln High, a wealthy public school with only 1 percent Black student enrollment, some students take two full years of *critical race studies*. The courses, taught by Jessica Mallare-Best, begin with training on racial identity, White supremacy, institutional racism, and racial empowerment, with the goal of providing *methods in which students can begin to be activists and allies for change*. The following year, students take two semesters of critical race theory—studying White fragility, intersectionality, *Whiteness as property*, *the permanence of racism*, *collective organizing*, and *being an activist*, with an eye toward training them to *do [their] part in dismantling White supremacy*. The abstract becomes concrete,

theory is transformed into action, and the young people of Portland come of age steeped in race analysis and revolutionary logic.[24]

Based on Rufo's analysis, no one should be surprised that problems arise when schools (1) indoctrinate children, (2) provide for them avenues in which to express activism, and (3) require their activities as credit for graduation.[25] When students are *molded* and then *emboldened*, is there any mystery as to why teenagers and young adults feel empowered and hit the streets of cities like Portland to cause mayhem?

Race has become the tantamount focal point in American education.[26] Authors and critical race theorists Delgado and Stefancic explain the phenomenon facing parents:

> Critical race theory is no longer new, but it continues to grow and thrive. . . . Critical race theory has exploded from a narrow subspecialty of jurisprudence chiefly of interest to academic lawyers into a literature read in departments of education, cultural studies, English, sociology, comparative literature, political science, history, and anthropology around the country. . . . During the past decade, critical race theory has splintered [into] new subgroups, which include a well-developed Asian American Jurisprudence, a forceful Latino-critical (LatCrit) contingent, and a feisty queer-crit interest group.[27]

Those who claim CRT is still only found in jurisprudential studies in law schools have not kept pace with current trends. Either that or there is a politically motivated widespread narrative released to distract attention from it. The reality is CRT "not only dares to treat race as central to the law and policy of the United States, it dares to look beyond the popular belief that getting rid of racism means simply getting rid of ignorance, or encouraging everyone to get along."[28] The reason is because the CRT movement "is a collection of activists and scholars interested in studying and transforming the relationship among race, racism, and power."[29]

The following sections illustrate select ongoing battles between parents and public schools. These examples can serve as exemplars to the extent that other states are dealing with the parents' fallout over CRT as well. The states included in the examples are Washington, North Carolina, and Oregon. For a complete and comprehensive list of states' legislative decisions pertaining to CRT, at the time of this writing, see appendix A.

The Battle over CRT in Washington State

Examples of how CRT has grown beyond higher education academe are replete. The first example is Seattle, Washington. Seattle's K-12, 2019

Math Ethnic Studies Framework includes examples of *Origins, Identity, and Agency*, *Power and Oppression*, and *History of Resistance and Liberation*. The framework also includes a section on *Reflection and Action*, as part of what their students were intended to know and required to actively demonstrate as knowledge by the time they graduate high school. The ethnic studies in mathematics is just part of the overall ethnic studies set of curricular frameworks, which have been added since 2017.[30]

In another example from the same framework, pertaining specifically to *Origins, Identity, and Agency* for ethnic studies in mathematics, the framework states: "Ethnic studies is [*sic*] the ways in which we view ourselves as mathematicians and members of broader mathematical communities. Mathematical theory and application is [*sic*] rooted in the ancient histories of people and empires of color."[31] Students are asked to question their own "mathematical identity,"[32] as if there is such a thing.

The K-12 Seattle Framework also includes definitions of the themes relating to *Power and Oppression*, as well as *Learning Targets* for K-12.

> Power and oppression, as defined by ethnic studies, as the ways in which individuals and groups define mathematical knowledge so as to see *Western* mathematics as the only legitimate expression of mathematical identity and intelligence. This definition of *legitimacy is then used to disenfranchise* people and communities of color. This *erases the historical contributions* of people and communities of color.[33]

Today's race activists in Washington, and elsewhere,

> decry the habits often associated with success as reflections of *whiteness*. Some even denounce habits such as punctuality, rationality and hard work as reflective of *racism* and white *privilege*. Mathematics and science have also been dismissed for being reflective of racism and white privilege.[34]

What follows are examples of the Seattle Public Schools' *Learning Targets* established in the framework for the K-12 students. These examples are not isolated incidents to Seattle. Rather, these are typical of what is taking place in other cities in Washington and other states in America.

Washington State K-12 Learning Targets. The *Learning Targets* for the K-12 students are prefaced with what students should be able to know or to do (SWBAT).[35] Therefore each SWBAT:

- "Identify how math has been and continues to be used to oppress and marginalize people of color."

- "Explain how math and technology and/or science are connected and how technology and/or science have been and continue to be used to oppress and marginalize people and communities of color."
- "Critique systems of power that deny access to mathematical knowledge to people and communities of color."
- "Identify the inherent inequities of the standardized testing system used to oppress and marginalize people and communities of color."
- "Explain how math has been used to exploit natural resources."
- "Explain how math dictates economic oppression."

The framework then takes students on a deep dive into mathematics experiences where students are encouraged to identify where mathematics oppresses people of color.[36] Students do this by questioning the following:

- "Who holds power in a mathematical classroom?"
- "Is there a place for power and authority in the math classroom?"
- "Who gets to say if an answer is right?"
- "What is the process for verifying the truth?"
- "Who is Smart? Who is not Smart?"
- "Can you recognize and name oppressive mathematical practices in your experience?"
- "Why/how do data-driven processes prevent liberation?"

The framework then asks the student to identify how math is manipulated to allow inequality and oppression to persist. This section does not only pertain to mathematics, it also bleeds into social justice.[37] For example, students are instructed to consider the following:

- "Who is doing the oppressing?"
- "Who does the oppression protect? Who does this oppression harm?"
- "Where is there opportunity to examine systemic oppression?"
- "How can math help us understand the impact of economic conditions and systems that contribute to poverty and slave labor?"
- "How does math contribute to how we value natural resources?"

After these series of questions, the framework then asks students to be able to suggest resolutions to oppressive mathematical practices. The framework asks, "How can we change mathematics from individualistic to collectivist thinking? How can we reframe our views of people/communities of color in mathematics?"[38] After solutions are explored, students are then challenged to consider how mathematics allows people "to acquire intellectual freedom."[39] This is accomplished as students "reflect on whether they can become advocates against oppressive mathematical practices,"[40] and "How can . . . stories be valued as data points to impact change."[41] Consider that through all of this exploration, students have not been asked to solve mathematics equations, or apply logical, mathematical thinking about real-world problems.

The Battle over CRT in North Carolina

The Fairness and Accountability in the Classroom for Teachers and Students task force, formed by Lt. Gov. Mark Robinson, "found 506 examples of political bias and teachings associated with critical race theory in school. These examples were submitted by teachers, students, and parents who said they witnessed bias in their local school systems through an online portal."[42] A detailed summary of the report was issued and found "incidents of bias that fell into six key categories: fear of retaliation, sexualization of children, critical race theory, white-shaming, biased news media or lessons plans, and the shaming of certain political beliefs."[43] This came as quite a surprise to many North Carolinians.

The report also included several examples of incidents that occurred on school campuses. For example, one school employee stated the school's "teacher of the year had *Black Lives Matter* decorations on her door and once wore a shirt that read *Blue Lives Murder*."[44] After the initial report, the 766-page document was presented to the North Carolina State Senate, where several of the reported incidents were read aloud. After reading several incidents aloud, state Senate leader Phil Berger proclaimed, "Don't tell me this doctrine [CRT] doesn't exist. Don't tell me that all these teachers and parents are just making this stuff up."[45]

The report was then passed on to North Carolina's Senate Education/Higher Education Standing Committee, where the chamber acted on and passed the lower house's *Ensuring Dignity and Nondiscrimination in Schools Act*. This act specifically

> prohibits the teachings of certain concepts, including critical race theory, which (along with other closely related ideologies) holds that America is inherently racist and that skin color is used to create and maintain social, economic, and political inequalities between white and nonwhite people.[46]

Recently, North Carolina's

> seventh-largest school system . . . adopted stricter new rules on how teachers can talk about race and history in their classrooms. The Johnston County school board approved revisions to the code of ethics policy . . . that say teachers could be disciplined or fired if they teach that American historical figures weren't

heroes, undermine the U.S. Constitution in lessons or say that racism is a permanent part of American life.[47]

Furthermore, "Instructional staff and other school system employees will not utilize methods or materials that would create division or promote animosity among students, staff and the community."[48]

The Battle over CRT in Oregon

The Oregon State Department of Education is promoting an optional course for its mathematics teachers. The course titled "A pathway to equitable math instruction: Dismantling racism in mathematics instruction . . . likens modern math instruction to the toxic characteristics of white supremacist culture."[49] The math course includes areas such as "white supremacy culture in math classrooms . . . reinforces the idea that there is only one right way to do math"[50] and exhorts teachers to "identify and challenge the ways that math is used to uphold capitalist, imperialist, and racist views."[51]

CRT appears in red and blue states. CRT is in private as well as public schools. This is in parochial schools and Christian schools.[52] "This is everywhere,"[53] according to Nicki Neily, a parent who observes the changes in education in her home state of Illinois. For an example of this author's conversation about CRT with Christian colleges, see appendix B.

POLICY AND LEGAL BATTLES

Nationally, there are policy and legal battles taking place between local school board members and their constituents over CRT. Parents are rising up to rally, protest, and speak their minds about what they perceive as racial indoctrination, under the guise of CRT. However, what many are now coming to realize is that CRT is not merely an acronym. Additional concerns are arising now that CRT has evolved additional terms and concepts. Groups like BLM understand the value of language and how adopting new terms helps to shape what people hear and believe. Language matters and constructed narratives are helpful in misleading people.

For example, many Americans are now waking up to the differences between the terms *equality* and *equity*. The advocates of racial indoctrination often resort to bait and switch tactics, which causes confusion among the general population. Another example of misleading the public is the claim made by proponents that concerns over CRT are just a "manufactured battle"[54] by critics and ignorant parents.

In case anyone thought that CRT, history, and antiracism activism were isolated to higher education in academe, Kendi's book *Stamped from the Beginning* has been rebranded by Jason Reynolds and published as a book for adolescents. The title for adolescents is *Stamped: Racism, Antiracism and You*.[55]

Sonja Cherry-Paul has done the same, but only for a much younger audience, with the book *Stamped for Kids*.[56] The claim is that all of Kendi's books are history and have nothing to do with CRT is untrue. Projects such as *Stamped* and the *1619 Project* are coming under increased scrutiny, and even getting banned.[57] This is occurring especially because the history begins and ends with whites being racists and that racism has always been a part of America. Such assertions are assumptions to justify a theory and amount to far less than historical analysis.[58] Nevertheless, a certain segment of the American populace has accepted Kendi's work and the work of other CRTs and antiracists as true.

Professor William Jacobson, of Cornell Law School, responded to attacks thrown at him for supporting Martin Luther King, King's call for character, and renewing the call for equality under the law. His opponents attacked him because they were seeking judicial decisions to guarantee equity and his support would have been helpful to that end.

In turning the tables, Jacobson's response to the attacks included the vindicating words, "Those of us attacked for speaking out for equality without regard for skin color will be vindicated, and those demanding race-based outcomes will be shamed."[59] Jacobson's declaration has become America's quandary. Swain and Schorr view the battle over CRT as one that necessarily involves policy. "Policy is where CRT can inflict the most damage, and so it is where we must concentrate much of our resistance efforts."[60]

Over time, public school teachers unions "confirmed, despite all the protestations otherwise, what parents already know,"[61] (and that) CRT has been embedded inside

> compelled professional training for teachers and classroom practice across the country. . . . These unions are not alone, as 5,000 teachers pledged to continue teaching CRT . . . they not only know that CRT is in the schools, they embrace it. In fact, they have participated in purging and rewriting curriculum for years.[62]

For an example of a state and local battle over CRT, which includes a teachers association, refer appendix C.

The Battles Escalate

McKinney School District in Texas has canceled a social studies academic elective because of a new law passed during 2021, banning "political activism and policy advocacy. . . . The new law also restricts classroom discussions on current events and bans teaching that anyone should feel discomfort or guilt about their race."[63] However, a club was formed out of interest in the elective course titled Youth and Government and was left unaffected.[64]

Noteworthy groups that have formed to fight the spread of CRT and its evolution include *Parents Defending Education*, the *Foundation Against Intolerance & Racism* (FAIR), *No Left Turn in Education, American Enterprise Institute, Heritage Foundation, Manhattan Institute*, the *Woodson Center, Hillsdale College*, and others.[65] The founder of *No Left Turn in Education*, Elana Yaron Fishbein, recently stated the rally-cry from members of these groups: "The schools have been hijacked. . . . Our kids are captive audiences. And they think that can do whatever they want with our kids."[66] One of the strategies of *Parents Defending Education* includes teaching parents

> how to become activists . . . but the group is also playing an active role. It has filed civil rights complaints against schools in Massachusetts for creating an affinity space for students of color after a string of attacks on Asians, and against districts in Minnesota, Missouri, and Ohio where administrators pledged to dismantle racism in schools.[67]

Recently, lawmakers in nearly two dozen states have introduced or enacted "legislation banning public schools from promoting critical race theory's core concepts, including race essentialism, collective guilt and racial superiority."[68] As of late 2021, "Activists and parents . . . launched 50 recall efforts . . . aimed at unseating 126 school board members. . . . And in a new development . . . rather than targeting a single member, these efforts often target multiple members or entire school boards."[69] On a frightening note, "Elementary school teachers, administrators and college professors are facing fines, physical threats, and fear of firing because of an organized push from the right to remove discussions of systemic racism."[70]

Activists and scholars are joining ranks to fight back against CRT policy. Swain and Schorr provide a list of excellent proposals for parents and teachers to resist CRT. Some of these proposals include the organization of grassroots efforts to affect local school board elections to the building of coalitions that reach all demographics concerned about CRT, to educating church leaders, and taking stands against big technology corporations that push agenda upon the American public. Refer to Appendix A, in *Black Eye for America.*

One organization that has been created by Carol Swain is *Unity Training Solutions*, whose goal is to unite "diverse people who seek harmony and are willing to commit themselves to work on common goals and common visions for their institutions."[71] Parents are taking heed and becoming more proactive.

PARENTS BECOMING PROACTIVE

Some California parents complained at a 2020 local Orange County Education Forum, where a panel was assembled to address local concerns about CRT being taught in their schools. One of the major concerns explicitly voiced by some parent attendees was their awareness that

> critical race theory teaches white children that they are oppressors and Black and Latino kids that they are perpetual victims. They have a point. Some badly fashioned curricula based on critical race theory separate and isolate groups, and imply that white students should feel guilty.[72]

The singling out of one race over others is a very risky and, to many, a mark of racism in-and-of-itself.

What most parents desire for their children is that they "learn facts rather than be indoctrinated into taking one side or another"[73] on racial issues. What this struggle demonstrated was that people disagreed with their opponents' sets of facts and lamented that those in power get to determine their own facts. What was clear from the meeting was that

> racism isn't an occasional aberration of individuals acting in biased or hateful ways, but entire systems that have built up over this nation's history that put people of color at a perpetual disadvantage and that will take purposeful action to remedy.[74]

The panel brought up inequities in culture and society. They addressed low-achieving black students and, rather than describe the lack of achievement on anything within the family structure, or choices made, the system in America is what failed these children. Low achievement for people of color, whether in schools or in the competitive economic sphere, is the result of a history of frameworks that put those groups at a disadvantage.

White people "get professional jobs that lift their incomes, then help their friends get hired at the same places—friends who are usually white. That's not intentional, hateful racism, but it is a system that acts in a racist way, day after day, across the country."[75] Critical race theorists believe that "students spend most of their schooling seeing . . . issues through the eyes of white people who had the power to create the institutions and tell most of the stories."[76]

To this end, "Students should be researching the very rich, though disturbing topic of this nation's racial history, learning both sides of controversial topics and debating those with others as they learn to reach informed and independent opinions."[77] This sounds reasonable, yet it is rejected as an objective approach, which proponents of CRT consider as evidence of white supremacists. The idea that there is an exclusive and objective approach, at a time when any and all answers to problems should be acceptable, is to recognize whiteness. In so doing, the neglect of acceptance and understanding of what is known as cultural "Black knowledge"[78] must be purposeful by whites and is the result of racism against blacks.

All of the back-and-forth about the problems associated with race and social justice have done little to reduce the concerns that students face academically. Skin color, social-emotional learning, and all of the talk of privilege and bias are falling on deaf ears, as American students fall farther and farther behind. The 2021 reading and mathematics scores indicated "more students are two or more grade levels below their actual grade level . . . than before the pandemic began."[79] This is according to "Curriculum Associates' November Understanding Student Learning report, which analyzed 3 million students' fall 2021 . . . scores against averages from 2017-19."[80]

States Getting Involved

States are fighting back against what they see as an onslaught of race-based academics, meant to capture a generation of children to their cause. To date, nearly two dozen states have either banned the teaching of CRT in their schools or are in the process of moving legislation to ban it.[81] For example, one school board in California blocked CRT districtwide, "banning what the board defined as fatally flawed ideology based on false assumptions about the United States."[82]

The Paso Robles Joint Unified School District (PRJUSD) passed a resolution prohibiting the teaching of CRT by a contentious 4-3 vote.[83] Table 6.1 includes select sample statements and restrictions placed on CRT and race-based education by the PRJUSD.

CRT is no longer just in schools. Swain and Schoor explain,

> Critical Race Theory now permeates our churches, military, and intelligence agencies, as well as our institutions of higher learning and even K-12. It needs to be stopped in its tracks by knowledgeable people imbued with courage and the lofty principles that made America the envy of the free world.[84]

Chris Arend, the school board president of PRJUSD, called CRT as "absolutely disgustingly racist ideology . . . developed with the intention of really driving a wedge between various groups in America, various ethnic groups, and to sue that to absolutely ruin our nation."[85] Evidence of this manifested itself when BLM flags were seen hanging in classrooms during the pandemic's virtual learning sessions, and with one middle school teacher, in particular, telling students "that the United States is a racist nation."[86]

Table 6.1 CRT and the Paso Robles Joint Unified School District 2021–2022 Resolution

Why CRT Is Not to be Taught in the PRJUSD	*Premises and Doctrinal Tenets That Cannot be Taught in the PRJUSD*
• CRT is an ideology based on false assumptions. • CRT involves a flawed, artificial distortion of the traditional definitions of racism. • CRT is divisive and assigns moral fault to individuals solely based on race and is therefore racist. • CRT assigns generational guilt and racial guilt for conduct and policies long in the past. • CRT is not required to be taught in the state of California. • CRT is rejected and will not constitute the basis for any instruction in the PRJUSD.	• Racism is racial prejudice plus power, a concept that is often used to argue (1) only individuals classified as white people can be racist because only white people control society and (2) individuals in ethnic minorities cannot be racist because they do not control society. • Racism is ordinary, the usual way society does business. • *Interest convergence* of *material determinism,* according to which the incentive to move away from racist policies depends primarily on the self-interest of the oppressor class, that is, whites. • An individual, by virtue of his or her race or sex, is inherently racist and/or sexist, whether consciously or unconsciously. • Individuals are either a member of the oppressor class or the oppressed class because of race or sex. • An individual is inherently morally or otherwise superior to another individual because of race or sex. • An individual should be discriminated against or receive adverse treatment due to the individual's race or sex, or an individual should receive favorable treatment due to the individual's race or sex. • An individual by virtue of his or her race or sex bears responsibility for actions committed in the past or present by other members of the same race or sex. • An individual should feel discomfort, guilt, anguish, or any other form of psychological distress on account of his or her race or sex. • Meritocracy or traits such as, but not limited to, a hard work ethic or the scientific method is racist or sexist or were created by members of a particular race to oppress members of another race. • The advent of slavery in the territory that is now the United States constituted the true founding of the United States, or the preservation of slavery was a material motive for independence from England.

Sources

- Paso Robles Joint Unified School District Board President. "Resolution 21-27: Prohibiting the teachings of Critical Race Theory." *Paso Robles Joint Unified School District.* June 17, 2021. Retrieved July 5, 2021, from https://agendaonline.net/public/Meeting/Attachments/DisplayAttachment.aspx?AttachmentID=1320720&IsArchive=0.
- Camille DeVaul. "PRJUSD votes to prohibit the teaching of critical race theory." The Paso Robles Press. August 11, 2021. Retrieved August 25, 2021, from https://pasoroblespress.com/news/education/prjusd-votes-to-prohibit-the-teaching-of-critical-race-theory/.

The Colorado Springs School District #49 school board voted to keep CRT from being part of its school instruction. But banning CRT does not mean it has banned all the ancillary programs that incorporate principles of race theory. A district can be in compliance but still allow all elements of the theory to seep in through supplemental materials.[87]

Two of the members of the Colorado Springs school board, Ivy Liu and Rick Van Wieren, went on record and stated although "educators should certainly teach about race and racism, they should not deliberately undermine family values, faith, or other principles."[88] Any policy or law that undercuts the family should be abolished. The state of Kentucky followed suit in tossing a controversial curriculum that included sexual content, suicide, and various racial content that referred to "Mexican kids in cages [and] angry White faces."[89] These concerns arose as students were using the Great Minds English-Language Arts *Wit and Wisdom* curriculum.[90]

CRT and Private Schools

The *woke* CRT schools are not just public schools. An increasing number of private schools are adopting CRT principles, supporting racial rhetoric, and being accused of indoctrinating students. A recent campaign mounted in New York City by parents targeted "multiple schools like Dalton, Grace Church, and others, which have caught headlines for pushing various ideas about race and identity."[91] At present, CRT is taught at nearly every one of the top fifty private schools in the nation.[92] CRT and antiracism are embedded in educational philosophies and curriculum and children are being indoctrinated—the results of which will appear problematic within the next decade.

As a measure of protest, signs were attached to vehicles and parked outside several schools, including Trinity and Brearley. These signs read *Diversity not Indoctrination*, *Teach How to think, Not What to Think*, and *Woke school? Speak out.*[93] An anonymous group of parents were responsible for the sign campaign and various other actions to combat what they saw as a "new orthodoxy . . . dividing communities based on immutable characteristics such as race, ethnic, gender, and sexual orientation."[94] The campaign seemed to cause incremental changes in the schools' practices.

Parent Efforts Make a Difference

The makeup of a school board is critical. When parents in the community have problems with their local school board, they have recourse to redress their grievances. These grievances are often limited to a short amount of time, during public comments, depending on the number of speakers on the agenda. In preparing for a presentation to a school board, Corey Lynn offers sage advice,

> When giving your 3-5 minute speech, don't let the school board interrupt you, shut you down, tell you to talk nicer or leave teachers' names out. You have a right to express yourself as you see fit, under the Constitution . . . if you have any supporting documents, bring those . . . and provide copies to the board members.[95]

However, a word of caution for parents. NSBA gained the ear of the Biden administration and the Department of Justice and petitioned for unruly parents to be considered as potential violent threats. Although they apologized in writing for the letter and language used, most parents who are against race-based curriculum are aware that threats by the school boards association and the Biden administration are not finished. Currently, names of potential threatening parents are being accumulated by the Department of Justice, even after apologies were offered by the NSBA.

An excerpt of the letter in question to the Biden administration, which apparently is the motivation for accumulating a list, reads in part,

> America's public schools and its education leaders are under an immediate threat. The NSBA respectfully asks for federal law enforcement and other assistance to deal with the growing number of threats of violence and acts of intimidation occurring across the nation.[96]

There is the perception that law enforcement is beginning to treat vocal parents and community dissenters as threats and *potentially* violent. In Virginia, on more than one occasion, people were escorted by force out of school board meetings and arrested, for the way they spoke to the board.[97] At the time of this writing, several parents had been arrested for violating board meeting protocols and demonstrating their frustration emotionally. These parents had been arrested for disorderly conduct and for expressing anger toward the school board members they elected.[98] In Loudon County, Virginia, the district has been accused by teachers and parents of creating a very hostile environment.[99]

What are parents to do? Those that can, either homeschool or take their children out of public schools and place them in private schools. Parents sensing a hopeless mission are resorting to another strategy. "From . . . April 2020 to the first week of October 2020, families pulling their children out of public schools to homeschool, more than doubled, which sits at nearly four times the overall average."[100] This represents "an increase of 2.5 million K-12 students being homeschooled in 2019, to 4.5-5.0 million by March 2021."[101]

So, for parents who either chose to keep their children in public schools or must keep them in these schools, fighting back against the concerns and indoctrination that present themselves through CRT, there should be a plan devised. Following are eight suggested steps that have been tried and proven to be effective. These are mere starting points and so much more could be suggested.

EIGHT STEPS FOR PARENT AWARENESS

First, parents must show up and speak up. Research issues thoroughly and become well-informed about CRT from origin to recent changes. Second, parents should form a group that can unite around their common cause. This cause should always have as its focus what is best for children and families in the district. Do not allow a few loud voices to command attention. Most Americans do not favor indoctrination of children and the belittling of students by race. Third, parents should attend board meetings to respectfully, lawfully, and peaceably protest.

Fourth, there should be parent-established and parent-led curriculum committees to review all curricula being used by teachers and not just the district-approved programs. Such a committee might relieve good teachers of the feeling they might have to resign, rather than teach racist materials.[102] Fifth, parents must be aware of the language shifts that districts undertake to obfuscate the fact that they are actually teaching CRT. Districts use other terms that are concepts from the theory. When they are called into question, districts deny their teachers are instructing the *theory* or deny it outright.[103] Sixth, use social media to your advantage by keeping in touch with the community regarding the violations that occur by teachers, school boards, administrators, and outside groups that are invited to campus. There are many excellent organizations available for parents to contact and from which to garner support. Some of these are found later in this chapter. In a word, the local organization is the best friend of communication, dissemination of information, and unity.

Seventh, parents should be willing to run for a school board seat, in order to reverse some of the policies that support CRT and racial divisions in public schools. They should also research methods of recalling board members who support CRT. Last, a community-organized group of parents should write letters to the editor of newspapers online and in print, share blogs of people who are of the same mindset, connect to online networks to share what works, and to discover strategies used elsewhere around the nation.

PARENTS SPEAKING UP AT SCHOOL BOARD MEETINGS

Opportunities to share with school boards occur at most public meetings. Nationally, some recent school board meetings were marked by forceful groups of dissenting, angry parents. Some individual parents were referred to as uncivil. Intense pressure became the norm at some meetings, while other board meetings were overwhelmed by the sheer numbers of concerned parents that attended. In some cases, large numbers of parents were instrumental in boards voting against the inclusion of CRT or canceling the controversial policies across entire districts. In other cases, not so much.

Many noteworthy recorded parent-board presentations went viral. The following list of ten such meetings represents an array of presentation styles. The reader is encouraged to access the links for their presentations, included in the endnotes section of this chapter.

- Black father shares an impassioned few minutes dissecting CRT.[104]
- Teacher addresses CRT instruction that occurs in teacher training institutions.[105]
- Teacher pleads with parents, students in the audience, and those watching online to speak up and take a stand against indoctrination in classrooms.[106]
- Black mother dismantles CRT and explains how its tenets and practices are deleterious to education.[107]
- Father, former school board member, passionately shares the problems within CRT with the school board.[108]
- Community Outreach Pastor shares public comments about race and CRT to the board of a large K-8 school district.[109]
- Parents attend a school board meeting and voice their opposition to CRT and other issues. The school board president addresses their concerns.[110]
- Former Ohio State Football Player addresses his concerns about CRT, even though the claims were that it was not currently being used in the district.[111]
- Parents demonstrating over CRT and the divisions it causes in schools.[112]
- Parents, teachers, and students speak up about CRT, indoctrination, and DEI.[113]

SOME HELPFUL TIPS IN THE BATTLE AGAINST CRT

Teacher and education counselor Christopher Paslay compiled a helpful list of resources for concerned parents, including other tools to assist in battling CRT.[114] Among the helpful tips, Paslay includes a section on two education approaches. These approaches are given the titles *identity-based* and *principle-based.* These are worth noting because the former is used by CRT and its advocates, while the latter principle is what most parents desire for their children. Paslay lists the characteristics of both approaches, which include:

- Identity-Based Approaches . . .
  - Focus on systems and collectivism
  - Make broad generalizations and stereotype entire groups of people
  - Are polarizing and based in dichotomy
  - Operate on a political level and are concerned with policy
  - Believe change comes through activism and political organizing
  - Believe quality of life stems from government
  - Believe identity is the primary determinant of success
- Principle-Based Approaches . . .
  - Focus on people and individuals
  - Are unifying and based in synergy
  - Are based in the American experiment of individual freedom and liberty
  - Believe change comes through personal skill building and self-improvement
  - Believe quality of life stems from personal choices and priorities
  - Believe principles and values are the primary determinant of success

A SILVER LINING

If the COVID-19 pandemic has a silver lining, that lining has brought about increased parental attention in monitoring their children's schoolwork. For example, Asram Nomani was recently interviewed by CNN, where she shared a curriculum that was used in public schools. She demonstrated several central tenets of CRT, as she read from the sources and exposed the focus on identity.[115] Another example, which was meant for younger children, was the book by author Anastasia Higginbotham, titled *Not My Idea: A Book about Whiteness (Ordinary Terrible Things).* This book directs students that they "can be white without signing on to whiteness."[116] The author includes an activity which teachers do not like to read aloud, and there is a good reason for this.

The activity page at the back of *Not My Idea* states a clear CRT tenet: "Whiteness is a bad deal. It always was."[117] The activity also contains the following:

> Contract. Binding you to WHITENESS. You get stolen land, stolen riches, special favors. WHITENESS gets to mess endlessly with the lives of your friends, neighbors, loved ones, and all humans of COLOR for purposes of profit. *Your*

soul. Sign below. The land, riches and favors may be revoked at any time for any reason.[118]

The image in the background signifies Satan by depicting a hooved creature and a pointed tail. Higginbotham's book is sort of a blend of a *Faustian Bargain* meets *The Devil and Daniel Webster.*[119] *Not My Idea* is found in at least fifteen states and in more than thirty public school districts nationwide.[120]

Rufo refers to increasing levels of parents' initiative, by exhorting those in the battle to remember that supporters of CRT

> must be confronted with and forced to speak to the facts. Do they support public schools separating first-graders into groups of oppressors and oppressed? Do they support mandatory curricula teaching that all White people play a part in perpetuating systemic racism? Do they support public schools instructing white parents to become *white traitors*, and advocate for *white abolition*? Do they want those who work in government to be required to undergo this kind of reeducation? How about managers and workers in corporate America? How about the men and women in our military? How about every one of us?[121]

According to Rufo, "There are three parts to a successful strategy to defeat the forces of critical race theory: governmental action, grass-roots mobilization, and an appeal to principle."[122] Those who would continue to make the claim that CRT is not being taught today in America's public schools are either ignorant of what is taking place nationally or they are purposely minimizing or obfuscating the facts, so as to deflect attention to pursue the goal of indoctrination of America's children's minds.

Parents need to keep up the pressure on local school boards. However, parents also need to hold administrators, principals, and teachers more accountable. Once their children's classroom doors close and school days begin, board members are often clueless about what takes place on any of their school's campuses on any given day.

When asked about CRT, Arkansas, United States History teacher Todd Sisson replied that "any history we read is an argument—it's just what someone else decided was most important to know about a person, event, or time period."[123] Notice the argument from subjectivity? No one should be surprised by this.

At Rogers New Technology High School, Sisson "incorporates some CRT concepts into his teaching and said the opinion won't impact his curriculum."[124] The fact that Sisson includes these concepts demonstrates CRT has already impacted his curriculum. However, Sisson's actions could be in violation of Arkansas law, which already legislates a ban on racial stereotyping and creating a divisive environment based on race. Yet, as with other activists, Sisson might just not care. The bottom line in the struggle over CRT is that more than one-half of the states have now limited what can be taught about race, and at least a dozen have banned CRT outright.[125]

THE NEXT PHASE OF CRITICAL RACE THEORY

CRT is thriving and changing national and international conversations about politics, education, religion, and gender and sex.[126] As a game-changer in America, "Critical race theories took part in . . . controversies . . . especially in three areas: capitalism, wealth accumulation, and distributive justice and domestic issues of power. They also addressed identity issues within critical race theory and intergroup coalitions."[127] Certainly, CRT has morphed over the years and continues to change. What has not changed are the primary CRT tenets about racism and whiteness in American society.

Authors Delgado and Stefancic point out that there are now many subdivisions within the critical theory and it is often difficult to pin down the theory to one particular concern, especially given that interest convergence and intersectionality play roles in the theory and its application. This enables CRT to escape some of the criticism placed against it. But parents should be on the lookout for these changes. The following is an example of why.

If LatCri (Latino/a Critical Race Theory) intersects with BlackCrit and also intersects with a person who also claims to be bisexual, or non-binary in gender designation, the problem then arises which critical theory best applies. Is such a person first black because of skin color, or does the person's current gender identity take precedence? The underlying tenet is still the same: there is an oppressed person—maybe oppressed in more than one area of life's intersections—and then there is the oppressor.

One can see how the critical theories can become quite intermeshed and change over time. Those that claim that CRT is not being taught are in the dark about what is actually taking place in culture. In reality, added into the CRT mix, the next phases of critical theory come down to "dynamic subdivisions, such as LatCrit and queer-crit studies [which] challenge civil rights activists to rethink the ways they conceptualize equality and civil rights."[128] More groups are associating themselves with CRT and finding out that by banding together, even with their differences in ideologies, there is strength in numbers. What they share in common is often greater than their differences.

In conclusion, critical theory, in general, is undergoing regular metamorphoses and is showing up in schools under many newer educational buzzwords, including the sex education programs districts are purchasing. The trend of emphasizing color over character continues as teacher advocates and CRT theorists explore shared interests and intersectionality—on the way to ensuring that striving for equity unites them, while enlarging the critical theory racial umbrella.

The only hope on the secular side is to return to the focus on the content of character and its development. Focusing on race with both eyes wide open does not bode well for the future of education in America. Teaching about racial issues in history is beneficial. But keeping one eye on the character development of children, at the same time, is most critical. The nation needs balance and there is none with CRT.

NOTES

1. Samuel Kim. "Critical race theory has its day in court." *Yahoo News*. August 3, 2021. Retrieved August 4, 2021, from https://www.yahoo.com/now/critical-race-theory-day-court-192100365.html.

2. Laura Meckler and Hannah Natanson. "As schools expand racial equity work, conservatives see a new threat in critical race theory." *The Washington Post*. May 3, 2021. Retrieved October 22, 2021, from https://www.washingtonpost.com/education/2021/05/03/critical-race-theory-backlash/.

3. Michael Ruiz. "Colorado school district bans critical race theory." *Yahoo News*. August 14, 2021. Retrieved August 15, 2021, from https://www.yahoo.com/now/colorado-school-district-bans-critical-020700461.html.

4. Eric Hananoki. "No left turn in education, a leading anti-critical race theory group, frequently pushes toxic rhetoric in media." *Media Matters*. June 22, 2021. Retrieved September 14, 2021, from https://www.mediamatters.org/education/no-left-turn-education-leading-anti-critical-race-theory-group-frequently-pushes-toxic.

5. Ronald Boone. "The Democratic Party is often violent, divisive and hypocritical; if it doesn't change, Trump will be back." *Baltimore Sun*. November 20, 2020. Retrieved October 28, 2021, from https://www.baltimoresun.com/opinion/op-ed/bs-ed-op-1122-democrats-their-own-worst-enemy-20201120-tybsvfh2vfcaxoua2xmqy6p27y-story.html.

6. Burgess Owens. "All the power to the parents vs. critical race theory." *New York Post*. November 1, 2021. Retrieved November 2, 2021, from https://nypost.com/2021/11/01/all-the-power-to-the-parents-vs-critical-race-theory/?fbclid=IwAR3IF1aQ2HrPMlnOxHwJmW_IB5Wmcx-KIU4NkSH3idBdCwfGO1BOnzIpMpU.

7. Ibid.

8. Anne Applebaum. "The answer to extremism isn't more extremism." *The Atlantic*. October 30, 2020. Retrieved October 28, 2021, from https://www.theatlantic.com/ideas/archive/2020/10/left-and-right-are-radicalizing-each-other/616914/.

9. Jeremiah Poff. "Loudoun school board members face threat of removal after parents collect sufficient signatures." *Washington Examiner*. November 10, 2021. Retrieved November 11, 2021, from https://www.washingtonexaminer.com/policy/loudoun-school-board-members-face-threat-of-removal-after-parents-collect-sufficient-signatures.

10. Terry Gross. "Uncovering who is driving the fight against critical race theory in schools." *NPR*. June 24, 2021. Retrieved June 27, 2021, from https://www.npr.org/2021/06/24/1009839021/uncovering-who-is-driving-the-fight-against-critical-race-theory-in-schools.

11. Tim Harris. "CNN's Chris Cuomo: Who says protests are supposed to be polite and peaceful?" *CNN*. June 4, 2020. Retrieved October 22, 2021, from https://www.realclearpolitics.com/video/2020/06/04/cnns_chris_cuomo_who_says_protests_are_supposed.html.

12. Attorney General Merrick Garland. "Justice Department address violent threats against school officials and teachers." *United States Department of Justice*. October 4, 2021. Retrieved October 22, 2021, from https://www.justice.gov/opa/pr/justice-department-addresses-violent-threats-against-school-officials-and-teachers. Cf. Gary Fields. "Garland says authorities will target school board threats." *AP News*. October 5, 2021. Retrieved October 22, 2021, from https://apnews.com/article/merrick-garland-school-boards-violence-daaff3f659981354b7a9a536db5cf2e2.

13. Caroline Downey. "South Carolina, Montana State school board associations sever ties with national organization." *National Review*. November 8, 2021. Retrieved November 9, 2021, from https://www.nationalreview.com/news/south-carolina-montana-state-school-board-associations-sever-ties-with-national-organization/.

14. Eric Hananoki. "No left turn in education, a leading anti-critical race theory group, frequently pushes toxic rhetoric in media." *Media Matters*.

15. Ibid.

16. Peter Wood. "Keeping the republic." *National Association of Scholars*. May 17, 2021. Retrieved May 19, 2021, from https://www.nas.org/blogs/article/keeping-the-republic.

17. Christopher Rufo. "The white backlash that wasn't." *The Tentacle*. October 4, 2021. Retrieved October 29, 2021, from https://www.thetentacle.com/2021/10/the-white-backlash-that-wasnt/.

18. Wood. "Keeping the republic." *National Association of Scholars*.

19. Stephen Sawchuk. "What is critical race theory, and why is it under attack." *EdWeek*. May 18, 2021, p. 3. Retrieved May 20, 2021, from https://www.edweek.org/leadership/what-is-critical-race-theory-and-why-is-it-under-attack/2021/05.

20. Ibid.

21. Alia Wong. "Kids develop views on race they they're young. Here's how some preschools are responding." *USA Today*. September 28, 2021. Retrieved September 29, 2021, from https://www.usatoday.com/story/news/education/2021/09/23/race-theory-preschool-how-to-teach-kids-about-racism/5796892001/.

22. Max Eden. "Concerned about your child's school? You might be a domestic terrorist." *Newsweek*. October 6, 2021. Retrieved October 6, 2021, from https://www.newsweek.com/concerned-about-your-childs-school-you-might-domestic-terrorist-opinion-1635751. Cf. Callie Patteson. "Parents take a stand against crackdown on CRT opponents." *New York Post*. October 5, 2021. Retrieved October 6, 2021, from https://nypost.com/2021/10/05/parents-pols-slam-fbi-probe-into-crt-related-harassment-in-schools/.

23. Katherine Cornell Gorka. "The great parent revolt." *The Heritage Foundation.* August 12, 2021. Retrieved October 28, 2021, from https://www.heritage.org/education/commentary/the-great-parent-revolt.

24. Christopher F. Rufo. "The child soldiers of Portland." *City Journal.* Spring 2021. Retrieved May 22, 2021, from https://www.city-journal.org/critical-race-theory-portland-public-schools?mc_cid=9ddf5edee7&mc_eid=dd2cd80aa4.

25. Christopher F. Rufo. "What I discovered about critical race theory in public schools and why it shouldn't be taught." *USA Today.* July 5, 2021. Retrieved July 6, 2021, from https://www.usatoday.com/story/opinion/voices/2021/07/06/critical-race-theory-schools-racism-origins-classroom/7635551002/?gnt-cfr=1.

26. Richard Delgado and Jean Stefancic. *Critical Race Theory: An Introduction.* 2nd edition. New York: New York University Press, 2012, pp. 6–7.

27. Ibid, pp. xvii, 3.

28. Ibid, p. xvii.

29. Ibid, p. 3.

30. Staff. "Ethnic studies at Seattle public schools." *Seattle Public Schools.* January, 2017. Retrieved August 6, 2021, from https://www.seattleschools.org/cms/One.aspx?portalId=627&pageId=53656040#.

31. Staff. "K-12 math ethnic studies framework 20.8.2019." *Seattle Public Schools.* 2019. Retrieved August 6, 2021, from https://www.k12.wa.us/sites/default/files/public/socialstudies/pubdocs/Math%20SDS%20ES%20Framework.pdf.

32. Ibid.

33. Ibid.

34. Joel Kotkin and Edward Heyman. "Critical race theory ignores anti-Semitism." *UnHerd.* August 9, 2021. Retrieved August 10, 2021, from https://unherd.com/2021/08/critical-race-theory-rewrites-history/.

35. Staff. "K-12 math ethnic studies framework 20.8.2019." *Seattle Public Schools.*

36. Ibid.

37. Ibid.

38. Ibid.

39. Ibid.

40. Ibid.

41. Ibid.

42. Misty Severi. "Critical race theory permeates North Carolina schools, task force says." *Washington Examiner.* August 27, 2021. Retrieved September 3, 2021, from https://www.washingtonexaminer.com/news/critical-race-theory-north-carolina-schools.

43. Ibid.

44. Ibid.

45. Ibid.

46. Ibid. Cf. North Carolina General Assembly. *House Bill 324: Ensuring Dignity & Nondiscrimination.* 2021-2022 Session. Retrieved September 8, 2021, from https://www.ncleg.gov/BillLookUp/2021/h324.

47. T. Keung Hui. "Here's how this NC school board says teachers must discuss race and history in class." *Raleigh News and Observer.* October 1, 2021. Retrieved

October 15, 2021, from https://www.newsobserver.com/news/local/education/article254684957.html?fbclid=IwAR2VVqgQOBKMRhJe3lGsPLdSI0EVy8GLIaYqvdqxny5tM3m6vVtVqakXmh8.

48. Ibid.

49. Jake Dima. "Oregon promoting teacher course on dismantling racism is mathematics." *Washington Examiner.* February 12, 2021. Retrieved August 18, 2021, from https://www.washingtonexaminer.com/news/oregon-math-course-racism-white-supremacy-teachers.

50. Ibid.

51. Ibid.

52. Mariana Rivas. "Fort Worth Christian School encourages students to see color when reading about race." *Fort Worth Star-Telegram.* November 8, 2021. Retrieved November 9, 2021, from https://www.star-telegram.com/news/local/crossroads-lab/article255525701.html.

53. Ryan Mills. "Parents find new allies in fight against racial indoctrination in schools." *National Review.* May 21, 2021. Retrieved June 15, 2021, from https://www.nationalreview.com/news/parents-in-fight-against-racial-indoctrination-in-schools/.

54. Maiysha Kai. "They're looking down upon children. The Root present: It's Lit! Talks teaching antiracism with Jason Reynolds." *The Root.* August 26, 2021. Retrieved September 12, 2021, from https://www.theroot.com/they-re-looking-down-upon-children-the-root-presents-1847564120?ref=SiteHype.com.

55. Ibid.

56. Ibid.

57. Brittany Bernstein. "Florida board of education approves rule banning 1619 project from classrooms." *National Review.* June 10, 2021. Retrieved September 27, 2021, from https://www.nationalreview.com/news/florida-board-of-education-approves-rule-banning-1619-project-from-classrooms/.

58. Peter W. Wood. *1620: A critical response to the 1619 project.* New York: Encounter Books.

59. Samuel Kim. "Critical race theory has its day in court." *Yahoo News.* August 3, 2021. Retrieved August 4, 2021, from https://www.yahoo.com/now/critical-race-theory-day-court-192100365.html.

60. Carol M. Swain and Christopher J. Schorr. *Black Eye for America: How Critical Race Theory Is Burning Down the House.* Rockville, MD: Be the People Books, 2021, pp. 69, 136. See Appendix B: *Model school board language to prohibit critical race theory.*

61. Elizabeth Schultz. "The left is lying: CRT is peddling hate in our schools." *Bacon's Rebellion.* August 4, 2021. Retrieved August 15, 2021, from https://www.baconsrebellion.com/wp/the-left-is-lying-crt-is-peddling-hate-in-our-schools/.

62. Ibid.

63. Jason Kao. "Texas' controversial new social studies law prompts McKinney school officials to cancel youth and government class." *The Texas Tribune.* August 17, 2021. Retrieved August 25, 2021, from https://goodwordnews.com/texas-school-cancels-classes-after-state-passes-controversial-social-studies-law/.

64. Ibid. Cf. Daniel Trotta (Leslie Adler, Ed.). "Texas schools remove children's books branded race theory." *Reuters*. October 6, 2021. Retrieved October 7, 2021, from https://www.reuters.com/world/us/texas-schools-remove-childrens-books-branded-critical-race-theory-2021-10-07/.

65. Mills. "Parents find new allies in fight against racial indoctrination in schools." *National Review*.

66. Tyler Kingkade, Brandy Zadrozny, and Ben Collins. "Critical race theory battle invades school boards—with help from conservative groups." *WPTV*. June 16, 2021. Retrieved June 17, 2021, from https://www.wptv.com/news/national/critical-race-theory-battle-invades-school-boards-with-help-from-conservative-groups.

67. Nicole Neily. "Letter to Office of Civil Rights Administrative Complaint." *Parents Defending Education*. May 12, 2021. Retrieved August 3, 2021, from https://defendinged.org/wp-content/uploads/2021/05/Wellesley-OCR_2.pdf. Cf. Tyler Kingkade, Brandy Zadrozny, and Ben Collins. "Critical race theory battle invades school boards—with help from conservative groups." *WPTV*. June 16, 2021. Retrieved June 17, 2021, from https://www.wptv.com/news/national/critical-race-theory-battle-invades-school-boards-with-help-from-conservative-groups.

68. Christopher F. Rufo. "Battle over critical race theory." *Wall Street Journal*. June 27, 2021. Retrieved June 28, 2021, from https://www.wsj.com/articles/battle-over-critical-race-theory-11624810791.

69. Kingkade, Zadrozny, and Collins. "Critical race theory battle invades school boards—with help from conservative groups." *WPTV*.

70. Russell Contreras. "Educators face fines, harassment over critical race theory." *Axios*. June 20, 2021. Retrieved June 20, 2021, from https://www.axios.com/teachers-harassment-fines-critical-race-theory-f0e6e7b2-d7cd-44f3-a30a-14f3acce5175.html.

71. Swain and Schorr. *Black Eye for America*, p. 77. Cf. Swain's organization at https://unitytrainingsolutions.com/.

72. Staff. "Editorial: What critical race theory is—and isn't—and why it belongs in schools." *Los Angeles Times*. August 8, 2021. Retrieved August 21, 2021, from https://www.latimes.com/opinion/story/2021-08-08/editorial-what-critical-race-theory-is-and-isnt-and-why-it-belongs-in-schools.

73. Ibid.

74. Ibid.

75. Ibid.

76. Ibid.

77. Ibid.

78. Pluckrose and Lindsay. *Cynical Theories*, p. 79.

79. Mariana Murdock. "New school data: 2021 math and reading scores reveal widening academic divide." *Yahoo News*. November 8, 2021. Retrieved November 8, 2021, from https://www.yahoo.com/news/school-data-2021-math-reading-121500474.html.

80. Staff. "Understanding student learning: Insights from fall 2021." *Curriculum Associates Research*. November 2021. Retrieved November 8, 2021, from https://www.curriculumassociates.com/-/media/mainsite/files/i-ready/iready-understanding-student-learning-paper-fall-results-2021.pdf.

81. Interactive Map. "States that have banned critical race theory." *World Population Review*. 2021. Retrieved October 13, 2021, from https://worldpopulationreview.com/state-rankings/states-that-have-banned-critical-race-theory.

82. Michael Ruiz. "California school board bans critical race theory." *Fox News*. August 12, 2021. Retrieved August 15, 2021, from https://www.foxnews.com/us/california-paso-robles-bans-critical-race-theory

83. Paso Robles Joint Unified School District Board President. "Resolution 21–27: Prohibiting the teachings of critical race theory." *Paso Robles Joint Unified School District*. June 17, 2021. Retrieved July 5, 2021, from https://agendaonline.net/public/Meeting/Attachments/DisplayAttachment.aspx?AttachmentID=1320720&IsArchive=0. Cf. Camille DeVaul. "PRJUSD votes to prohibit the teaching of critical race theory." *The Paso Robles Press*. August 11, 2021. Retrieved August 25, 2021, from https://pasoroblespress.com/news/education/prjusd-votes-to-prohibit-the-teaching-of-critical-race-theory/.

84. Swain and Schorr. *Black Eye for America*, p. 4.

85. Ruiz. "California school board bans critical race theory." *Fox News*.

86. Ibid.

87. Ibid.

88. Ibid.

89. Liz Moomey. "Robbed them of their innocence. KY school district tosses controversial curriculum." *Lexington Herald Leader*. September 29, 2021. Retrieved September 30, 2021, from https://www.kentucky.com/news/local/education/article254586327.html.

90. *Great Minds Wit and Wisdom K-8 English-Language Arts Curriculum*. https://greatminds.org/english.

91. Sam Dorman. "Billboards outside liberal NYC prep schools call out woke lesson plans: Diversity not indoctrination." *Fox News*. June 7, 2021. Retrieved June 7, 2021, from https://www.foxnews.com/us/nyc-private-school-woke-billboards.

92. Brian Flood. "Critical race theory taught at many of America's 50 most elite K-12 private schools, according to new study." *Fox News*. November 10, 2021. Retrieved November 11, 2021, from https://www.foxnews.com/media/critical-race-theory-americas-50-most-elite-private-k-12-schools. Cf. "Interactive Map." *Critical race training in education*. Retrieved November 10, 2021, from https://criticalrace.org/.

93. Sam Dorman. "Billboards outside liberal NYC prep schools call out woke lesson plans: Diversity not indoctrination." *Fox News*.

94. Ibid.

95. Corey Lynn. "How the challenge a school board in 3-5 minutes." *Corey's Digs*. July 7, 2021. Retrieved September 5, 2021, from https://www.coreysdigs.com/solutions/how-to-challenge-a-school-board-in-3-5-minutes/?__cf_chl_jschl_tk__=pmd_HUPbdRiDprvzIDyqdt8D57_AI_tKevrwTHHqUNC76Ug-1632066506-0-gqNtZGzNAhCjcnBszQml.

96. Viola M. Garcia and Chip Slaven. "Federal Assistance to Stop Threats and Acts of Violence Against Public Schoolchildren, Public School Board Members, and Other Public School District Officials and Educators." *National School Boards*

Association. September 29, 2021. Retrieved October 13, 2021, from https://nsba.org/-/media/NSBA/File/nsba-letter-to-president-biden-concerning-threats-to-public-schools-and-school-board-members-92921.pdf.

97. Emma Mayer. "Virginia school board hearing on critical race theory turns chaotic, two arrested." *Newsweek*. June 23, 2021. Retrieved July 6, 2021, from https://www.newsweek.com/virginia-school-board-hearing-critical-race-theory-turns-chaotic-two-arrested-1603500. Cf. Ryan W. Miller. "Shouting matches, arrests and fed up parents: How school board meetings became round zero in politics." *USA Today*. July 7, 2021. Retrieved July 8, 2021, from https://www.usatoday.com/story/news/education/2021/07/03/critical-race-theory-makes-school-board-meetings-political-ground-zero/7785802002/.

98. Asra Nomani. "Parents respond to DOJs School Board Memo." Fox News. *YouTube*. October 7, 2021. Retrieved October 12, 2021, from https://youtu.be/yelEkGIACdo.

99. Caroline Downey. "Loudoun County Teacher: District has created very hostile environment over equity initiatives." *National Review*. June 11, 2021. Retrieved September 27, 2021, from https://www.nationalreview.com/news/loudoun-county-teacher-district-has-created-very-hostile-environment-over-equity-initiatives/.

100. Lynn. "How to challenge a school board in 3-5 minutes." *Corey's Digs*.

101. Ibid.

102. Skyler Frazier. "Manchester school officials detail race, equity curriculum following teacher' resignation." *Journal Inquirer*. September 28, 2021. Retrieved September 29, 2021, from https://www.journalinquirer.com/towns/manchester/manchester-school-officials-detail-race-equity-curriculum-following-teachers-resignation/article_53a463ce-2063-11ec-8832-afcd40f6cc65.html.

103. Buck Sexton. "Interview with Tom Fitton, President of Judicial Watch." *YouTube*. October 26, 2021. Retrieved November 1, 2021, from https://www.youtube.com/watch?v=HIekNn2UqCM.

104. "Watch Black father blast critical race theory at board meeting in viral video." *YouTube*. June 18, 2021. Retrieved September 9, 2021, from https://www.youtube.com/watch?v=m66rcHzWaPU.

105. "VA teacher blasts school board for forcing critical race theory in classrooms." *Rumble*. March 13, 2021. Retrieved July 7, 2021, from https://rumble.com/velvnx-va-teacher-blasts-school-board-for-forcing-critical-race-theory-in-classroo.html.

106. "Fairfax teacher tells parents and students how to fight critical race theory in the LCPS SB meeting." *YouTube*. June 8, 2021. Retrieved September 18, 2021, from https://www.youtube.com/watch?v=8Xwo3y1vnGo.

107. "Black mom delivers scorching takedown of critical race theory at school board meeting." *Rumble*. May 12, 2021. Retrieved September 19, 2021, from https://rumble.com/vgxaad-black-mom-delivers-scorching-takedown-of-critical-race-theory-at-school-boa.html.

108. "The tip of the iceberg." *Twitter*. June 22, 2021. Retrieved August 30, 2021, from https://twitter.com/YALiberty/status/1407361053776912387.

109. David Kaplan. "BCSD decides to not implement critical race theory." *Bakersfield Now*. October 3, 2021. Retrieved October 4, 2021, from https://bakersfieldnow.com/news/local/bcsd-decides-to-not-implement-critical-race-theory.

110. Charlotte Stefanski. "Muncie school board president addresses critical race theory, social emotional learning." *Muncie Star Press*. October 12, 2021. Retrieved October 13, 2021, from https://www.thestarpress.com/story/news/education/2021/10/12/muncie-school-board-president-addresses-crt-sel-misinformation/6101114001/.

111. "Parents present critical race theory concerns during public comments at local school board meeting." NBC4 News. *YouTube*. July 8, 2021. Retrieved October 13, 2021, from https://www.youtube.com/watch?v=CoCrE7bA8NI.

112. "Parents stand up to proposed CRT curriculum at school board meeting." Young America's Foundation. *YouTube*. May 27, 2021. Retrieved October 4, 2021, from https://www.youtube.com/watch?v=kiqF23eYHqw.

113. "Parents accuse school board of trying to indoctrinate students with controversial critical race theory." 11Alive News. *YouTube*. May 18, 2021. Retrieved October 3, 2021, from https://www.youtube.com/watch?v=v-fKU4ZEZL4.

114. Christopher Paslay. *A Parent's Guide to Critical Race Theory*. Self-published, 2021, pp. 59–68. Cf. "Parent's Guide and Resources to Fight Critical Race Theory." United States Parents In-volved in Education (USPIE). May 24, 2021. Retrieved March 5, 2022 from https://uspie.blog/2021/05/24/parents-guide-and-resources-to-fight-critical-race-theory/.

115. Asra Nomani and Kazique Prince. "Critical Race Theory." CNN. *YouTube*. October 12, 2021. Retrieved October 13, 2021, from https://youtu.be/LJFsXycWBLE.

116. Christopher Paslay. "Not my idea: Toxic children's book teaches whiteness is evil." Chalk and Talk. *YouTube*. July 5, 2021. Retrieved October 12, 2021, from https://www.youtube.com/watch?v=e-x-BC6aEZk.

117. Ibid.

118. Ibid.

119. Richard L. Cravatts. "Teaching school children the evil of whiteness." The Times of Israel. July 18, 2021. Retrieved October 12, 2021, from https://blogs.timesofisrael.com/teaching-school-children-the-evil-of-whiteness/.

120. Ibid.

121. Rufo. "Critical race theory: What is it and how to fight it?" *Imprimis*, 50(3): 4–5.

122. Ibid, p. 5.

123. Worth Sparkman. "Arkansas AG: Teaching critical race theory could violate law." *Axios*. August 18, 2021. Retrieved August 19, 2021, from https://www.axios.com/arkansas-attorney-general-critical-race-theory-could-violate-law-95035fd5-f418-409e-bf6c-bc3520dc09bd.html.

124. Ibid.

125. Ibid.

126. Delgado and Stefancic. *Critical Race Theory*, p. 113.

127. Ibid, p. 114.

128. Ibid, p. 113.

Appendix A

States' Legislative Decisions Regarding CRT[1]

1. ALABAMA

"A bill has been introduced to ban CRT in elementary, secondary, and higher education across the state, but has not yet been taken up by the legislature." "The Republican-majority state board of education voted to codify a resolution banning schools from teaching 'concepts that impute fault, blame, a tendency to oppress others, or the need to feel guilt or anguish to persons solely because of their race or sex.'"

2. ALASKA

"No state-level action or bill introduced," and "the state of Alaska has not passed any laws regarding the teaching of CRT at any level."

3. ARIZONA

"Governor . . . signed a bill banning CRT in elementary schools and state-run agencies. The colleges and universities in Arizona don't appear to have adopted CRT to the same extent as major institutions in other states, but have begun to ramp up their initiatives into diversity, equity and inclusion." The law restricts "how teachers can discuss race and sex in the classroom. If educators or schools are found to be in violation of this law, the school district could be fined up to $5,000."

4. ARKANSAS

"Republican legislators withdrew their bill that would have prohibited teaching that promotes 'division' between groups or 'social justice.'"

5. CALIFORNIA

"California has adopted many aspects of CRT at all levels of education . . . the state Board of Education passed an ethnic studies curriculum based in large part on CRT that applies to all public schools. It also mandates anti-Zionism, which many critics cite as explicitly anti-Semitic . . . the California Board of Education adopted the long-anticipated Ethnic Studies Model Curriculum (ESMC) . . . rooted in the neo-Marxist framework known as Critical Theory—is less about fostering children's critical thinking skills and more about pushing children to become social justice activists." In terms CRT specifically, "No state-level action or bill introduced."

6. COLORADO

"No state-level action or bill introduced."

7. CONNECTICUT

"No state-level action or bill introduced."

8. DELAWARE

"No state-level action or bill introduced."

9. FLORIDA

"While the state Board of Education has banned CRT in public schools . . . many of Florida's public universities have embraced CRT in the form of mandatory training for faculty, staff, and incoming students . . . Governor . . . joined the Florida Board of Education to announce new teaching standards banning elements of Critical Race Theory (CRT) in the state's public schools." "The state board of education voted to approve a rule that prohibits schools from teaching critical race theory and the 1619 Project."

10. GEORGIA

"Governor-appointed state board of education adopted a resolution against lessons that 'indoctrinate' students or 'promote one race or sex above another.' The resolution also opposes awarding credit for student service learning with advocacy groups. These restrictions have not been codified into rules at this time."

11. HAWAII

"No state-level action or bill introduced."

12. IDAHO

"Bans public institutions from teaching particular elements of Critical Race Theory (CRT) and forcing students to accept it. It also bans public funding for any related curriculum and 'limiting the ways that teachers can discuss race and gender and banning what the legislation called tenets of critical race theory.' Idaho becomes the first state in the nation to enact prohibitions against CRT in public education."

13. ILLINOIS

"No state-level action or bill introduced."

14. INDIANA

"No state-level action or bill introduced."

15. IOWA

"Governor . . . signed a law limiting the ways that teachers can discuss race and gender."

16. LOUISIANA

"Bill has been withdrawn or stalled indefinitely or legislative session has ended with no further action on the measure." "Bill was voluntarily deferred

. . . that would ban teaching of 'divisive concepts,' after criticism from other Louisiana lawmakers and state education officials."

17. KENTUCKY

"Legislators have pre-filed two bills for the 2022 session that would prohibit teaching certain concepts related to race, sex, and religion, and would subject teachers who violate the law to disciplinary action."

18. KANSAS

"No state-level action or bill introduced."

19. MAINE

Bill introduced that would "prohibit public school teachers from engaging in political, ideological or religious advocacy in the classroom. Bill has been withdrawn or stalled indefinitely or legislative session has ended with no further action on the measure."

20. MASSACHUSETTS

"No state-level action or bill introduced."

21. MICHIGAN

"Legislators introduced a bill that would direct school boards to ensure that curriculum does not include critical race theory, the 1619 Project, or anti-American and racist theories. Bill has been proposed or is moving through state legislature."

22. MISSISSIPPI

"No state-level action or bill introduced."

23. MISSOURI

A bill was introduced that would "ban teaching of critical race theory and use of specific curricula, including the 1619 Project. The Missouri legislative session ended in May. Bill has been withdrawn or stalled indefinitely or legislative session has ended with no further action on the measure."

24. MONTANA

"At the request of Superintendent of Public Instruction . . . Montana Attorney General . . . issued an opinion in May that prevents schools from asking students to reflect on privilege and bans teaching that assigns characteristics to individuals based on their race or sex. The opinion is legally binding."

25. NEBRASKA

"No state-level action or bill introduced."

26. NEVADA

"No state-level action or bill introduced."

27. NEW HAMPSHIRE

"Governor signed the state budget into law. The budget bill included language banning teachers from discussing race, gender, and other identity characteristics in certain ways in class. This provision was added to the budget after a separate bill seeking to ban the teaching of 'divisive concepts' died."

28. NEW JERSEY

"No state-level action or bill introduced."

29. NEW MEXICO

"No state-level action or bill introduced."

30. NEW YORK

“Lawmakers pre-filed a bill for the 2021-22 legislative session that would prevent teaching that individuals bear collective responsibility for acts committed by members of their race, that individuals should feel guilt because of their race, or that individuals should receive discriminatory treatment based on their race. It would also ban requiring students to study the 1619 Project. Bill has been pre-filed for next legislative session.”

31. MARYLAND

“No state-level action or bill introduced.”

32. MINNESOTA

“No state-level action or bill introduced.”

33. NORTH CAROLINA

Governor vetoed “his state’s proposed ban on certain classroom discussions about racism. The bill would have prevented teachers from promoting 13 concepts related to race or sex, including that meritocracy is racist or sexist, or that the United States was created to oppress members of one race or sex. Bill has failed, been withdrawn, or stalled indefinitely.”

34. NORTH DAKOTA

“No state-level action or bill introduced.”

35. OKLAHOMA

Governor “signed a law limiting the ways that teachers can discuss racism and sexism in class, including banning Critical Race Theory from public schools . . . The bill does not ban . . . teaching certain parts of history. The bill says that no teacher shall require or make part of a course that one race or sex is inherently superior to another race or sex.”

36. OHIO

"Legislators introduced two bills: One would prohibit discussion of certain topics related to race and sex and forbid schools from awarding credit for student service learning with advocacy groups. If teachers promote any banned ideas, their classes cannot count toward graduation requirements for the students present. The other would prevent classroom conversations regarding *divisive concepts*. Bills have been proposed or are moving through state legislature."

37. OREGON

"Oregon has spent the better part of the past decade infusing equity into every level of education in the state. No state-level action or bill introduced."

38. PENNSYLVANIA

"Bill introduced that would limit how teachers can discuss racism and sexism and ban schools from hosting speakers or assigning books that advocate 'racist or sexist concepts.'"

39. RHODE ISLAND

"Bill introduced . . . that would prohibit the teaching of 'divisive concepts' related to race or sex. A House committee recommended that the bill be held for further study. Bill has been withdrawn or stalled indefinitely or legislative session has ended with no further action on the measure."

40. SOUTH CAROLINA

"Under a section included in the state's budget bill, schools and districts are prohibited from using state funding to teach that certain races or sexes are superior to others, or that individuals have certain traits, experiences, or responsibilities because of their race or sex. Bill signed into law. Two other bills banning critical race theory and the 1619 Project in schools failed to advance before the end of the legislative session."

41. SOUTH DAKOTA

"Legislators withdrew a bill they had introduced that would ban schools from using materials that encourage the overthrow of the U.S. government or promote social justice for particular groups. Bill has been withdrawn or stalled indefinitely or legislative session has ended with no further action on the measure. Governor signed the '1776 Pledge' which opposes critical race theory in schools."

42. TENNESSEE

Governor signed into law a bill that "limits how teachers can discuss racism and sexism in the classroom. Tennessee became one of the states passing laws against teaching CRT in K-12 education in . . . shortly after Idaho passed their law. The Department of Education still has a strong dedication to equitable outcomes. Despite no CRT mandates at the state level for public institutions, Tennessee's higher education system is infused with CRT at all levels. . . . bans CRT in primary education, upon the penalty of funding cuts."

43. TEXAS

"State legislature passed a bill that prohibits schools from awarding credit for student service learning with advocacy groups or requiring teachers to discuss controversial issues . . . banning the teaching of CRT and its fundamental assumptions in public schools. However, many of its institutions of higher learning have conducted recent changes to implement mandatory training for faculty, staff, and students . . . most public and many private colleges and universities in Texas have fully embraced CRT, anti-racism, equity, diversity, and inclusive excellence."

44. UTAH

"At the request of the legislature, the Utah State Board of Education approved a new rule in June that would limit how teachers can discuss racism and sexism." Utah has also "taken steps to curtail CRT in primary education, which puts it in conflict with its higher education system that mandates CRT in all public universities, and goes as far as many more prominent states to advance elements of CRT in college curricula."

45. VIRGINIA

"The fight over CRT has exploded into the national news in Loudon County and other school districts in Virginia . . . districts and administrators seem to have doubled down on equity, anti-racism, and other aspects of CRT in the curriculum. . . . The Virginia Department of Education has reimagined the wording on its website, for instance by replacing 'dismantling systems of oppression' with *dismantling inequities*. It publishes an entire dashboard full of anti-racist and diversity resources . . . for school districts, through the Office of Equity and Community."

46. VERMONT

"No state-level action or bill introduced."

47. WASHINGTON

"Mandates that Washington's 40 public colleges and universities conduct training sessions and assessments for both faculty and staff around diversity, equity, inclusion and anti-racism starting in the 2022-23 academic year . . . requires Critical Race Theory (CRT) training for all school staff, board directors, teachers, and administrators in public schools across the state."

48. WEST VIRGINIA

"Legislators introduced two bills that would prohibit schools from teaching *divisive concepts* relating to race and sex. Bills have been withdrawn or stalled indefinitely or legislative session has ended with no further action on the measure."

49. WISCONSIN

A proposed bill would "prevent teachers from promoting *race or sex stereotyping* and withhold 10% of state aid from schools that violate this prohibition. It would also require that schools publish a list of all curricula they use."

50. WYOMING

"No state-level action or bill introduced."

51. PUERTO RICO

"No state-level action or bill introduced."

NOTE

1. Staff. "Map: Where critical race theory is under attack." *Education Week*. October 15, 2021. Retrieved October 19, 2021, from https://www.edweek.org/policy-politics/map-where-critical-race-theory-is-under-attack/2021/06. Cf. Staff. "Critical race training in education." *Legal Insurrection Foundation*. 2020–2021. Retrieved October 18, 2021 from https://critica lrace.org/.

Appendix B

Christian Colleges and CRT

In 2020, a set of questions was sent to two large, prestigious, and historically Christian colleges. What follows are the questions and the institutions' response to selected questions summarized. The names of the colleges and the persons involved in the correspondence will be kept anonymous.

There were seven questions asked. Each is included here. The suggestion was made that Question 3 serve as the initial conversation starter. Agreement ensued and the colleges replied. Directly following the list of seven questions are the two colleges' replies to the pre-selected query.

THE QUESTIONS POSED TO TWO SELECT CHRISTIAN COLLEGES

- 1. What is the difference between racial *equality* and racial/socioeconomic *equity*, and is it the church's responsibility to ensure each?
- 2. Are people born with implicit bias? Is it only whites who have it?
- 3. Do you agree with the premises of CRT and Intersectionalism? Why, or why not?
- 4. Is the United States fundamentally and systemically racist? If so, can you specify where these exist in practice or law today?
- 5. Does white fragility actually exist, as explained in Robin DiAngelo's book by the same title? How does one know he or she is fragile? Can this fragility apply to any race?
- 6. Do the doctrines and practices of BLM remove itself from a Christian's support and involvement (e.g., destruction of the nuclear family, LGBT support, violence, anti-white, and anti-Christian rhetoric about Christianity being a white man's religion, etc.?) Why, or why not?

- 7. Can a Christian subscribe to the notion of Kendi's antiracism, in good conscience? Explain.

RESPONSES TO SELECTED QUESTION 3

ABC College's Statement

Over the past few years, the ABC college—like many organizations, institutions, and corporations—has been asked to comment and issue public statements on current events and public figures. The ABC College is an educational institution firmly grounded in the truths of Christianity and a biblical worldview. Our faculty teach that the disciplines of Politics, Philosophy, and Economics provide the framework to help students explore who we are as human beings: what and how we believe (Philosophy), how we live together and govern ourselves, despite our differences (Politics), and how money and resources influence human flourishing (Economics).

These principles, while brought to life by current issues, are not changed by the events of the day. They are timeless. Our mission is to teach students how to contextualize and think well about the issues of the day in pursuit of truth not to moralize and refuse to consider other positions.

The XYZ College is not in the business of condoning or disavowing controversies of the day. Rather, we seek to ensure an environment of academic freedom that allows our students and faculty to craft their own opinions, discerning for themselves how to live out their values. The XYZ college statement on academic freedom provides more detail on our commitment to fostering intellectual exchange and individual freedom.

Summary Response to ABC and XYZ College Statements

The responses did not answer the direct question, which tells me a lot. I have not heard or seen a biblical or Christian apologetic, defending CRT. I can only assume that academic freedom means more to a "Christian college" than maybe it ought to. As a researcher, I enjoy a good debate over issues. But here is the problem I have presently.

It is not enough to defend academic freedom, while a professor is speaking on behalf of the college. If there is an error in the theory or error in the sociology that contradicts biblical and Christian worldview, who then is using the academic freedom platform to correct the errors? Truth is more important than theory.

Knowledge built on truth is powerful. Academic freedom today is dissimilar to free speech. The past several years have seen support for CRT gaining traction nationally, and any criticism from professors often results in them being fired or canceled.

One of the slippages in Christian Higher Education is that there are *experts* in some academic fields of the colleges of ABC and XYZ, many of whom were trained by *woke* universities, and humanities departments at those universities. Some of these professors have not spent equivalent time in biblical theology and formational Christian worldview development. They then move into a Christian college environment and attempt to Christianity with culture.

This is not actually academic freedom. Rather, I consider it a form of compromise of truth for the sake of cultural relevance. CRT and Christianity come from two different worldviews. Are both given the same level of attention theologically and theoretically? I look forward to continued discussions regarding these matters.

Appendix C

Teachers' Associations and the Progressive Agenda: Washington State

Teachers' associations and unions exist all across America. Some of these groups actually have good working relationships between their districts, their communities, and the teachers. Some of the more progressive groups artfully obfuscate critical issues and use politics to advance their agenda, both by financial support and protest. Not all districts in the state are the same, and local contracts are what guide all local teachers.

In the state of Washington, for example, the Washington Education Association (WEA) released their *Teaching Truth* document, which provides *Tips for Teachers in a Tumultuous Time*.[1] The document begins with the statement,

> Educators are experts on making sure our students learn honesty about who we are, integrity in how we treat others, and courage to do what's right. Recent broad-ranging attacks on how we teach and what we teach has created confusion about how we can safely continue teaching accurate and updated curricula to help our students understand our past and present in order to create a better future.[2]

Observe the phrase *learn honesty about who we are*. There is an honest approach to submit students to a progressive agenda. Therefore, the honesty that is acceptable comes from the teacher and the *updated curricula*. Who we are is presented by those who want students to know who they, the teachers, are. No other honesty, which is viewed as disagreement, is tolerated.

Readers should notice also that the association calls those with questions and disagreements about what is being taught and how as broad-ranging attacks. This is not a tolerant approach from teachers and their union, which expects the same privilege extended to them. Tolerance for curriculum and instructional methods that are wrong to the parents are not broad-ranging attacks. What the association is missing is what is taking place in the classrooms. What actually takes place amounts to broad-ranging and calculated attacks upon children's minds and hearts.

An analysis of the rest of the document reveals a statement and answer format. These statements are written mostly in a defensive fashion, ensuring that teachers feel confident in moving forward a progressive agenda in Washington State public schools. Here are some examples, followed by a brief critique of each.[3]

- You do not singlehandedly need to justify or defend the curricula.
  - *We are aware that parents are sending emails to educators asking questions about what exactly we are teaching regarding equity, anti-racism, LGBTQ inclusion, sexual health education, and more. As an educator, you do not have to reply to these. It is also fine to reply to the parents that you are teaching the curricula as designated by your district and the state . . .*

Teachers are literally instructed not to reply to parents about their concerns regarding curriculum. If they do reply, teachers are instructed to place all responsibility upon the district. Parents must hold the teachers accountable, since teachers are now developing activists with the assistance of curricular frameworks. Not only are they teaching values contrary to most parents, but they are encouraging students to become activists for causes in the present, in order to change the future.

- Note that the First Amendment does not extend into the classroom.
  - *That means, unless otherwise stated in our union contracts, we have to refrain from taking political positions or espousing personal beliefs. That includes in our speech, classroom decorations, and displays.*

It is most obvious that this statement is merely in the document to fulfill a legal requirement on paper. Teachers who are members of BLM, or belong to the alphabet soup of sexual and gender distinctions, are not quiet when discussing the curriculum with students. They often share with their students their personal narratives. This sharing serves as a means to securing empathy toward normalization of what many parents consider improper education and to which they did not provide written opt-in acknowledgments or opt-out permission.

The hypocrisy and contradiction to this legal statement are found in another statement of the document, where the question arises by a Washington classroom teacher about hanging a BLM flag in a classroom.

- What about my classroom Black Lives Matter flag?
  - *Stating that Black Lives Matter is stating the truth—that we lift up our Black students and work to ensure they have equitable access to education and resources. Some non-Black people have harmfully and wrongfully assumed that Black Lives Matter is a political statement or suggests unconditional support for an organization and its actions. WEA maintains that Black Lives Matter is appropriate, and indeed needed, in our schools.*

There are misleading and false statements in the WEA document, and here is an example of one of misleading and contradictory statement. First, *All Lives Matter* (ALM) flags and posters are not allowed in classrooms, because of the exclusivity of focusing only on black lives. Such flags would be considered political and harmful to the message of exclusivity to a racial group. Yet, ALM is inclusive of all, whereas BLM is exclusive of all but black lives. This gives the community the message that there is exclusive support. If one is not deemed political, then either is the other.

ALM is an equally true statement and includes all other races and genders, whether claimed or biological. If BLM is not political, then ALM is the best message to teach in public schools that claim inclusion is one of the educational and social focal points.

There is ample evidence that BLM is indeed a political organization. There is also more than enough evidence to conclude it is an emerging racial cult, complete with tenets and beliefs. The political power is wielded by threats and cancellations of groups and individuals that disagree with their organization. All one has to do is to listen to any video interview by one or more of the leaders, their followers, and examine the BLM website. Race and politics are the ways to deconstruct current political, economic, and institutional structures, and Marxism is a means by which this deconstruction is justified.

The fact that BLM is considered necessary and appropriate for Washington State schools, there is also tacit support for BLM flags and posters to hang in classrooms and for teachers to share the political beliefs of the group, including invitations to outside speakers to come to campus. Furthermore, state and local tax funding is now paying for diversity, equity, and inclusivity directors in districts and on school campuses. State legislatures pass laws, meaning politics are involved in moving forward with the progressive movement to capture hearts and minds of Washingtonians.

So, the political act of flying a BLM flag in a classroom is a violation of the WEA statement against taking political positions or espousing personal beliefs, including speech, classroom decorations, and displays. The only caveat is whether the teachers' contract explicitly states that teachers can speak their personal beliefs on a subject, even if BLM is not an official Political Action Committee (PAC).

- I have been told by my administration that I cannot teach Critical Race Theory. How does that impact me?
  - *Educators should not teach curricula that are explicitly prohibited by their administration. . . . Critical race Theory is taught in universities and law schools, but at the PK-12 and community college levels we teach age-appropriate lessons that help our students understand and communicate across differences and portray a holistic and accurate picture of our nation's history.*

Here again is another misleading statement of distraction. Adapting CRT to age-level appropriateness is exactly what is taking place. There are terms that come directly from the morphing of CRT that children learn about in class. Certainly, no teacher is standing in front of the classroom saying *Today we will be learning college level Critical Race Theory*. That is ridiculous. However, students are hearing how they can identify racism and learn to become antiracists. They are learning about how whites are oppressors and blacks are oppressed. They also come away with the teacher's positions on indigenous lands being stolen by colonizers that white have implicit bias and are born that way and that there is white privilege. All of these have direct connections to CRT but are presented to students in age-appropriate lessons.

Swain and Schorr agree when they write,

> One of our points of emphasis concerns the spread of CRT throughout the educational arena. In K-12 schools, I particular, CRT rarely presents itself as CRT; rather, it hides behind euphemistic labels such as *antiracism*, *educational equity*, and *cultural competency*. Such methods are plainly deceitful. CRT advocates market themselves as engaged in a noble effort to combat systemic racism and to bring about a fair and just distribution of resources, in the process rooting out pernicious explicit or implicit—i.e., conscious or unconscious—racial biases.[4]

Like their ideological forbearers, CRT proponents aim to overthrow the social order of behalf of the oppressed . . . . From this vantage point, social institutions—economic, social, security, religious, cultural, etc.—are all described as elements of capitalist oppression. Marxists consequently advocate upending the social order and reconstituting society along socialist lines. "Concepts such as colorblindness, assimilation, and merit are dismissed as cynical means by which whites maintain their power and privilege in American society."[5]

In teaching a holistic approach to students, BLM curricula and *The 1619 Project* are part of what the WEA refers to as knowledge which is better for students and that they deserve to learn about accurate racial history over *out-dated, redlined accounts of the past history curriculum.*

"Because politics contains a personal dimension, it should come as no surprise that critical race theorists have turned critique inward, examining the interplay of power and authority within minority communities and movements."[6]

NOTES

1. Staff. Teaching truth: Tips for teachers in a tumultuous time." *Washington Education Association.* August 12, 2021. Retrieved August 15, 2021, from https://www.washingtonea.org/file_viewer.php?id=48973&fbclid=IwAR2kJ-ufDmCxBv5OkKe7EVCyMxFFAIkpv2moaVTXwmTgxaKQdnpzG30g7H8.
2. Ibid.
3. Ibid.
4. Carol M. Swain and Christopher J. Schorr. Black Eye for America: How Critical Race Theory Is Burning Down the House. Rockville, MD. Be the People Books, 2021, p. 12.
5. Ibid.
6. Richard Delgado and Jean Stefancic. *Critical Race Theory: An Introduction*, 2nd edition. New York: New York University Press, 2012, p. 57.

Other Works by this Author

Ernest J. Zarra III has authored fourteen books, including the additional Rowman & Littlefield titles:

- *When the Secular Becomes Sacred: Religious Secular Humanism and its Effects upon American Public Learning Institutions* (2021);
- *Detoxing American Schools: From Social Agency to Academic Urgency* (2020);
- *America's Sex Culture: Its Impact upon Teacher Student Relationships Today* (2020);
- *The Age of Teacher Shortages: Reasons, Responsibilities, Reactions* (2019);
- *Generacion Z: La Generacion con Derechos* (2019);
- *Assaulted: Violence in Schools and What Needs to be Done* (2018);
- *The Teacher Exodus: Reversing the Trend and Keeping Teachers in the Classrooms* (2018);
- *The Entitled Generation: Helping Teachers Teach and Reach the Minds and Hearts of Generation Z* (2017);
- *Helping Parents Understand the Minds and Hearts of Generation Z* (2017);
- *Common Sense Education: From Common Core to ESSA and Beyond* (2016);
- *The Wrong Direction for Today's School: The Impact of Common Core on American Education* (2015); and
- *Teacher-Student Relationships: Crossing into the Emotional, Physical, and Sexual Realms* (2013).

Index

About the Author

Ernest J. Zarra III, PhD, is retired assistant professor of Teacher Education at Lewis-Clark State College. Zarra has five earned degrees and holds a PhD from the University of Southern California, in teaching and learning theory, with cognates in psychology and technology. He has a storied forty-two-year career in teaching at all levels, with most of his classroom experience in the teaching of seniors' US government and politics and economics.

Ernie is a former Christian College First Team All-American soccer player, high school and club soccer coach, and former teacher of the year for a prestigious California public school. He was awarded the top student in graduate education from the California State University at Bakersfield, California. He is the father of two outstanding, professional, and accomplished adult children, a daughter and a son.

Dr. Zarra has written fourteen books, several of which earned awards. He is the author of more than a dozen journal articles and several Op-Eds. His writings have appeared in *RealClear Education*, *The National Association of Scholars*, of which he is a member, and peer-reviewed professional journals of education. He has designed professional development programs, is a national conference presenter, is former district professional development leader for the largest high school district in California, is a full-time and adjunct university instructor, and is a member of several national honor societies. He also participated as a speaker of the Idaho Speakers Bureau, as well as presenter in the Lewis-Clark Presents program, bringing special topics to high school students.

Originally from New Jersey, he and his wife Suzi, also a retired California public school teacher, live in Washington State and enjoy spending time with family, cooking, church ministry, yard work, and finding energy to keep up with their two grandchildren.

CPSIA information can be obtained
at www.ICGtesting.com
Printed in the USA
LVHW110714170522
718970LV00001B/112

9 781475 864137